ISLAMIC SURVEYS 2

A HISTORY OF ISLAMIC LAW

N.J. COULSON M.A.

Professor of Oriental Laws at the School of Oriental and African Studies, University of London.
Of Gray's Inn, Barrister-at-Law.
Sometime Scholar of Keble College, Oxford.

SECOND INDIAN REPRINT 2013

Edinburgh University Press Ltd

Universal
Law Publishing Co. Pvt. Ltd.
NEW DELHI - INDIA

First Published : 1964
Reprinted : 1971
Paperback edition : 1978
reprinted : 1990, 1991, 1994
First Indian Reprint : 1997
Second Indian Reprint : 2013

ISBN : 978-93-5035-359-2

Published by
Universal
Law Publishing Co. Pvt. Ltd.
NEW DELHI - INDIA

A-58, G.T. Karnal Road Industrial Area,
(Near Azadpur Metro Station), Delhi-110033
Tel. : 011-47082254, 27458529, 27215334 Fax : 011-27458529
e-mail: unilaw@vsnl.com
• Showroom : C-27, Connaught Place, New Delhi-110001
e-mail: sales@unilawbooks.com
• Website : **www.unilawbooks.com**
Join us on Facebook
www.facebook.com/unilawbooks

Under special arrangement with
EDINBURGH UNIVERSITY PRESS LTD.
22 George Square, Edinburgh EH8 9LF

ACIP record for this book is available from the British Library

Printed in India at Chaman Offset Printers, New Delhi.

FOREWORD

In 1939 the prospect of a war which would involve many Asian nations made men in positions of responsibility in Britain suddenly aware of the meagre number of our experts in Asian languages and cultures. The Scarbrough Commission was set up, and its report led to a great expansion of Oriental and African studies in Britain after the war. In the third decade after 1939 events are making clear to ever-widening circles of readers the need for something more than a superficial knowledge of non-European cultures. In particular the blossoming into independence of numerous African states, many of which are largely Muslim or have a Muslim head of state, emphasises the growing political importance of the Islamic world, and, as a result, the desirability of extending and deepening the understanding and appreciation of this great segment of mankind. Since history counts for much among Muslims, and what happened in 632 or 656 may still be a live issue, a journalistic familiarity with present conditions is not enough; there must also be some awareness of how the past has moulded the present.

This series of "Islamic surveys" is designed to give the educated reader something more than can be found in the usual popular books. Each work undertakes to survey a special part of the field, and to show the present stage of scholarship here. Where there is a clear picture this will be given; but where there are gaps, obscurities and differences of opinion, these will also be indicated. Full and annotated bibliographies will afford guidance to those who want to pursue their studies further. There will also be some account of the nature and extent of the source material.

to those who want to pursue their studies further. There will also be some account of the nature and extent of the source material.

While the series is addressed in the first place to the educated reader, with little or no previous knowledge of the subject, its character is such that it should be of value also to university students and others whose interest is of a more professional kind.

The transliteration of Arabic words is essentially that of the second edition of *The Encyclopaedia of Islam* (London, 1960, continuing) with three modifications. Two of these are normal with most British Arabists, namely, *q* for *ḳ*, and *j* for *dj*. The third is something of a novelty. It is the replacement of the ligature used to show when two consonants are to be sounded together by an apostrophe to show when they are to be sounded separately. This means that *dh*, *gh*, *kh*, *sh*, *th* (and in non-Arabic words *ch* and *zh*) are to be sounded together; where there is an apostrophe, as in *ad'ham*, they are to be sounded separately. The apostrophe in this usage represents no sound, but, since it only occurs between two consonants (of which the second is *h*), it cannot be confused with the apostrophe representing the glottal stop (*hamza*), which never occurs between two consonants.

W. Montgomery Watt
GENERAL EDITOR

CONTENTS

INTRODUCTION

The Role of Legal History in Muslim Jurisprudence

LAWYERS, according to Edmund Burke, are bad historians. He was referring, of course, to a disinclination rather than an inaptitude on the part of early nineteenth-century English lawyers to concern themselves with the past: for contemporary jurisprudence was a pure and isolated science wherein law appeared as a body of rules, based upon objective criteria, whose nature and very existence were independent of considerations of time and place. Despite the influence of the historical school of Western jurisprudence, whose thesis was that law grew out of, and developed along with, the life of a community, Burke's observation is still today generally valid. Legal practitioners, of course, are interested only in the most recent authorities and decisions; and English law, it may be remarked, has declared the year 1189 to be the limit of legal memory for certain purposes. But more particularly, current Western jurisprudence as a whole relegates the historical method of enquiry to a subsidiary and subordinate role; for it is primarily directed towards the study of law as it is or as it ought to be, not as it has been.

Muslim jurisprudence, however, in its traditional form, provides a much more extreme example of a legal science divorced from historical considerations. Law, in classical Islamic theory, is the revealed will of God, a divinely ordained system preceding and not preceded by the Muslim state, controlling and not controlled by

Muslim society. There can thus be no notion of the law itself evolving as an historical phenomenon closely tied with the progress of society. Naturally the discovery and formulation of the divine law is a process of growth, systematically divided by traditional doctrine into several distinct stages. Master-architects were followed by builders who implemented the plans; successive generations of craftsmen made their own particular contribution to the fixtures, fittings, and interior decor until, the task completed, future jurists were simply passive caretakers of the eternal edifice. But this process is seen in complete isolation from the historical development of society as such. The role of the individual jurist is measured by the purely subjective standard of its intrinsic worth in the process of discovery of the divine command. It is not considered in the light of any external criteria or in its relationship to the circumstances of particular epochs or localities. In this sense the traditional picture of the growth of Islamic law completely lacks the dimension of historical depth.

Since direct access to revelation of the divine will had ceased upon the death of the Prophet Muḥammad, the Sharīʿa, having once achieved perfection of expression, was in principle static and immutable. Floating above Muslim society as a disembodied soul, freed from the currents and vicissitudes of time, it represented the eternally valid ideal towards which society must aspire. To call Muslim jurisprudence idealistic is not to suggest that the terms of the law itself lack practical considerations realistically related to the needs of society; nor is it to imply that the practice of Muslim courts never coincided with this ideal. Both such propositions are demonstrably false. It is simply that Muslim legal philosophy has been essentially the elaboration and the analysis of Sharīʿa law *in abstracto* rather than a science of the positive law emanating from judicial tribunals. In short, the function of Muslim jurisprudence has always been, with one notable but limited exception, to tell the courts what they ought to do, rather than attempt to prophesy what they will in fact do.

Inherent, then, in Islamic law—to use the term in the sense of the laws which govern the lives of Muslims—is a distinction between the ideal doctrine and the actual practice, between the Sharīʿa law as expounded by the classical jurists and the positive law administered by the courts; and this provides a convenient basis for historical enquiry, which would proceed, simply, along the lines of the extent to which the practice of the courts has coincided with or deviated from the norms of the Sharīʿa. Muslim legal literature, however, has shown little interest in such an approach. Biographical chronicles of the judiciary in particular areas, descriptions of non-Sharīʿa jurisdictions and similar works, are not lacking; but they cannot be regarded as systematic or comprehensive accounts of the legal practice, much less as attempts to compare the latter with the doctrine of the scholars. Occasional protests against the legal practice by individual jurists provide the exceptions to the general attitude of resignation which the majority assumed. The standards of the religious law and the demands of political expediency often did not coincide; and perhaps the arbitrary power of the political authority induced the jurists to adopt a discretionary policy of ignoring rather than denying. But however that may be, the nature of Muslim legal literature, coupled with the absence of any system of law-reporting, naturally makes any enquiry along the lines indicated a task of considerable difficulty. Light has been shed on certain aspects of the problem by Western scholarship, but the extent to which the ideal law has been translated into actuality in a given area at a given period remains a grave lacuna in our knowledge of Islamic legal history.

From these brief remarks on the nature of the Sharīʿa, it will be evident that the notion of historical process in law was wholly alien to classical Islamic jurisprudence. Legal history, in the Western sense, was not only a subject of study devoid of purpose; it simply did not exist. Two developments in the present century, however—developments of a wholly different origin and nature but possessing, as will be seen, a link of profound significance—require a radical revision of this traditional attitude. In the first place Joseph Schacht (who would generously ascribe the initiative in the approach he has adopted to that great Islamist of a previous generation, Ignaz Goldziher) has formulated a thesis of the origins of Sharīʿa law which is irrefutable in its broad essentials and which proves that the classical theory of Sharīʿa law was the outcome of a complex historical process spanning a period of some three centuries; further development of this thesis by Western scholarship has shown how closely the growth of Islamic law was linked to current social, political and economic conditions. In the second place the notion of the Sharīʿa as a rigid and immutable system has been completely dispelled by legal developments in the Muslim world over the past few decades. In the Middle East particularly the substance of Sharīʿa family law as applied by the courts has been profoundly modified and to a large degree successfully adapted to the needs and the temper of society.

Islamic legal history, then, does exist. The Sharīʿa may now be seen as an evolving legal system, and the classical concept of law falls into its true historical perspective. This classical exposition represents the zenith of a process whereby the specific terms of the law came to be expressed as the irrevocable will of God. In contrast with legal systems based upon human reason such a divine law possesses two major distinctive characteristics. Firstly, it is a rigid and immutable system, embodying norms of an absolute and eternal validity, which are not susceptible to modification by any legislative authority. Secondly, for the many different peoples who constitute the world of Islam, the divinely ordained Sharīʿa represents the standard of uniformity as against the variety of legal systems which would be the inevitable result if law were the product of human reason based upon the local circumstances and the particular needs of a given community. In so far, then, as the historical evolution of Sharīʿa law falls into the three main stages of the growth, the predominance and the decline of the classical concept of law, the process may be measured in terms of these two criteria of rigidity and uniformity.

During the formative period of the seventh to ninth centuries diversity of legal doctrine in the different localities of Islam was gradually reduced and the mobility of the law progressively restricted, as the movement towards the classical theory gained ground. In the tenth century the law was cast in a rigid mould from which it did not really emerge until the twentieth century. Perhaps the degree of rigidity which the doctrine attained has been unduly exaggerated, particularly in spheres other than that of the family law; and the notion of a uniform Sharīʿa is seriously qualified by wide variations of opinion between different schools and individual jurists. But a rift certainly developed between the terms of the classical law and the varied and changing demands of Muslim society; and, where the Sharīʿa was unable to make the necessary accommodations, local customary law continued to prevail in practice, and the jurisdiction of non-Sharīʿa tribunals was extended. From this state of coma, fast approaching *rigor mortis*, the Sharīʿa was roused and revived by legal modernism. Comparable to the effect of Equity on the moribund mediaeval

English common law, this movement has freed the congealed arteries of the Sharīʿa. In the claim of the modernists the Sharīʿa can be adapted to support the social upheavals and progress of modern times. Increasing mobility in the law, therefore, is the modern trend; and since the measure of adaptation of the traditional law is conditioned by the varying reaction of the different areas to the stimuli of modern life, the inevitable result is an increasing diversity of legal practice in the Muslim world.

Fundamental indeed is the distinction between modern Muslim legal philosophy and classical jurisprudence. According to the classical tradition law is imposed from above and postulates the eternally valid standards to which the structure of state and society must conform. In the modernist approach law is shaped by the needs of society; its function is to answer social problems. Thus expressed the distinction is, in broad terms, parallel with the conflict in modern Western jurisprudence between the exponents of *ius naturae* and the sociological school. But Islamic legal modernism in fact represents an interesting amalgam of the two positions. Social engineering, to use the phrase of Dean Pound, the American leader of the school of functional jurisprudence, is a fitting description of modernist activities. Yet the needs and aspirations of society cannot be, in Islam, the exclusive determinant of the law; they can legitimately operate only within the bounds of the norms and principles irrevocably established by the divine command. And it is precisely the determination of these limits which is the unfinished task of legal modernism.

The clash, therefore, between the allegedly rigid dictates of the traditional law and the demands of modern society poses for Islam a fundamental problem of principle. If the law is to retain its form as the expression of the divine command, if indeed it is to remain Islamic law, reforms cannot be justified on the ground of social necessity *per se*; they must find their juristic basis and support in principles which are Islamic in the sense that they are endorsed, expressly or impliedly, by the divine will. As long as the theory of classical Muslim jurisprudence was predominant such support was difficult to find. Here it is, then, that the connection between modernist legal activities and the results of the researches of Western orientalists becomes readily apparent.

In its extreme form legal modernism rests upon the notion that the will of God was never expressed in terms so rigid or comprehensive as the classical doctrine maintained, but that it enunciates broad general principles which admit of varying interpretations and varying applications according to the circumstances of the time. Modernism, therefore, is a movement towards an historical exegesis of the divine revelation. Western scholarship has demonstrated that Sharīʿa law originated as the implementation of the precepts of divine revelation within the framework of current social conditions, and thus provides the basis of historical fact to support the ideology underlying legal modernism. Once the classical theory is seen in its historical perspective, as simply a stage in the evolution of the Sharīʿa, modernist activities no longer appear as a total departure from the one legitimate position, but preserve the continuity of Islamic legal tradition by taking up again the attitude of the earliest jurists and reviving a corpus whose growth had been artificially arrested and which had lain dormant for a period of ten centuries.

Modernist activities, therefore, can find their most solid foundation in a correct appreciation of the historical growth of Sharīʿa law. As this movement gathers momentum and a new era in Muslim jurisprudence is ushered in, legal history assumes a role of vital and previously unparalleled significance. The Muslim jurist of today cannot afford to be a bad historian.

Part One

THE GENESIS OF SHARĪ'A LAW

CHAPTER I

QUR'ĀNIC LEGISLATION

'OBEY God and His Prophet.' In this Qur'ānic command lies the supreme innovation introduced by Islam into the social structure of Arabia: the establishment of a novel political authority possessing legislative power.

Prior to the advent of Islam the unit of society was the tribe, the group of blood relatives who claimed descent from a common ancestor. It was to the tribe as a whole, not merely to its nominal leader, that the individual owed allegiance, and it was from the tribe as a whole that he obtained the protection of his interests. The exile, or any person hapless enough to find himself outside the sphere of this collective responsibility and security, was an outlaw in the fullest sense of the term, his prospects of survival remote unless he succeeded in gaining admittance into a tribal group by a species of adoption or affiliation known as *walā'*.

To the tribe as a whole belonged the power to determine the standards by which its members should live. But here the tribe is conceived not merely as the group of its present representatives but as a historical entity embracing past, present, and future generations. And this notion, of course, is the basis of the recognition of a customary law. The tribe was bound by the body of unwritten rules which had evolved along with the historical growth of the tribe itself as the manifestation of its spirit and character. Neither the tribal *shaykh* nor any representative assembly had legislative power to interfere with this system. Modifications of the law, which naturally occurred with the passage of time, may have been initiated by individuals, but their real source lay in the will of the whole community, for they could not form part of the tribal law unless and until they were generally accepted as such.

In the absence of any legislative authority it is not surprising that there did not exist any official organisation for the administration of the law. Enforcement of the law was generally the responsibility of the private individual who had suffered injury. Tribal pride usually demanded that inter-tribal disputes be settled by force of arms, while within the tribe recourse would usually be had to arbitration. But again this function was not exercised by appointed officials. A suitable *ad hoc* arbitrator (*ḥakam*) was chosen by the parties to the dispute, a popular choice being the *kāhin*, a priest of a pagan cult who claimed supernatural powers of divination.

This general picture of the primitive customary tribal law of Arabia in the sixth century requires some qualification as regards the settled communities of Mecca and Medina. Mecca, the birthplace of the Prophet Muḥammad and a flourishing centre of trade, possessed a commercial law of sorts, while Medina, an agricultural area, knew elementary forms of land tenure. In Mecca, moreover, there appear to have existed the rudiments of a system of legal administration. Public arbitrators were appointed and other officials were charged with the task of recovering compensation in cases of homicide or wounding. Yet in both these centres, just as among the Bedouin tribes, the sole basis of law lay in its recognition as established customary practice.

The year 622 saw the establishment of the Muslim community in Medina. The Arab tribes or sub-tribes (with some temporary exceptions) accepted Muḥammad as the Prophet or spokesman of God, and regarded themselves and his Meccan followers as constituting a group of a new kind wherein the bond of a common religious faith transcended tribal ties. While Muḥammad's position gradually developed into one of political and legal sovereignty, the will of God as transmitted to the community by him in the Qur'ānic revelations came to supersede tribal custom in various respects. To assess the nature and scope of the legislation which the Qur'ān contains and its impact upon the form and substance of the existing customary law is the purpose of the remainder of this chapter.

In the evolution of a society the technical process of legislation is a secondary stage. Reducing into terms of rights and obligations an accepted standard of conduct and providing remedies in the event of its infringement, it presupposes the existence of this accepted standard. Naturally enough, therefore, the religious message of the founder-Prophet of Islam, the purpose of which included the establishing of certain basic standards of behaviour for the Muslim community, precedes, both in point of time and emphasis, his role as a political legislator. Accordingly, the so-called legal matter of the Qur'ān consists mainly of broad and general propositions as to what the aims and aspirations of Muslim society should be. It is essentially the bare formulation of the Islamic religious ethic.

Most of the basic notions underlying civilised society find such a mode of expression in the Qur'ān. Compassion for the weaker members of society, fairness and good faith in commercial dealings, incorruptibility in the administration of justice are all enjoined as desirable norms of behaviour without being translated into any legal structure of rights and duties. The same applies to many precepts which are more particular, and more peculiarly Islamic, in their terms. Drinking of wine and usury (*ribā*) are both simply declared to be forbidden (*ḥarām*) in practically the same terms. But no indication of the legal incidents of the practices is contained in the Qur'ān. In fact wine-drinking later became a criminal offence punishable by flogging while usury was a purely civil matter, the transaction being a type of invalid or unenforceable contract. This clearly demonstrates the distinct attitudes of the religious prophet and the political legislator. Both are obviously concerned with the consequences of an act or omission; but, while the legislator sees those consequences in terms of practical sanctions enforceable by human agencies, the prophet sees them as the attainment of merit or fault in the sight of God. The ultimate sanction visualised for the infringement of the Qur'ānic provisions is always the blessing or wrath of God. For example, those who wrongfully exploit the property of orphans, says the Qur'ān, "only swallow down the fires of hell into their stomachs and shall burn in the flame". While political legislation considers social problems in terms of the effects of an individual's behaviour upon his neighbour or upon the community as a whole, a religious law looks beyond this to the effect that actions may have upon the conscience and eternal soul of the one who performs them. In short, the primary purpose of the Qur'ān is to regulate not the relationship of man with his fellows but his relationship with his Creator.

While the Qur'ānic legislation, then, is predominantly ethical in quality, the quantity is not great by any standards. It amounts in all to some six hundred verses, and the vast majority of these are concerned with the religious duties and ritual practices of prayer, fasting, and pilgrimage. No more than approximately eighty verses deal with legal topics in the strict sense of the term. The first laws of a society are naturally couched in brief and simple terms—as was the case with the Twelve

Tables of Roman law. But unlike the Twelve Tables the Qur'ān does not attempt to cover, in however rudimentary a form, all the basic elements of a given legal relationship. Although the regulations which are of a more specifically legal tone cover a great variety of subjects, ranging from women's dress to the division of the spoils of war, and from the prohibition of the flesh of swine to the penalty of flogging for fornication, they often have the appearance of *ad hoc* solutions for particular problems rather than attempts to deal with any general topic comprehensively.

This piecemeal nature of the legislation follows naturally perhaps from the circumstances in which the Qur'ān was revealed; for the official compilation of the Qur'ān, which did not appear until some years after the death of the Prophet, represents an arbitrary arrangement of short passages which had been uttered by the Prophet at various times and in various places throughout his lifetime—or at least, as far as the legal verses are concerned, during the ten years of his residence at Medina. An example of this type of regulation which catered for the exigencies of the moment is provided by the verse (xxxiii. 37) which abolishes the pre-Islamic custom of adoption, under which an adopted child had the legal status of the adopter's own child; for this was designed to settle the controversy which arose from the marriage of the Prophet to the divorced wife of his adopted son Zayd. Similarly the Qur'ānic verses which lay down the penalty of eighty lashes for the offence of a false accusation of unchastity (*qadhf*) were revealed following imputations of adultery against the Prophet's wife, 'Ā'isha.

Certain topics, it is true, are dealt with at considerable length. But even here there is no single comprehensive exposition of the topic. It was simply that certain problems of a recurring nature gave rise to a series of regulations, disjointed in point both of time and substance, on the same general subject, and these, when gathered together from their various positions in the Qur'ān, afford some semblance of a detailed treatment. Without doubt it is the general subject of the position of women, married women in particular, which occupies pride of place in the Qur'ānic laws. Rules on marriage and divorce are numerous and varied, and, with their general objective of the improvement of woman's status, represent some of the most radical reforms of the Arabian customary law effected in the Qur'ān. The import of two outstanding rules in this context may be briefly noticed.

As regards marriage the Qur'ān commands that the wife alone shall receive the dower (*mahr*) payable by the husband. While payments to the wife herself were sometimes made in pre-Islamic times, the basic concept of marriage under some forms of the customary law was that of a sale of the woman by her father, or other near male relative, who received, *qua* vendor, the purchase price paid by the husband. The effect of this simple Qur'ānic rule, then, is to transfer the wife from the position of a sale-object to that of a contracting party who, in return for her granting the right of sexual union with herself, is entitled to receive the due consideration of the dower. She is now endowed with a legal competence she did not possess before. In the laws of divorce the supreme innovation of the Qur'ān lies in the introduction of the "waiting period" (*'idda*). Prior to Islam a husband could discard his wife at a moment's notice. His repudiation (*ṭalāq*) of his wife, a right naturally stemming from his position as a purchaser of her, operated as an immediate and final severance of the marital relationship. The Qur'ān now virtually suspended the effect of the repudiation until the expiry of the "waiting period", which was to last until the wife had completed three menstrual cycles or, if she proved pregnant, until delivery of the child. This period is primarily designed, according to the express terms of the Qur'ān itself, to provide an opportunity for reconciliation, and during it the wife is entitled to financial support from the husband.

Reforms such as these obviously go a long way towards ameliorating the position of the wife. But they are designed to remedy only particular aspects of the marital relationship: they do not attempt to create an entirely novel structure of family law or to eradicate the basic concepts of existing customary practices. Marriage remains a contract in which the husband, as a quasi-purchaser, occupies the dominant position. He also retains his basic right (which, as has been pointed out, is a natural corollary of that concept) unilaterally to terminate the marriage. "The men are overseers over the women", says the Qur'ān, "by reason of ... the property which they have contributed" (i.e. the dower and maintenance). But this patriarchal scheme of society is now subjected to the tempering influence of the ethical standard of fair treatment for women. The oft-repeated injunction to "retain wives honourably or release them with kindness" finds its practical implementation in legal rules which mitigate for women the rigours of that society and remove its harshest features. In short, the Qur'ānic regulations modify in certain particulars rather than supplant entirely the existing customary law.

Perhaps the best illustration of the various aspects of the Qur'ānic laws to which we have referred is provided by the regulations concerning inheritance. In pre-Islamic times the rules of inheritance were designed to consolidate the strength of the individual tribe as an effective participant in the popular sport of tribal warfare. Patrilineal in structure, the tribe was formed of those who traced their descent from the common ancestor exclusively through male links.[1] Accordingly, in order to keep property within the tribe, rights of inheritance belonged solely to the male agnate relatives (*'aṣaba*) of the deceased. Furthermore, it was the "nearest" such relative alone who inherited, the order of priority being the descendants of the deceased, followed by his father, his brothers and their issue, his paternal grandfather, and finally his uncles and their descendants. Although there is some evidence that property was occasionally bequeathed, outside this scheme, to close relatives such as parents and daughters, the general rule was that females had no rights of succession; nor had minor children—on the ground, presumably, of their inability to participate in military activities.

The first Qur'ānic reference to this subject is a typically ethical injunction which urges a person who is on the point of death to "bequeath equitably to his parents and kindred". This provision obviously qualifies, in general, the system of exclusive inheritance by the male agnate relatives and in particular recognises the capacity of women relatives to succeed. As such it reflects the transition effected by Islam from a society based on blood relationship to one based on a common religious faith; and in this new society the individual family has replaced the tribe as the basic unit.[2]

Later circumstances, however, necessitated the translation of this general injunction into more positive and practical rules. Following the death of many Muslims in the battles fought against the unbelievers, a series of Qur'ānic revelations allotted specific fractions of the deceased's estate to individual relatives. Of the nine relatives so entitled six are women—the wife, the mother, the daughter, the germane, consanguine and uterine sisters—and the remaining three are male relatives who would either never have inherited at all under the old system (i.e. the husband and the uterine brother) or would have been excluded by a nearer agnate (i.e. the father, who would not have inherited in competition with a son of the deceased). Although the Qur'ān does not expressly recognise the claims of the male agnate relatives as such, it enacts that where the deceased is survived by sons and daughters the share of the son shall be double that of the daughter; and a similar principle applies when the heirs are the deceased's brothers and sisters. The obvious intention, then, of the Qur'ānic rules is not to sweep away the agnatic system entirely but merely to modify it, with the particular objective of improving the position of female relatives, by superimposing upon the male agnates an additional class of new heirs. Once again the legislation is by way of a supplement to, not a substitute for, the existing customary law.

For those who were pledged to conduct their lives in accordance with the will of God the Qur'ān itself did not provide a simple and straightforward code of law. As a legislative document, the Qur'ān raises many problems; but we are not for the moment concerned with the manifold and complex questions of the interpretation of the Qur'ān and its precise implications which were to occupy the minds of later and more sophisticated generations. There were, however, two basic problems which must have been of immediate concern to the contemporaries of the Prophet themselves.

In the first place there was the question of the effect, in terms of practical measures, of the essentially ethical standards established by the Qur'ān. Usury had been simply prohibited. But it is hardly too cynical to suggest that the potential lender or borrower might be at least as interested in the effect of his dealings on his pocket or his person as he would be in the prospect of eternal damnation.[3]

In some cases the legal implications of an ethical

norm were self-evident. On the subject of homicide and physical assaults, for example, the Qur'ān lays down the standard of just retribution in the maxim "an eye for an eye and a life for a life". Under the pre-Islamic customary law a rough system of private justice, dominated by the notion of vengeance, had prevailed in these matters. The loss of a tribal member was to be avenged by the infliction of a corresponding loss upon the culprit's tribe who were collectively responsible for the action of one of their members. Until satisfactory vengeance had been wreaked, the soul of the victim could not rest in peace; and, since the natural tendency was for a tribe to set an exaggerated value on the member it had lost, two or more lives might be claimed in revenge for a single victim. The Qur'ānic maxim thus radically altered the legal incidents of homicide. Henceforth only one life—the life of the killer himself—was due for the life of the victim, and the distinction is marked by a change of terminology, the term *tha'r* (blood revenge) being replaced by that of *qiṣāṣ* (just retaliation). It is once again noteworthy, however, that the basic structure of the existing law is left unchanged. Homicide remains an offence which falls into the category of civil injuries rather than that of public offences or crimes, for it is the relatives of the victim who have the right to demand retaliation, accept compensation or pardon the offence altogether. It is still a matter for private justice, but that justice is now to be meted out in accordance with the moral standard of just and exact reparation for loss suffered, the maxim of a life for a life itself stemming from the broader religious principle that all Muslims are equal in the sight of God.

But the legal implications of the Qur'ānic precepts were by no means always as self-evident as in the case of homicide. Polygamy, restricted to a maximum of four wives concurrently, is expressly permitted, but at the same time husbands are enjoined to treat co-wives equally and not to marry more than one wife if they fear they will be unable to do so. Does this represent a legal condition attaching to polygamous unions, and if so what is the remedy for its breach? Or is the duty of impartial treatment simply a matter for the conscience of the individual husband? These and similar questions would soon require an answer from those whose task it was to apply the law of God.

The second and even more obvious problem arises from the omissions in the Qur'ānic legislation. On many legal topics, of course, the Qur'ān is completely silent. But this would occasion no difficulty, at least for the early Muslim community, inasmuch as the existing customary law would continue to apply in these respects. It is a natural canon of construction, and one in full accord with the general tenor of the Qur'ān, that the *status quo* is tacitly ratified unless it is expressly emended. Again the rules in the Qur'ān on certain subjects may be extremely rudimentary. There is the repeated injunction, for example, to pay alms (*zakāt*), to the extent a person can afford, to those in need. Simple rules like this naturally proved inadequate as society progressed, and they were later developed into an elaborate system of taxation which specified the amount payable, the property subject to the tax and the order of priority among beneficiaries. But this does not constitute an omission, in our sense, in the Qur'ān. Nevertheless, in certain respects the Qur'ān formulated novel rules which were manifestly incomplete in themselves. An outstanding instance is provided by the rules of inheritance previously discussed. While the injunction to make out bequests in favour of near relatives had clearly been superseded by the system of fixed shares, this begged the obvious and unanswered question as to whether any power at all of testamentary disposition still remained, and if it did to what extent and in favour of whom it could be exercised.

How these lacunae were filled, and how the other problems to which we have alluded were solved, will be indicated in the chapters that follow. Here we have been attempting an objective assessment of the Qur'ān itself as a legislative document, and enough has now been said to show that it does not expressly provide solutions for all the legal problems inherent in the organisation of a society. The principle that God was the only lawgiver and that his command was to have supreme control over all aspects of life was clearly established. But that command was not expressed in the form of a complete or comprehensive charter for the Muslim community. Later events, indeed, were to show that the Qur'ānic precepts form little more than the preamble to an Islamic code of behaviour for which succeeding generations supplied the operative parts.

CHAPTER 2

LEGAL PRACTICE IN THE FIRST CENTURY OF ISLAM

THE period up to the year A.D. 750 witnessed the transformation of Islam from a small religious community in Arabia to a vast military empire which on one side threatened the frontiers of Latin Christendom in the Pyrenees and on the other stood astride the northern approaches to the Indian sub-continent. Within the span of a century the Islamic empire had embraced a great complexity of races, cultures and religions; its political dominion had spread over territories as different as those which were formerly subject to the highly developed civilisations of Byzantine and Persian rule and those which supported the more primitive societies of the Arab peoples and the Berber tribes of North Africa. Little imagination is needed to appreciate the tremendous problems of administrative organisation which faced the Arab rulers as a result of the military conquests and the social and economic upheavals which followed in their wake. Nor was Islam free from internal political troubles in this period, when disputes concerning the right of succession to leadership produced a period of civil war, a series of revolts, and the formation of political factions hostile to the central power. This rapidly moving background of momentous historical events determined the course of legal development during the first century of Islam.

As long as Muḥammad was alive he was naturally regarded as the ideal person to settle disputes. Later generations falsely ascribed to Muḥammad a great corpus of legal decisions, and the extent of his extra-Qur'ānic law-making is the subject of the greatest single controversy in early Islamic legal history. This problem, however, will be more conveniently discussed at a later stage. Suffice it to say here that Muḥammad must have been faced during his rule at Medina with a variety of legal problems, particularly those which, as we have noted, arose out of the terms of the Qur'ān itself. Recourse to a pagan arbitrator, or *kāhin*, had been specifically denounced in the Qur'ān and Muḥammad had been elevated to the position of judge supreme, with the function of interpreting and explaining the general provisions of the divine revelation.

One example of his varied rulings of this nature will be sufficient. In the matter of inheritance the Qur'ān had introduced radical but ambiguous innovations. A series of rulings by Muḥammad clarified the position. First the relationship between the new heirs named in the Qur'ān and the old heirs of the customary law was established by the simple rule that the Qur'ānic heirs should first be given their share and then the residue should go to the nearest *'aṣaba* relative. Secondly Muḥammad made it clear that the bulk of an estate must necessarily devolve in accordance with this scheme by restricting the power of testamentary disposition to one-third of the net assets. Finally the principle of the inviolability of the proportionate claims of the legal heirs was enshrined in the rule: "No bequest in favour of an heir".

Regulations of this nature marked the beginnings of the growth of a legal structure out of the ethical principles contained in the Qur'ān. But Muḥammad made no attempt to elaborate anything like a code of law on this basis. He was content to proffer *ad hoc* solutions as problems arose.

For some thirty years after the death of Muḥammad

in 632 Medina remained the focal point of Muslim activity. Here the vital issue was that of succession to the political authority of Muḥammad. At first it was natural that the influence of those most closely associated with him should prevail, and the office of Caliph—"successor" to the Prophet—was held in succession by four of Muḥammad's most intimate companions: Abū-Bakr, 'Umar, 'Uthmān and 'Alī.

During this period military expeditions, meeting with increasing success, expelled the Byzantine forces from Syria and Egypt and overran Persia; and such conquests posed novel problems for these Caliphs. To 'Umar is attributed the foundation of the rudiments of a fiscal regime when, in 641, he instituted the *dīwān*, or pay-roll register, to facilitate the distribution of stipends. Similarly his decision not to divide out the conquered territories among the soldiery but to retain them in the public ownership of the Muslim community, exacting a land-tax (*kharāj*) from the occupier, inaugurated a new concept of land tenure. But the principal concern of the authorities lay with the internal organisation of the community.

Upon the Caliphs and their advisers fell the duty of further implementing the Qur'ānic provisions in the same spirit as their former leader. Once again instructive examples of this activity are provided by the subject of inheritance. Why this particular sphere of the law should have proved of such importance in Medina is easily explained. The new Qur'ānic scheme of inheritance represented the transition from a tribal society to a society in which the individual family was the unit and in which the rights of relatives other than the male agnate relatives were recognised. Epitomised, therefore, in the problems to which it gave rise is the tension created between the old and the new orders. Moreover, the solution of these problems was a matter of practical urgency: for the increasing influx of booty to the treasury created an intense preoccupation with the newly acquired wealth and provoked a legal activity concerning its devolution on death, which was matched only by the concern for its distribution among the living.

To ʿAlī is ascribed the device of proportionately reducing the fractional shares allotted by the Qur'ān when these add up to more than a unity. From the somewhat arresting circumstances in which it occurred the case is known as the *Minbariyya* (the Pulpit case). While delivering a sermon in the mosque ʿAlī was interrupted by a questioner from the congregation who asked what happened to the wife (normal share $\frac{1}{8}$) when the deceased husband had also left two daughters ($\frac{2}{3}$), a father ($\frac{1}{6}$) and a mother ($\frac{1}{6}$). ʿAlī, we are told, replied without any hesitation: "The wife's one-eighth becomes one-ninth". And the shares of the other relatives, of course, were abated in proportion.

For other problems, and other judges, the solution was not so readily reached. Where the deceased was survived only by his maternal and paternal grandmothers Abū-Bakr adjudged the whole estate in the first instance to the maternal grandmother, on the ground, presumably, that, since the Qur'ān does not specifically mention grandmothers, the mother's mother, but not the father's mother, could be regarded as the mother of the deceased. But when ʿAbd-ar-Raḥmān ibn-Sahl raised the question of reciprocity and pointed out that the person from whom the present propositus would have inherited as an agnate had been excluded and all had been given to the person from whom the present propositus, as a daughter's son, would never have inherited, Abū-Bakr revised his decision and gave both the grandmothers equal shares.

Probably the most striking illustration of the conflict

between the old and the new orders of cosiety is reflected in the celebrated case of the *Himariyya* (the Donkey case). The deceased had left a husband, mother, two full brothers and two uterine brothers. 'Umar, in accordance with the rule of first satisfying the Qur'ānic shares, gave the husband 2, the mother 6 and the uterine brothers 3, thus exhausting the estate and leavnig nothing for the residuary heirs, the full brothers. These latter, despite vigorous protestations of their pre-eminence as agnatic heirs and bitter complaints that they had in effect been ousted by the non-agnatic half-brothers, were forced to depart empty-handed. Since there was no dispute about the rightx of the husband and the mother the case resolved itself into a straightforward competition for the 3 residue between the heirs of the old customary law and the new Qur'ānic heirs, and 'Umar had preferred the claims of the latter. The full brothers, however, later appealed against the decision on the ground that at least they had the same mother as the deceased and therefore possessed the very same quality of relationship which was the exclusive basis of the uterine brothers' right of inheritance. Accepting the logic of this argument, 'Umar allowed them to share equally with the uterine brothers in the 3. The case takes its name from the way in which the full brothers explained that they wished to claim *qua* uterines and waive their character of agnates. "Assume", they said, "that our father does not count. Consider him a donkey (*himar*)."

From the readiness of the Caliphs Abu-Bakr and 'Umar to take advice it is evident that the right of interpreting the Qur'ānic regulations was not the privilege of any special official body but could be exercised by anyone whose piety or social conscience dictated such a course. Zayd ibn-Thānit, the former secretary of Muhammad, is one whose name is often associated with views solving the arithmetical complexities of the laws of succession. Since they now wore the mantle of the political, if not the religious, authority of the Prophet, the Caliphs were naturally regarded as eminently qualified judges. But there is no reason to suppose that other close associates of Muḥammad did not fulfil this role, in accordance with the established custom of the parties to a dispute selecting their own arbitrator.

Naturally enough, however, the Caliphs alone had the power of positive legislation, a power implied by the Qur'ānic verse: "Obey God, his prophet and those in charge of your affairs". Such power seems occasionally to have been exercised during the Medinan period by way of a supplement to the Qur'ān—to lay down, for example, the penalty for wine-drinking. This was fixed, apparently, at forty lashes by Abū-Bakr, and later at eighty lashes by ʻUmar and ʻAlī, the latter drawing a rough parallel with the offence of *qadhf* (false accusation of unchastity) for which the Qur'ān had fixed the same penalty. Again, circumstances obviously called for the regulation of matters altogether outside the purview of the Qur'ānic provisions. ʻUmar's fiscal laws have already been mentioned, and the general power of defining offences and the punishment therefor, in the interests of public security, was certainly used. But the precise nature and scope of this legislative activity remains clouded in obscurity.

During the Medinan period, then, the principles of the Qur'ānic legislation were developed by the Prophet and his successors to the degree that was required by the practical problems confronting the Muslim community in Medina. In a spirit of compromise typified by the case of the *Ḥimāriyya*, a population deeply attached to its traditional values had come to terms with the dictates of its new religious faith.

Events now took place which brought about a profound change in the character of Islam. As military conquests produced a growing awareness of political power the immediate force and impact of the distinctive message of Islam began to wane and the old Arab tribal ideas reasserted themselves. After the acknowledgement of Muʿāwiya as Caliph in 661 and the foundation of the Umayyad dynasty, members of the old aristocracy set eagerly about the task of consolidating the vast territorial gains. From their new seat of government at Damascus the Empire builders wielded their political power in the name of Islam; but while the Medinan Caliphs had been the servants of the religion the Umayyads were its masters. Damascus became the centre of an organisation for administering the affairs of the conquered provinces and their populations—the occupying Arab forces no less than the original inhabitants; and this produced a legal development of such broad dimensions that it made the activities of the Medinan period seem parochial in comparison.

The basic policy of the Umayyads, dictated by necessity, was the preservation of the existing administrative structure in the provinces. Umayyad practice thus naturally absorbed many concepts and institutions of foreign origin. The legal status of non-Muslim subjects in Islam was modelled largely on the position of the non-citizen groups in the Eastern Roman empire. By the contract of *dhimma*, which embodied the notion of *fides* in Roman law, the Jewish and Christian communities, or *dhimmīs*, paid a poll tax in return for the guarantee of protection and the preservation of their rights under their own personal law administered by their rabbinical and ecclesiastical tribunals. Although the foundations of this policy were laid earlier, the detailed regulations concerning the *dhimmīs* were the work of the Umayyads.[4] Similarly they elaborated and systematised the tax laws inaugurated by ʿUmar.

One particular administrative office taken over by

the Umayyad regime was that of the Byzantine market inspector, or *agoronomos*. This official, bearing the equivalent Arabic title of *ʿāmil as-sūq*, possessed limited powers of jurisdiction concerning such things as weights and measures used in the market and petty offences committed there. At a later stage he was entrusted with the peculiarly Islamic function of *ḥisba*, or the duty of safeguarding the proper standards of religious morality. Accordingly he now took the title of *muḥtasib*, but still retained the market-place jurisdiction as a legacy of his historical origin.

Such adoption of existing administrative machinery naturally opened the door to a wider reception of foreign elements in the substantive law proper. Because of the lack of contemporary sources the precise measure of this influence cannot be known, but it must have been considerable. It extended from details of legal terminology—for example, the term *tadlīs*, with the root consonants *DLS* and meaning the fraudulent concealment of defects in merchandise, is an Arabicized form of the Byzantine Greek *DoLoS*—to that important part of property law known as *waqf*, that is, religious trust or charitable settlement; for this institution stemmed largely from the Byzantine system of *piae causae*. Over the whole of the Umayyad period standards and norms of foreign law (Sasanian Persian as well as Roman law) gradually infiltrated into legal practice, so that Muslim jurisprudence in the mid-eighth century could take them for granted when conscious knowledge of their origin had been lost.

Among the army of officials created by the Umayyad administration was the *qāḍī*, a judge of a special kind. Like all other officials he was the delegate of the local governor and had the particular task of settling disputes; administrative efficiency could no longer tolerate the old system of *ad hoc* arbitrators. But at first this judicial function is a subordinate, almost a merely incidental, part of administrative work.[5] In the early days we find the chief of police and the Master of the Treasury acting as *qāḍīs*. In A.D. 717 the Egyptian *qāḍī* ʿIyāḍ was also the official in charge of the granary. Not until towards the end of the Umayyad period, it would appear, were *qāḍīs* exclusively concerned with judicial business. And with the loss of their character as jacks-of-all-trades the first traces of a professional pride appear. Khayr ibn-Nuʿaym, after a term of office as *qāḍī* of Egypt, was appointed to the Records Office. On being appointed *qāḍī* for a second term he refused to adjudicate a suit brought by the governor ʿAbd-al-Mālik ibn-Marwān, and this provoked from the latter the comment: "Perhaps you are angry with us for making you a scribe after you had been a *qāḍī*". This same *qāḍī* refused to continue in office when the governor intervened to set free a soldier whom the judge had imprisoned while awaiting further evidence that he had committed slander. Khayr ibn-Nuʿaym also held the office of *qāṣṣ*, or instructor on religious precepts and precedents. This was often a joint appointment with that of *qāḍī*, and the redoubtable Khayr seems to have considered it a fit and proper task for a judge.

As subordinate officials the *qāḍīs* were, of course, bound by the orders of the political authority. But such directives as were issued to them were of an essentially administrative nature. Thus Muʿāwiya, while effective governor of Egypt in 657, ordered that the compensation due in cases of wounding and assault should be recovered by the pay-roll officer making the necessary deductions from the stipends of the offender's tribe in instalments spread over three years. In addition there are several recorded instances of judges seeking and receiving the advice of their political superiors on points of law. But the Umayyad Caliphs and governors seem to have been generally content to leave such matters to their *qāḍīs*. As a result the general uniformity that prevailed in the sphere of public law (e.g. fiscal law and the treatment of the non-Muslim communities), which was the subject of regulation from the central government, was matched by a corresponding diversity in private law.

There were two principal reasons for this diversity. Firstly, the basic feature of the *qāḍī*'s work was the application of the local law and this varied considerably throughout the territories of Islam. Society in Medina, for instance, remained faithful to the traditional concepts of Arabian tribal law under which the arranging of marriage alliances was the prerogative of the male members of the family. No woman, therefore, could contract a marriage on her own account but had to be given in marriage by her guardian. In Kūfa, on the other hand, a town in Iraq which had started as a military encampment, the admixture of diverse ethnic groups in a predominantly Persian milieu produced a cosmopolitan atmosphere to which the standards of a closely knit tribal society were alien. Woman occupied a less inferior position and in particular had the right to conclude her own marriage contract without the intervention of her guardian.[6]

The second reason behind the diversity in Umayyad legal practice was the simple fact that the power of the individual judge to decide according to his own personal opinion (*ra'y*) was to all intents and purposes unrestricted. No real unifying influence was exerted by the central government and there was no hierarchy of superior courts whose binding precedents might have established the uniformity of a case law system. Nor can it be said that the Qur'ānic laws provided a strong unifying element. Apart from their limited scope, whether or not the Qur'ānic norms were applied at all depended simply upon the degree of knowledge and piety possessed by the individual judge. But even for the pious *qāḍīs* the interpretation of the Qur'ānic provisions was largely a matter of personal discretion, so that, apart from the simple and basic rules, their application often added to rather than subtracted from the prevailing diversity in legal practice. Two examples from the laws of marriage and divorce will illustrate this.

The first case arises from uncertainty in the text of the Qur'ān itself. One of the variant readings which had existed in early days concerned the rights of a finally repudiated wife during her *'idda* or "waiting period". While the official text of the Qur'ān (lxv. 6), addressed to husbands, reads: "Lodge them where you lodge according to your circumstances", the text transmitted by Ibn-Mas'ūd, an eminent companion of the Prophet who had lived in Kūfa, contained the additional words: "Lodge them where you lodge *and bear their expenses* ..."[7] Accordingly the practice in Kūfa was to allow such a repudiated wife full maintenance during her *'idda* period, while elsewhere she had the bare right to the shelter of the husband's roof.

Our second example illustrates the diversity of opinion which obtained, even among the judiciary of one particular locality, on the question of the precise legal implications of a general moral injunction of the Qur'ān. Verses of the Qur'ān (ii. 236, 241) urge husbands to make "a fair provision" for wives they have repudiated. Ibn-Ḥujayra, *qāḍī* of Egypt 688–702, considered such provision, which came to be called *mut'a*, to be obligatory. He fixed the amount at three *dīnārs* and arranged for its recovery by ordering the pay-roll official to make the necessary deduction from the husband's stipend. On the other hand, a later *qāḍī*, Tawba ibn-Namir, opined that the Qur'ānic injunction was directed only to the husband's conscience. When a husband refused his request to provide a *mut'a* for his repudiated wife, Tawba "fell silent, for he did not consider that it was legally binding upon the husband"; although in a later case, where this same husband appeared as a witness, Tawba refused to accept his testimony, on the ground that he was not to be numbered "among the virtuous and the pious". Under Tawba's successor, Khayr ibn-Nu'aym, *mut'a* once again became a strict legal obligation.

A typical picture of the activities of the later Umayyad judges is provided by al-Kindī's account of Tawba ibn-Namir's term of office in Egypt (733–737). It is the picture of a hard-working official (who forbade his wife, under pain of divorce, to talk of judicial business during his leisure hours) faced with a great variety of law suits and generally enjoying a discretion bounded only by the dictates of common sense. Although the normal standard of legal proof was two witnesses, Tawba would accept the evidence of one witness coupled with the oath of the plaintiff as to the truth of his claim in "trifling matters". He rejected the evidence of witnesses whom he considered biased because of inter-tribal enmity between the parties, or of those persons whose conduct he regarded as morally blameworthy—as we have just seen in the case of the husband who refused to pay *mut'a*. The absence of any rigidity in the law allowed Tawba to deal with each case on its individual merits. When the plaintiffs sought his permission to sell a *mukātab* slave (one who has contracted to purchase his freedom by instalments) on the ground that the slave had defaulted in his payments, Tawba was prepared to grant the slave one year's grace to make up the arrears. Only when the slave expressed his doubts as to his ability to keep up future payments and declared himself willing to be sold at once did Tawba authorise the sale. With a similarly unfettered discretion Tawba dismissed an action brought by slave dealers to rescind the purchase of slaves on the ground that the vendors had failed to disclose hidden defects in the slaves. "If you yourselves are selling", Tawba addressed them, "you are silent about faults, but when you have bought a faulty slave you wish to return him to the vendor. You are all the same." These two decisions embody principles which did not survive the later systematisation of the law but which are remarkably parallel to certain notions of Equity introduced into English law in late mediaeval times. From a comparative standpoint it may be said that Islamic equity here preceded Islamic law.

But Tawba's activities were not confined to the settlement of disputes. In 736 he instituted a register of *waqfs*—religious trusts or charitable endowments. Before this such properties had been under the exclusive control of private administrators or the beneficiaries. "I cannot see", said Tawba, "that the ultimate purpose of these charitable gifts is other than the benefit of the poor and needy. I therefore think that I should take charge of *waqfs* to protect their interests." Such initiative naturally enhanced the importance of the *qāḍī*'s office. From the minor and subordinate role of legal secretary to the local governor he was gradually acquiring the prestige of an elevated rank in the hierarchy of public servants.

By the end of the Umayyad period the *qāḍīs* had advanced far from their original position as official arbitrators. They had become an integral and important part of the administrative machine, no longer controlled by, but themselves controlling, the customary law and by their decisions adapting it to meet the changing circumstances of society. An illuminating example of this aspect of their work, although it occurred slightly after the Umayyad period, is provided by a decision of Abū-Khuzayma, *qāḍī* of Egypt 761–769.

The plaintiffs, members of the tribe of Banū 'Abd-Kulāl, were the near kinsmen of a girl who had been contracted in marriage by her paternal uncle. They sought annulment of the marriage on the ground that the husband belonged to a tribe which was inferior to the Banū 'Abd-Kulāl and was therefore not the equal of his wife. Although such inequality of status between spouses was a recognised ground for annulment, Abū-Khuzayma refused to accede to the plaintiffs' demands. "Since the girl was married by her guardian", he declared, "the marriage must stand." The right of marriage guardianship, which had been exercised under the old customary law by the tribe collectively, was now vested in the closest male relative—in this case the paternal uncle who had, by consenting to the union, waived his right to insist upon equality of status. In contemplation of the law the family had now replaced the tribe as the unit of society.

Under the Umayyads, then, the basic material of the local customary law had been modified by the elaboration of the Qur'ānic rules, overlaid by a corpus of administrative regulations and infiltrated by elements of foreign legal systems. The process of growth had been haphazard, the fusion of these heterogeneous materials being largely fortuitous and depending ultimately upon the discretion of the individual judge. Within this complex mass of legal material, produced by administrative officials such as the police and the market inspector as well as the *qāḍīs*, the specifically religious or Qur'ānic element had become largely submerged. Certainly the authorities had demonstrated their concern for the application of the Qur'ānic rules. Yūnus ibn-'Aṭiyya, we are informed, owed his appointment as *qāḍī* of Egypt in 704 to the favourable impression he made on the governor when summoned to court with a group of scholars to discuss the problem of the legal rights of a divorced wife during the *'idda* period. But the sharp focus in which the Qur'ānic laws had been held in the Medinan period was now lost and their image blurred by the expanding horizons of activity.

Few societies in history can have been subject to such swift changes and been so ill-equipped to deal with them as were the Muslim Arabs. That Umayyad legal practice achieved a workable synthesis of the diverse influences at work in the Islamic empire was a real achievement. Under the pressure of events problems had materialised and multiplied too rapidly for systematic thought, and solutions were necessarily based on the demands of immediate expediency. The task of the Umayyads had been to establish a practical system of legal administration, not a science of jurisprudence; and in this they had succeeded.

CHAPTER 3

JURISPRUDENCE IN EMBRYO: THE EARLY SCHOOLS OF LAW

COMMUNITIES, like shopkeepers, have their periods of stocktaking, when the momentum of events slackens to afford a breathing space and the opportunity to review the present position in the light of original aims and objectives. Such a time came for Islam in the early decades of its second century (from A.D. 720 on). Its auditors showed a hypercritical tendency to exaggerate the losses and undervalue the gains, and found the account sadly deficient in the balance.

Politically the process of review resulted in a mounting wave of hostility towards current governmental policy. The Umayyads stood condemned as rulers who, in their thirst for worldly power, had lost sight of the fundamental principles of the religion. Discontent was fostered by the complaints of the Persian and other non-Arab converts (known as *mawālī*) against the racial discriminations of the Arab dominion and was exploited by those whose ambition was to seize power for themselves. The troubled conscience of Islam looked for its salvation in a return to the pious administration of the Medinan Caliphs who now, in contrast to their successors, were seen as "the rightly-guided ones" or *ar-Rāshidūn*.

Legally the same process of review led to the conclusion that the practices of the Umayyad courts had failed properly to implement the spirit of the original laws of Islam propounded in the Qur'ān. Pious scholars began to give voice to their ideas of standards of conduct which would represent the fulfilment of the true Islamic religious ethic. Grouped together for this purpose in loose studious fraternities they formed, in the last decades of Umayyad rule, the early schools of law.

These two streams of anti-Umayyad criticism, political and legal, naturally converged when the Umayyad dynasty was finally overthrown and the 'Abbāsids came to power in A.D. 750. The legal scholars were publicly recognised as the architects of an Islamic scheme of state and society which the 'Abbāsids had pledged themselves to build, and under this political sponsorship the schools of law developed rapidly.

Islamic jurisprudence thus began not as the scientific analysis of the existing practice of courts whose authority was accepted, but as the formulation of a scheme of law in opposition to that practice. The first scholar-jurists were men of religion rather than men of law, concerned, almost exclusively, with the elaboration of the system of ritual practices. Their interest in the field of legal relationships strictly so called was a subsequent development, deriving its major impetus from the political ideals of the 'Abbāsids, and their approach to law, therefore, was initially that of religious idealists. Such an activity of academic speculation contrasted sharply with the pragmatism of Umayyad legal tradition and marked a new point of departure.

Historical circumstances had thus produced a distinction between the legal doctrine expounded by the scholars and the legal practice of the courts. Under the early 'Abbāsids a large measure of integration of the two elements was achieved. Representatives of the schools of law were appointed to the judiciary and employed by the government as legal advisers. Abū-Yūsuf (d. 799) was an outstanding scholar who filled both these roles. He was appointed chief *qāḍī* by the

Caliph Hārūn (786–809) and composed, at the request of the latter, a treatise on fiscal and penal law. But in later times the rift between doctrine and practice widened and became the central feature of Islamic legal history. In this chapter, however, we are concerned only with the doctrine and its development in the early schools of law.

Of the many schools of law which flourished in the different provinces of Islam at this time those of Medina and Kūfa were to prove the most important and enduring, and to these two schools our attention will be confined. Although legal thought in Kūfa was generally in advance of that in Medina—the result, to some extent, of the fact that Kūfa was the school officially sponsored by the central ʿAbbāsid government—the basic method, and the broad lines of development which ensued, were common to both schools.

The starting-point was the review of local practice, legal and popular, in the light of the principles of conduct enshrined in the Qur'ān. Institutions and activities were individually considered, then approved or rejected according as to whether they measured up to or fell short of these criteria. Thus, one of the methods of paying the troops in Umayyad times was by a kind of cheque which entitled the holder to draw a specified amount of grain from the Government granaries after the harvest. Speculation on the basis of the fluctuating price of grain produced an activity of buying and selling these cheques which was disapproved by the scholars. It fell, they opined, under the general prohibition of usury (*ribā*) contained in the Qur'ān. For the Qur'ānic prohibition of gambling had become merged with the prohibition of *ribā* to give the latter a much wider import than simple usury or interest on capital loans. It was now interpreted to cover any form of profit or gain which was unearned, in the sense that it resulted from chance, and which could not be precisely calculated in advance by the contracting parties. Accordingly, to counteract this speculative traffic in army pay cheques, the legal rule was formulated that a purchaser of foodstuffs could not re-sell before he had taken physical delivery of them. Although confined to foodstuffs in Medina the rule was extended in Kūfa to apply to all moveable goods.

An example of a customary contract which passed the scrutiny of the early scholars was the barter of *'ariyya*, or unripe dates on the palm, against their calculated value in dried dates. Although there is an obvious element of risk and uncertainty in a contract of this kind, it was not of such a degree as to prove objectionable, *qua ribā*, to the early scholars.

From this piecemeal review of existing practice a body of Islamic doctrine was gradually formed in the early schools. It had originated in the personal reasoning, or *ra'y*, of individual scholars, but as time passed its authority was rested on firmer foundations. With the gradual growth of agreement between the scholars of a particular locality the doctrine was expressed as the consensus of opinion in the school. Then, as the consensus remained firmly established over the course of the years, the concept of the *sunna* of the school appeared. *Sunna*, literally "beaten path", had originally meant the actual customary practice, whether of pre-Islamic tribes or of seventh-century Muslims; but in the jurisprudence of the eighth century it had come to bear a different connotation. In the language of the scholars *sunna* was now the ideal doctrine established in the school and expounded by its current representatives. From its very nature it obviously did not coincide with the *sunna* of Umayyad courts.

In the development of jurisprudential method in early 'Abbāsid times two main tendencies emerged.

First, in the interests of consistency and coherence of the doctrine, reasoning became more systematic, and arbitrary opinion, or *ra'y*, gradually gave place to analogical deduction, or *qiyās*. Among the earliest instances of the use of analogy, in a naturally somewhat rudimentary manner, was the fixing of the minimum amount of dower payable by the husband on marriage as ten *dirhams* in Kūfa and three *dirhams* in Medina. A parallel had been drawn between the loss of virginity as a result of marriage and the amputation of the hand as the penalty for theft; for the sums mentioned were the value which the stolen goods had to reach, in Medinan and Kufan doctrine respectively, before the penalty of amputation was applicable.

Practical considerations, however, often necessitated a departure from strict analogical reasoning. Where the jurists made equitable concessions or preferred some other criterion to analogy—as, for instance, the criterion of the public interest in the rule that the joint perpetrators of a homicide could all be put to death in retaliation for the life of their single victim—this was called *istiḥsān* or "preference". It represented a return to the freedom of *ra'y*, and in fact the two terms were at first used synonymously. But *istiḥsān* represents a more advanced stage in the development of legal thought since it presupposes as normal the method of reasoning by analogy.

The second trend in early jurisprudence was a growing emphasis on the notion of *sunna* or established doctrine. In order to consolidate the idea of tradition the doctrine was represented as having roots stretching back into the past, and the authority of previous generations was claimed for its current expression. Although such authority was at first anonymous, increasing formalism soon attached the specific names of former pious personages to the doctrine. It was projected backwards through intermediate links to the early generations of Muslims. 'Umar, for example, was frequently represented as the originator of Medinan *sunna*, and Ibn-Mas'ūd held a similar position in Kūfa. Eventually and inevitably the process ended in claiming the authority of the Prophet himself for the doctrine. Although there was involved in this process a certain amount of material which had genuinely originated in the early days of Islam, and which Umayyad legal practice or oral tradition had preserved, the great mass of the alleged doctrines of the ancients were anachronistic ascriptions. Legal as well as political aspirations now sought to revive the pristine purity of Islam in the Medinan period. In cutting right through the Umayyad period and representing the doctrine as having its roots in the earliest days, the jurists forged a link of continuity with the time of the "rightly-guided" rulers.

It was at this stage, *circa* A.D. 770, that opposition to the generally accepted legal method in the early schools materialised. Its distinguishing feature was a rigidly doctrinaire attitude both in regard to the substance of the law and the jurisprudential basis on which it rested. While the majority of the scholars were prepared to accept current legal practice into their scheme of law unless an explicit principle of the Qur'ān was thereby flagrantly violated, the doctrinaire group advocated a much stricter and a much more meticulous adherence to the Qur'ānic norms. Their rigid interpretation, for example, of *ribā* resulted in the rule that the barter of certain commodities—gold, silver and staple foodstuffs—against a commodity of the same species was only permissible when the offerings on both sides were exactly equal in weight or quantity and when delivery on both sides was immediate. Early Medinan doctrine had allowed the exchange of gold ore against a smaller weight of gold coinage, the difference covering the cost of minting. But to the doctrinaire group this constituted *ribā* and was therefore prohibited. This approach naturally resulted in the law of the doctrinaire group assuming a highly negative character, in essence if not in form, to the degree that it lost touch with practical needs and circumstances. It is difficult to see any point or purpose in a transaction where 'Umar takes 20 lb. of Zayd's wheat in exchange for 20 lb. of his own wheat in the same session.

But it was in the matter of the juristic basis of the law that the conflict between the majority and the doctrinaire group was most clearly defined. Pursuing to its systematic conclusion the tendency in the early schools to project the *sunna* backwards into the past, the opposition movement saw the precedents of the Prophet himself as the supreme and overriding authority for law. The logical appeal of this thesis was undeniable, and in the desire to establish it many rulings and decisions were falsely ascribed to the Prophet. These are contained in stories or reports of what Muḥammad said or did on a particular occasion, which are usually known in English as "Traditions" (this technical sense being distinguished by a capital in the present work) and in Arabic as *ḥadīth*, *akhbār*, etc. Those who put into circulation such reports, however, should not be regarded as malicious forgers. Rather, in the *bona fide* belief that their doctrine expressed the correct Islamic standard, they were convinced that the Prophet would so have acted had he been faced with the relevant problem. From this it was a short step to asserting that he had in fact so acted, and affixing to the Tradition a formal chain (known as the *isnād*) of authorities, who had supposedly transmitted the report from Muḥammad through succeeding generations to the present time. Thus, while certain of the legal Traditions may preserve the substance of the actions and words of Muḥammad, particularly in non-controversial matters, this genuine core became overlaid by a mass of fictitious material. It should finally be stressed that there was no suggestion, at this stage, that the Prophet was other than a human interpreter of the divine revelation; his authority lay in the fact that he was closest, in time and spirit, to the Qur'ān and as such was the ultimate starting-point of the Islamic *sunna*.

Under the influence of the doctrinaire opposition the current doctrine in the early schools was gradually modified. Many of the stricter rules advocated by the opposition—such as those concerned with *ribā*—won a general acceptance, and there was a growing tendency to claim the authority of the Prophet for the doctrine and to express it in the form of Traditions. But though this brought an increasing awareness of the potential conflict of principle between the authority of Muḥammad and the contemporary consensus of opinion among the local scholars, no attempt was as yet made to resolve this conflict in a systematic manner. In the jurisprudence of the years 770–800 the reasoning of individual scholars, local consensus and the reported precedents of Muḥammad lay in uneasy juxtaposition. This stage of legal development is mirrored in the first written compendium of law produced in Islam—the *Muwaṭṭa'* of the Medinan scholar Mālik ibn-Anas (d. 796). Three examples from this important text, all taken from the section on contracts, provide evidence of the influences and the trends in jurisprudence to which we have alluded.

Mālik recognises the general prohibition against *muzābana* contracts—the barter of unripe fruits on the tree against the same species of dried fruits—but at the same time recognises the validity of the barter of *'ariyya*, or unripe dates on the palm, against dried dates. Both these conflicting rules are expressed in the form of Traditions from the Prophet. The evidence of the *isnāds* shows that the general prohibition of *muzābana* was the first rule to be expressed as a precedent of Muḥammad.[8] We conclude, therefore, that the prohibition of *muzābana* contracts resulted from the stringent interpretation of *ribā* adopted by the doctrinaire group. Medinan doctrine came to accept this rule but qualified it by admitting the particular barter of unripe dates which had long been established practice in Medina and which was now also expressed in the form of a Tradition. In this Tradition the transaction is described as a "special dispensation" (*rukhṣa*) and Mālik attempts to explain it on this basis by arguing that the barter of unripe dates is a transaction which has its own peculiar legal incidents and, as such, is to be numbered amongst other exceptions to general rules which exist in the law of contracts. Later doctrine sought to explain the anomaly more satisfactorily by restricting the transaction to the case where the owner of a palm tree takes unripe dates from the person who has the usufructuary right to the date crop. This is justified by the immediate needs of the owner of the crop for edible dates and the interests of the owner of the tree in ridding himself of the intrusions of others on to his land. But there is no reason to suppose that the transaction allowed by the early Medinan scholars, including Mālik, was of such a particular and restricted form. The *Muwaṭṭa'* here simply reflects the stage of a rough and uneasy compromise between the comparatively liberal and practical outlook of the earliest scholars and the rigid approach of the doctrinaire group.

Mālik's invariable practice is to begin his discussion of a legal topic by quoting relevant Traditions or precedents. On a particular problem involved in the sale of slaves he first quotes an alleged statement of ʿUmar. "If a slave who has property is sold, the property of the slave belongs to the seller unless the buyer stipulates that it shall belong to him." Mālik then states that "the rule upon which we are all agreed in Medina" is that such a stipulation by the buyer is valid and effective, of whatever nature and value the property of the slave may be, and whether its precise amount is known or unknown. This is so, he says, "because a master does not pay . . . taxes on his slave's property; if a slave has a slave girl, his sexual relations with her are permissible by virtue of his owning her; a slave who is set free . . . takes his property with him; and if a slave becomes bankrupt his creditors take his property but have no recourse against the slave's master for any part of his debts."

Medinan doctrine, then, as Mālik is at some pains to show by these four illustrations, was that the legal ownership of a slave's property vested in the slave himself and not in his master. And it is on this basis that the slave's property may be validly transferred, along with the slave himself in the same transaction, to the buyer. For if the master were the true owner of the slave's property, a transfer of the slave and his property for one lump price would infringe one of the basic principles of sale of which Mālik was fully aware and which he accepted, namely, that where two or more distinct articles are the objects of a single sale, the price of each should be individually known and determined, otherwise the transaction is void for uncertainty (*gharar*). Kufan doctrine, holding that a slave was incapable of ownership, regarded the slave and his property as two distinct articles belonging to the master, and therefore did not admit the transfer of both for one price unapportioned between the two. For Mālik, on the other hand, the slave and his property naturally form one sale-object which can be validly transferred for one price if such is the intention of the parties. But if this intention is not made manifest by the appropriate stipulation the seller of the slave will be presumed to have exercised his power, as master, to appropriate the slave's property for himself.

'Umar's alleged dictum, therefore, presupposes both the recognition of the precise nature of the slave's capacity to own property and the application of the doctrine of uncertainty to composite sales, this last being part of the increasingly strict interpretation of *ribā* previously described. As such, the rule must be of relatively late origin; it was not the starting-point of Medinan doctrine but the succinct expression of an advanced stage in its elaboration and development.

"Each of the parties to a contract of sale has the option against the other party as long as they have not separated." This alleged statement of the Prophet expresses the doctrine known as *khiyār al-majlis*, which gives the parties to a contract, duly completed by offer and acceptance, the right to repudiate the agreement during the session (*majlis*) of the bargain. Having quoted the Tradition, Mālik comments: "Here in Medina we have no such known limit and no established practice for this", and the points he then proceeds to discuss show that for Mālik a contract was binding as well as complete immediately mutual agreement had been reached. This is one of the many occasions on which the law expressed in the reported precedents of the Prophet or later authorities was rejected by the early Medinan scholars when it ran counter to their currently accepted doctrine.

The *Muwaṭṭa'*, then, was written at a time when the concern to ascertain the basis of the authority of the law had led to its growing expression, both by the majority of the scholars as well as the opposition group, as precedents established by the early Islamic authorities and by the Prophet himself. Mālik's chosen method of composing his treatise was first to report such precedents as were known, and then to consider them, interpret them, and accept them or otherwise in the light of his own reasoning and the legal tradition of Medina. His supreme criterion was the local consensus of opinion, and there was nothing so sacrosanct about Traditions from the Prophet or other precedents that enabled them to override this authority in cases of conflict. The *Muwaṭṭa'* is essentially a manual of the doctrine currently endorsed by "the Establishment" in Medina.

Before leaving the *Muwaṭṭa'* we may finally remark upon the close connection between the development of the law and its literary expression. The *Muwaṭṭa'* is divided into "books", based on the major divisions of the law, on marriage, contracts, penal law, etc.; but each book consists of a seemingly haphazard and disjointed collection of individual topics and rules. Law was thus recorded exactly as it had grown up, through the piecemeal review of particular aspects of Umayyad legal practice. Later literature, although certainly dealing with each topic in more logical sequence, preserved the fragmentary form of the *Muwaṭṭa'*. Islamic legal treatises do not first expound general principles and follow them with their detailed applications, but consist of a succession of separate and isolated topics. Such a legal method naturally produced its own legal concepts. There is, for example, no notion of Contract, in the English sense, where general principles governing agreement are applied to the manifold forms such agreement may assume: instead there is a law of contracts, on the Roman pattern, in which individual types of transactions are each governed by their own particular rules. In fact the whole technique of law in Islam was, until modern times, profoundly influenced by the methodology of its originators in the eighth century.

Although the legal method in Kūfa and Medina was basically the same, the systems of law which the two schools created from it differed to no small degree.

Their common ground lay in the explicit provisions of the Qur'ān and in such precedents of the Prophet and the early Caliphs as had been preserved in Umayyad legal practice; and to a great extent the implications which the two schools drew from this basic material were the same. But outside this restricted field the freedom of personal reason enjoyed by the scholars inevitably produced different results, certain of which have already been noted. In particular, legal thought was naturally influenced by prevailing local conditions, and many of the differences between Medinan and Kufan doctrine are explained, as the following examples will show, by the different societies of the two centres.

Although the schemes of inheritance adopted by both schools shared the same fundamental rules, in so far as this subject had been regulated in some detail by the Qur'ān, the precedents of the Prophet and those of his immediate successors, there arose significant differences on points which had not been so settled. Where no Qur'ānic heir or agnate relative (*'aṣaba*) had survived the propositus, the Kufan jurists admitted non-agnate relatives (e.g. daughters' and sisters' children) to succession. Such relatives (known as *dhawū 'l-arḥām*) were never allowed to inherit in Medina. Both these views may be said to be reasonable interpretations of the Qur'ān, the Medinan view resting on the fact that such relatives were not specifically granted rights of succession by the Qur'ān, and the Kufan view on the fact that, by recognising the rights of women relatives, the Qur'ān implied the rights of relatives connected with the propositus through them. But it was the natural tendency in the patrilineal society of Medina to deny such relatives rights of inheritance; while it was equally natural for society in Kūfa to admit their rights. For women enjoyed a higher estimation in the cosmopolitan society of Kūfa, one concrete result of which—their capacity to contract their own marriage—has already been observed. In short, the Qur'ān was interpreted by both schools in the light of existing social circumstances.

Class consciousness in Kūfa, stemming from the variegated nature of its society, where Arab and non-Arab Muslims were in intimate contact, and from the tradition of social stratification in the Sasanian Persian empire, produced the doctrine of marriage equality (*kafā'a*).[9] This doctrine, which required the husband to be the equal of his wife (or her family) in various specified respects, including lineage, financial standing and profession, had no parallel in early Medinan law and is not mentioned at all in Mālik's *Muwaṭṭa'*. Class distinctions were not so keenly felt in the closely knit society of Medina.

Certain variations in the legal systems of the two schools show how the bond of traditional Arabian society—that of blood relationship—no longer had the same importance for the jurists of Kūfa as it had for those of Medina. Both schools recognise the principle of collective responsibility for the payment of compensation in cases of homicide or wounding, and they both call the group which shoulders this burden the *'āqila*. But in Medina this group is made up of the fellow-tribesmen of the offender, while in Kūfa the *'āqila* are those who have a common interest with the offender arising out of profession or simple neighbourhood—the soldiers in the same unit, for example, or the merchants who occupy premises in the same market. Similar considerations account, at least partially, for differences in the rules of pre-emption, or the right to step into the shoes of a purchaser of real property and take the property from the vendor on the agreed terms. The interest of the pre-emptor in the property sold, which grounded the right, could be in Kūfa his own ownership of property adjoining the property sold. In Medina the right of pre-emption did not belong to a neighbour but only to the co-owner, who, under the customary methods of property tenure, would normally be a blood relative of the vendor.

Apart from such differences in the details of the law the whole outlook and attitude of the scholars was conditioned by their respective environments. A conservative attachment to tradition is the hallmark of the early Medinan jurists, while their Kufan colleagues, living in a newly formed society which had no such roots in the past, were animated by a spirit of free enquiry and speculation.

Again, the school of Kūfa was geographically more open to, and mentally more receptive of, the influence of foreign legal systems. Abū-Ḥanīfa (d. 767), in his time the leading authority of Kufan jurisprudence, held that a person could not be subject to interdiction—or control by a guardian over his dealings with his property—after he had reached the age of twenty-five. This was the recognised limit for guardianship of property (*curatio*) under Roman law. The legal status of slaves in Medina reflected their position as accepted members of the family group in Arabian society; *inter alia* they were capable, as we have seen, of owning property. In Kūfa their position was strictly regulated on the basis that, being themselves owned, they could have no rights of ownership; and this systematic attitude stems as much from the influence of Roman law as it does from the rigid class distinctions of Kufan society.

Besides these considerable differences between the legal systems of the two schools, divergent doctrines were held by individual scholars within each school. Two outstanding jurists in Kūfa, for example, Abū-Yūsuf (d. 798) and ash-Shaybānī (d. 804), were not the kindred spirits that their traditional title of "the two companions" might imply; they had, in fact, little in common apart from their pupilage under Abū-Ḥanīfa. Abū-Yūsuf, as chief *qāḍī*, was an eminently practical man who was intimately connected with political circles. Ash-Shaybānī was by inclination an academic lawyer who, although he was a judge for a brief spell, found his true metier in prolific writings expounding his legal doctrine.

The distinct personalities of the two jurists appear in their treatment of the law of *waqf* (charitable endowment), one of the many respects in which their opinions were at variance. Ash-Shaybānī regulates the incidents of *waqf* by drawing systematic parallels with the law of gift. *Waqf*, he argued, is a gift of the corpus of the property to God and of the usufruct thereof to the beneficiaries. Hence his rule that delivery of the property to the administrator is essential for the validity of the *waqf*. Abū-Yūsuf's doctrine, on the other hand, was largely affected by the practical consideration that the creation of *waqfs* should be facilitated and encouraged. To this end he ruled that the mere declaration of the founder, without any delivery, was sufficient to constitute a valid *waqf*; and an even more obvious indication of his attitude lies in his view that the founder may reserve a life interest for himself in the income of the *waqf*.

With the advent of the literary period in law came a change in the constitution of the early schools. Notions of local allegiance were now superseded by the personal authority of the authors of the first legal treatises. The Medinan school became the Mālikī school, and the school of Kūfa the Ḥanafī school; for the faithful pupil ash-Shaybānī attributed the authority for all his writings to his former master Abū-Ḥanīfa. Later generations were to exaggerate the role played by the nominal founders of the two schools. Ash-Shaybānī was the true founder of Ḥanafī law; later doctrine clung to his support, says Sachau,[10] "as ivy entwines the powerful trunk of the oak". Similarly it was Mālik's pupil, Ibn-al-Qāsim, who laid the real systematic foundations of Mālikī law.

Increasing diversity of doctrine, then, is the outstanding feature of legal development in the second half of the eighth century. Local and partisan affiliations had produced a fragmentary scheme of law; several schools—for Medina and Kūfa were but two of many—rivalled each other as the true expression of an Islamic code of conduct, and within each school controversy had given rise to variant opinions and the formation of splinter groups.

As early as 757 Ibn-al-Muqaffa', a secretary of state, had recognised the dangers inherent in such diversity, and had urged the Caliph al-Manṣūr to resolve conflicts by his command and to unify the law by a comprehensive enactment. But the opportunity thus to impose unity in the law from without had been lost, and once the schools of law were firmly established such an approach was no longer feasible. For 'Abbāsid policy had endorsed the idea that the Caliph was the servant of the law, not its master; legal authority was vested in the scholar-jurists and not in the political ruler. Furthermore, conflicts of principle had now become too fundamental to admit of any such peremptory solution. The issue between "the Establishment" in the early schools and the doctrinaire opposition had crystallised in a conflict between those who maintained the right of jurists to reason for themselves (*ahl ar-ra'y*) and those who advocated the exclusive authority of precedents from the Prophet (*ahl al-ḥadīth*, Traditionists).

Clearly some unifying process was necessary to save the law from total disintegration. Equally clearly the impetus for such a process had to come from within the law itself and its qualified exponents. The hour produced the man—in the person of Muḥammad ibn-Idrīs ash-Shāfi'ī.

CHAPTER 4

MASTER ARCHITECT: MUḤAMMAD IBN-IDRĪS ASH-SHĀFIʻĪ

BORN in A.D. 767 ash-Shāfiʻī at first played the role of a critical spectator rather than an active participant in the evolving drama of Islamic law. From his periods of study and deliberation in the principal centres of jurisprudence—Mecca, Medina, Iraq and Syria—he had acquired an intimate knowledge of all the leading protagonists, but he refused to ally himself with any one cause. Standing aloof from local and particular allegiances he was able to comprehend the whole complex panoramic scene with a breadth of outlook and depth of perception that produced an altogether new dimension in legal thought. He eventually appears on the stage as the *deus ex machina* of his time, who seeks to unravel the tangled threads of multiple controversies and propound a solution to create order out of existing chaos.

In the field of technical legal method generally ash-Shāfiʻī consolidated and improved upon the advances achieved by his older contemporary ash-Shaybānī, the outstanding jurist of Kūfa. Prior to this time the process of "Islamicising" the law—the moral evaluation of acts and relationships in the light of the religious standards—had fully occupied the attentions of the scholars. An apt illustration of the more advanced and more technically legal approach of ash-Shāfiʻī is provided by his treatment of a group of alleged statements of the Prophet which censure interference by a third party when a contract is in the course of negotiation—for example, "Let no one sell to a person what he has already agreed to sell to another".

The scholars of the early schools had simply declared such interference to be prohibited without attempting to consider its specifically legal implications. Ash-Shāfi'ī, on the other hand, reduces the problem to terms of the material damage such conduct might cause to the contracting parties. Before mutual agreement has been reached, he argued, no legal damage can result because no legal obligations have been created. Equally, no damage can result once the contract is binding; for "if a man purchases a suit of cloth for ten *dīnārs* and the contract is binding, no damage accrues to the first vendor if a third party offers to sell to the purchaser (a similar suit) for nine *dīnārs*, because the contract for ten *dīnārs* is binding and cannot be repudiated". Such interference, therefore, reasoned ash-Shāfi'ī, was only prohibited in the period between the completion of the contract and its becoming binding—i.e. during the session (*majlis*), when both parties had the right to repudiate a concluded agreement; for inducement so to repudiate, as where a third party offers the same commodity at a cheaper price, might cause loss to the original vendor should he be unable to find another purchaser, and loss to the original purchaser if the second sale did not materialise.[11]

Such reasoning has, of course, its obvious deficiencies in comparison with later standards. Inducement to break a binding contract can certainly result in damage—for example, to confine ourselves to the limited instance given by ash-Shāfi'ī, where the purchaser in breach proves bankrupt. Moreover, ash-Shāfi'ī wholly ignored the question of the precise legal remedies available to the frustrated party. Nevertheless his approach represents a considerable step forward in legal reasoning. A structure of law properly so called was beginning to arise upon the foundations of the essentially ethical standards of conduct which had been formulated by the early schools.

Ash-Shāfi'ī's influence upon the substance of the law, however, fades into comparative insignificance beside his impact in the realm of jurisprudential method. Here, the grandeur of the role he assumed and the force of intellect he brought to bear upon its implementation mark him out as the colossus of Islamic legal history. His supreme purpose was the unification of the law, his method of neutralising the forces of disintegration the exposition of a firm theory of the sources from which law must be derived. The *Risāla*, composed in Cairo where he spent the last five years before his death in 820, contains the matured essence of ash-Shāfi'ī's legal theory. From the brief analysis which follows it will be seen to be drawn in simple, yet bold and uncompromising, lines. It was an innovation whose genius lay not in the introduction of any entirely original concepts, but in giving existing ideas a novel connotation and emphasis and welding them together within a systematic scheme.

According to ash-Shāfi'ī there are four major sources or roots (*uṣūl*) of law. The first of these is naturally the Qur'ān. But, while there had never been any dispute about the binding force of its legal rules, the Qur'ān had, argued ash-Shāfi'ī, a deeper significance as the primary source of law than his predecessors had recognised. For the Qur'ān, apart from its substantive provisions, also indicated the means by which this limited material was to be interpreted and supplemented. In particular, the repeated command to "obey God and his Prophet" established the precedents of Muḥammad as a source of law second only to the word of God himself.

Ash-Shāfi'ī's emphasis upon the authority of the Prophet as a lawgiver is the mainstay and the dominating theme of his doctrine. But here he did not simply reassert the thesis of the doctrinaire opposition (*ahl al-ḥadīth*, or party of Tradition) in the early schools. For them the authority of the Prophet had been that of the person best qualified to interpret the Qur'ān, a *primus inter pares* but none the less a human interpreter;[12] and it was for this reason that scholars like Mālik had felt free to reject the Prophet's rulings on the ground that their intrinsic merits were outweighed by other juristic considerations, *inter alia* the fact that they were not in accordance with the terms of the Qur'ān.[13] Ash-Shāfi'ī, however, adduced a further and decisive argument. Expounding, for the first time consistently, a notion which before him had been but vaguely mooted, he insisted that the Prophet's legal decisions were divinely inspired. For ash-Shāfi'ī this was the inescapable significance of the Qur'ānic command to obey God and his Prophet and the similar injunction to follow "the Book and the Wisdom (*ḥikma*)"; for this last term could mean only the actions of Muḥammad. The recognition of the Traditions (*ḥadīth*, precedents of the Prophet) as a source of the divine will complementary to the Qur'ān is the supreme contribution of ash-Shāfi'ī to Islamic jurisprudence. His arguments proved irrefutable, and once they were accepted Traditions could no longer be rejected by objective criticism of their content; their authority was binding unless the authenticity of the report itself could be denied.

Sunna, therefore—in the sense of the divinely inspired behaviour of Muḥammad—is the second source of law in ash-Shāfi'ī's scheme. In the early schools, as we have seen, *sunna* had signified essentially the local tradition of the individual school. By replacing this concept of a tradition, which had, for Islam as a whole, a multiplicity of starting points, with that of a tradition which stemmed from one single origin—the actions of Muḥammad—ash-Shāfiʿī aspired to eradicate a root cause of diversity between the several centres and instil uniformity into the doctrine. In short, he argued, there could be only one genuine Islamic "tradition". And yet ash-Shāfiʿī was not propounding any completely novel idea. There had been a growing tendency for the early schools, through the projection backwards of the doctrine, loosely to represent their *sunna* as rooted in the practice of the Prophet. Ash-Shāfiʿī exploited this tendency, confirming its correctness as a matter of principle by his thesis of the divine nature of the Prophet's authority, and arguing, as a matter of form, that the Prophet's practice could be properly ascertained and established only by a Tradition. His doctrine thus achieves a subtle synthesis of the apparently contradictory attitudes of "the Establishment" in the early schools and the opposition groups.

Although nominally the *sunna* (or practice of Muḥammad) was for ash-Shāfiʿī the second source of law, in fact it was bound to assume a primary importance. The Qur'ān was to be interpreted in the light of the *sunna*, and since the function of the *sunna* was to provide an explanatory commentary on the Qur'ān it was naturally vested with a superseding authority. Ash-Shāfiʿī's insistence upon this overriding role of the *sunna* of Muḥammad, and his outright rejection of any arguments which tended to jeopardise it, can best be seen in his approach to the question of apparent contradictions in the substance of the divine revelation.

By ash-Shāfiʿī's time the fictitious ascription of decisions to the Prophet had produced a considerable conflict between the terms of individual Traditions. Primarily concerned as he was to establish uniformity of doctrine, ash-Shāfiʿī devoted much of his energy to the resolution of such conflict. His first principle was to attempt to reconcile the terms of the conflicting Traditions, on the ground, for example, that one represented a particular exception to a general rule propounded in the other. Failing this, one Tradition could be preferred because it had a stronger chain of authority. Finally, all other things being equal, ash-Shāfi'ī resorted to the assumption of the repeal or abrogation (*naskh*) of the earlier rule by the later one.

As applied to conflicts between the Qur'ān and the Traditions, ash-Shāfi'ī's doctrine of abrogation is based on the rule that the Qur'ān can only be abrogated by the Qur'ān and the *sunna* only by the *sunna*. The *sunna* cannot abrogate the Qur'ān because its function is to interpret the Qur'ān, not to contradict it. Equally the Qur'ān cannot abrogate the *sunna* because to recognise this possibility would be to nullify the explanatory role of the *sunna*. If a prior precedent of the Prophet was in fact contradicted by a later Qur'ānic revelation, then, argued ash-Shāfi'ī, there would certainly exist a further *sunna* in conformity with this later revelation.

An illustration of this relationship between the twin sources of the divine will, as expounded by ash-Shāfi'ī, is provided by a problem concerning bequests. Three texts are involved: the Qur'ānic verse which commands the making of bequests in favour of near relatives, the Qur'ānic verses which allot specific portions of the estate (*farā'iḍ*) to relatives, and the Tradition in which the Prophet states: "No bequest in favour of an heir". The obvious conflict between the verse of the bequests and the Tradition cannot be resolved by assuming that either one directly abrogates the other. The Tradition explains the "*farā'iḍ* verses" by ordaining that the balance established by them between the claims of different relatives must not be disturbed by an additional bequest to any one of their number—and therefore indicates that the system of specific portions had abrogated the verse of bequests, at least as far as those relatives who were actually entitled to specific portions were concerned.

The rule that the *sunna* cannot be abrogated by the Qur'ān embodies the essence of ash-Shāfiʿī's position. To admit that the *sunna* could be so abrogated would be to acknowledge, in an even stronger form, the principle of the earlier scholars which it was ash-Shāfiʿī's aim to eradicate—namely, that the authority of Traditions could be challenged on the ground that they contradicted the spirit of the Qur'ān.

Ijmāʿ, or consensus, is ash-Shāfiʿī's third source of law. Again he takes up an existing notion and gives it a new connotation designed to achieve uniformity in the law. Denying that the agreement of the scholars of a particular locality had any authority, he argues that there could be only one valid consensus—that of the entire Muslim community, lawyers and lay members alike. Obviously ash-Shāfiʿī did not regard such consensus as in any way an important source of law; its scope was in fact restricted to matters which, like the performance of the daily prayer, affected each and every Muslim personally. While ash-Shāfiʿī admitted that, in theory, the Muslim community as a whole could never agree upon anything contrary to the Qur'ān or the *sunna*, he also realised that the formation or ascertainment of such an agreement had ceased to be practical once Islam had spread outside the boundaries of Medina. His doctrine on this point is therefore essentially negative, designed to the end of rejecting the authority of a local or limited consensus and thus eliminating the diversity of law which resulted therefrom.

The fourth and final source of law for ash-Shāfiʿī is reasoning by analogy, or *qiyās*. In its widest sense, the use of human reason in the elaboration of the law was termed *ijtihād* ("effort" or "exercise" *sc.* of one's own judgement), and covered a variety of mental processes, ranging from the interpretation of texts to the assessment of the authenticity of Traditions. *Qiyās* or analogical reasoning, then, is a particular form of *ijtihād*, the method by which the principles established by the Qur'ān, *sunna*, and consensus are to be extended and applied to the solution of problems not expressly regulated therein. The role of juristic reasoning is thus completely subordinate to the dictates of divine revelation. Analogical deduction must have its starting-point in a principle of the Qur'ān, *sunna*, or consensus, and cannot be used to achieve a result which contradicts a rule established by any of these three primary material sources.

Although ash-Shāfiʿī's predecessors were well acquainted with analogical reasoning, they had also employed more arbitrary forms of reasoning called *ra'y* ("juristic speculation") and, in more advanced terminology, *istiḥsān* ("juristic preference"). This inevitably produced a variety of doctrines. By repudiating these undisciplined forms of reasoning and insisting on the exclusive validity of strictly regulated analogical reasoning ash-Shāfiʿī is again systematically pursuing his goal of uniformity. Differences of opinion might still result, but would be cut to a minimum. Ash-Shāfiʿī recognises this in a statement which will serve as a concise summary of his legal theory and of the purpose which inspired it. "On points on which there exists an explicit decision of God or a *sunna* of the Prophet or a consensus of the Muslims, no disagreement is allowed; on the other points scholars must exert their own judgement in search of an indication in one of these three sources. . . . If a problem is capable of two solutions, either opinion may be held as a result of systematic reasoning; but this occurs only rarely."[14]

Islamic legal scholarship has adequately recognised

ash-Shāfiʿī's role as the father of Muslim jurisprudence. Indeed his position in the science of Sharīʿa law has been compared to that of Aristotle in the realm of philosophy. Yet, as we have attempted to show, ash-Shāfiʿī's genius did not lie in the introduction of any completely novel concepts, but in giving existing ideas a new orientation, emphasis and balance, and in forging them together, for the first time, into a systematic scheme of the "roots" of law. Seeking to suppress the process of disintegration in current jurisprudence, his theory set the authority of law on a much higher plane by transforming the local and limited elements in the jurisprudence of the early schools into concepts of an application and validity universal for Islam. At the same time ash-Shāfiʿī's scheme embodied a compromise between divine revelation and human reason in law and thus endeavoured to reconcile the basic conflict of principle in the early schools between the "party of Tradition" (*ahl al-ḥadīth*) and the "party of reasoning" (*ahl al-raʾy*). It was a legal theory which expressed, with irrefutable logic, the innate aspirations of Muslim jurisprudence. Expounded with an extraordinary force of persistence and singleness of purpose, it was assured of success. Future jurisprudence, as we shall see, considerably modified ash-Shāfiʿī's ideas of the relationship between the component parts of his theory; but his fundamental thesis—that the terms of the divine will were more precisely indicated than had hitherto been recognised, that the supreme manifestation of God's will lay in the *sunna* or practice of Muḥammad, and that the function of human reason in law was subsidiary and complementary—was never after him seriously challenged. In ash-Shāfiʿī's work lies a confluence of the different streams of activity in early Muslim jurisprudence; now harnessed together they flowed inexorably forward along the channel he had defined.

CHAPTER 5

CONCLUDING STAGES OF GROWTH

IN the century which followed the death of ash-Shāfiʿī the *sunna* of the Prophet became the focal point of attention and legal development was conditioned, almost exclusively, by the reaction of the scholars to this central pillar of ash-Shāfiʿī's teaching. Measured by the standard of ash-Shāfiʿī's own views, initial reactions varied from lukewarm acceptance to over-zealous support. But none rejected ash-Shāfiʿī's doctrine outright—or if they did, contemporary literature did not see fit to transmit their names to posterity—and by the year 900 Muslim jurisprudence as a whole had succeeded in absorbing the master's teaching in a generally acceptable form.

The outstanding feature of this period is the growth of a separate science of Traditions with a literature of its own. Specialist scholars devoted themselves to the process of collecting, documenting and classifying Traditions. They were not jurists in the full sense of the term but rather law reporters, who provided the raw material which it was the task of the lawyers then to evaluate and integrate within the wider scheme of jurisprudence.

Voyages of discovery in search of Prophetic precedents unearthed a vast bulk of material. Muslim scholarship was intensely conscious of the possibility of fabrication; but now that Muḥammad's decisions were recognised as divinely inspired, the substance itself of a Tradition could no more be challenged by objective criticism than the text of the Qur'ān itself. Only the chain of transmission (*isnād*) of the report could be questioned, and it was, accordingly, on this basis that the intricate structure of rules for assessing the authority of Traditions was built.

Reliability of Traditions was thus formally determined by the recognised criteria governing the validity of evidence given in the courts. For the testimony of a witness to be acceptable he had to possess the quality of moral integrity (*'adāla*), and legal doctrine had already evinced an increasing strictness in this record. An Egyptian *qāḍī*, for example, *circa* A.D. 795, had refused to accept the testimony of a person, who had been previously renowned for his moral integrity, because he had excitedly applauded the performance of a singing girl. But such rigorous standards could not always govern the acceptance or otherwise of Traditions. A witness, and consequently a reporter, was presumed to possess moral integrity until the contrary was established, and the accepted practice of screening witnesses for this purpose (*tazkiya*) could hardly be effectively applied to reporters of Traditions in bygone generations. Moreover, a reporter of a Tradition could not be challenged, as a witness could, on the ground that his evidence was biased. For these reasons the parallel between legal testimony and the transmission of Traditions is a superficial one, and the canons of Tradition-criticism, as established by Muslim scholarship, cannot provide any real test of authenticity.

Once the trustworthiness of their reporters was established, Traditions were classified in varying grades of authority according to the strength of their *isnāds*. If the continuity of transmission was broken—i.e. where two successive links in the chain of reporters could not historically have been in contact with each other—this naturally detracted from, although it did not necessarily wholly destroy, the authority of the Tradition. Apart from such considerations the simple criterion was the number of transmitters in each generation. The scale of authority began with the report of a single individual (*khabar al-wāḥid*), rose to the "well-known" (*mash'hūr*) Tradition, and culminated in the "widely transmitted" (*mutawātir*) report, where the number of transmitters in each generation was large enough to dispel any suspicion of fabrication or complicity.[15]

During the latter part of the ninth century, scholarship in this field produced several compilations of Traditions which claimed to have sifted the genuine from the false. Two such manuals in particular, those of al-Bukhārī (d. 870) and Muslim (d. 875), have always enjoyed a high reputation in Islamic jurisprudence as authentic accounts of the practice of the Prophet.

This would therefore seem to be the most appropriate point at which to explain, in such measure as space permits, the attitude which has been adopted in this book towards the controversial problem of the authenticity of Traditions from the Prophet.

We take the view that the thesis of Joseph Schacht is irrefutable in its broad essentials and that the vast majority of the legal dicta attributed to the Prophet are apocryphal and the result of the process of "back-projection" of legal doctrine as outlined above. At the same time, as has already been pointed out, the Qur'ān itself posed problems which must have been of immediate concern to the Muslim community, and with which the Prophet himself, in his role of supreme political and legal authority in Medina, must have been forced to deal. When, therefore, the thesis of Schacht is systematically developed to the extent of holding that "the evidence of legal traditions carries us back to about the year A.H. 100 [*sc.* A.D. 719] only", and when the authenticity of practically every alleged ruling of the Prophet is denied, a void is assumed, or rather created, in the picture of the development of law in early Muslim society. From a practical standpoint, and taking the attendant historical circumstances into account, the notion of such a vacuum is difficult to accept. This is not to suggest that the chain of transmission, or the *isnād*, of this Tradition or that is authentic, for this is, in the great majority of cases, demonstrably not so; but it is suggested that the substance of many Traditions, particularly those which deal with the obvious day-to-day problems arising from the Qur'ānic laws, may well represent at least an approximation to a decision of the Prophet which had been preserved initially by general oral tradition. If this practical premise is accepted then it is a reasonable principle of historical enquiry that an alleged ruling of the Prophet should be tentatively accepted as such unless some reason can be adduced as to why it should be regarded as fictitious.

A discussion of "the case of the six slaves" may serve to clarify the issues involved. The restriction of the power of testamentary disposition to one-third of the deceased's net assets has been mentioned previously as a ruling of the Prophet called for by the urgent and practical nature of the problem. Schacht, on the other hand,[16] states that this rule was of Umayyad origin and gives two reasons for this conclusion. The first is that "the Umayyad origin of the restriction is explicitly stated" in Mālik's *Muwaṭṭa'*, where it is recorded that, when a man on his death-bed manumitted the six slaves which were his only property, Abān ibn-ʿUthmān, governor of Medina, drew lots between them and set free only the winning two. Secondly, the Tradition with its full *isnāds* going back to the Prophet "dates only from the second century [of Islam], because ash-Shāfiʿī states that it is the only argument which can be adduced against the doctrine of Ṭāwūs on another problem of legacies; whether the alleged doctrine of Ṭāwūs is authentic or not, the Tradition cannot have existed in the time of the historical Ṭāwūs who died in A.H. 101 [A.D. 720]".

With respect, these two arguments by no means conclusively establish the Umayyad origin of the rule. The first report of Mālik simply records the decision of an Umayyad governor. It does not state explicitly that Abān first formulated the rule. Nor, it may be argued, does it even imply this. For the *Muwaṭṭa'* is essentially a compendium of current Medinan law and is not primarily concerned to establish the origins of that law. The simple statement, occurring *passim* in the *Muwaṭṭa'*, that a rule is the subject of current practice and agreement, provides not merely a sufficient, but often the supreme, juristic basis for the rule concerned.

Before assessing the merits of Schacht's second argument it is necessary to consider in greater detail the context in which the Tradition occurs in ash-Shāfi'ī's *Risāla.*[17] Ash-Shāfi'ī is here concerned with the general problem of resolving conflicts between individual Qur'ānic passages by the presumption that one passage repeals or abrogates the other. Such a presumption may be drawn from the Qur'ān itself or, failing this, from the *sunna* or practice of the Prophet. The latter is the case in the matter of inheritance, for, argues ash-Shāfi'ī, the repeal of the injunction to make bequests in favour of near relatives by the system of the fixed shares allotted to them is indicated by the Prophet's words: "No bequest in favour of an heir". But, ash-Shāfi'ī goes on, though the obligation to make bequests to those relatives who do in fact inherit may have lapsed, it might still apply in favour of relatives who are not heirs. Ṭāwūs is then named as one who was in favour of this latter view, and who drew from it the further conclusion that it was not permissible to make bequests to persons other than relatives. This last conclusion is then refuted by ash-Shāfiʿī on the ground of the Tradition concerning the six slaves; for this indicated that a gift (of their freedom to slaves) made in death-sickness was to be regarded as a legacy, and the slaves, the recipients of the "legacy", could not have been relatives of their master.

Schacht's second argument, then, that the Tradition did not exist in Ṭāwūs's time because, if it had, he could not have maintained the view he did, is only valid if we assume (a) that Ṭāwūs would necessarily be aware of an existing Tradition, (b) that he would interpret it in exactly the same way as ash-Shāfiʿī did, and (c) that he would consider himself bound by it. Each one of these suppositions is open to serious objection.

At a time when the Prophet's practice, if it was preserved at all, was orally transmitted and when contact between scholars was anything but close, to suggest that Ṭāwūs was unaware of an existing Tradition is not to question his scholarly merit or assiduity. Next, he may have been aware of the Tradition but failed to draw from it the conclusions which were drawn by ash-Shāfiʿī, for Ṭāwūs, as quoted by ash-Shāfiʿī, was concerned with the problem of the recipients of legacies, not their amount; and to attribute to him the same capacity for systematic thought as ash-Shāfiʿī is to place him in a position some hundred years in advance of his time. In fact the Tradition, on the face of it, concerns gifts in death-sickness, not legacies. It is by no means axiomatic that the two transactions should have the same legal incidents and ash-Shāfiʿī himself, as has been noted above, found it necessary to establish the parallel as the first stage in his line of reasoning. It may, however, be objected that it is fanciful to suppose that the implications of the Tradition would not have been evident to Ṭāwūs and his contemporaries. In this case it is no more fanciful to suggest that Ṭāwūs, even so, did not regard the Prophet's action as opposed to his view, either because the gift of freedom to slaves, as members of the family household, was not in the same category as legacies to total strangers, or because the prohibition against legacies in favour of strangers only applied where the deceased was in fact survived by relatives who were not entitled to inherit; and there was no indication that this was so in the case of the six slaves. Finally, if Ṭāwūs indeed knew of the Tradition and fully agreed with the interpretation of ash-Shāfiʻī, he would not necessarily consider himself bound by it; for he lived at a time when, as has already been explained, the authority of the Prophet as the interpreter of the Qur'ān was by no means considered paramount or exclusive.

Because of the possibility that one of the above situations could reasonably apply (and ash-Shāfiʻī himself, of course, must have assumed this), Schacht's second argument by itself is inconclusive. In this particular instance, however, the fact still remains that the case of the six slaves first appears in the *Muwaṭṭa'* as a decision of Abān and that some years later there exists a record of an identical decision being given by the Prophet. The unlikelihood of there having been, historically, two such cases merits the conclusion that one of the anecdotes is false; and it would be in accord with the general trends of legal development in this period to conclude further that this particular decision of Abān was projected backwards and fictitiously ascribed to the Prophet. But, even if we go so far—and this is certainly the crucial point—it by no means follows that the one-third rule itself was of Umayyad origin.

There exists a further well-known Tradition to the effect that Saʻd ibn-Abī-Waqqāṣ sought the advice of the Prophet as to how much of his property he should bequeath to charity when his only relative was a daughter, and that the Prophet set the limit at one-third. This Tradition is not open to the same objections as the case of the six slaves; and it would be arbitrary, to say the least, to assume that, simply because many other alleged decisions of the Prophet are fictitious, this one also is. We cannot, of course, positively know whether or not Ṭāwūs was aware of this Tradition. But his view of the recipients of legacies, as ash-Shāfi'ī records it, is only intelligible if we assume that he must have recognised some limit to testamentary dispositions, and he cannot have ignored the question of precisely what limit. Ash-Shāfi'ī himself, at any rate, quite obviously knew of and accepted the one-third rule from a source other than the six slaves case; for having quoted the case he begins his argument against the view of Ṭāwūs as follows. "Thus the indication of the *sunna* is that the Prophet's grant of freedom (to the two slaves) at the time of death constitutes a bequest." What could provide such indication for ash-Shāfi'ī if not the limitation of one-third?

From the available evidence, then, the following development may be reasonably assumed. In regulating a problem posed by the Qur'ānic rules themselves the Prophet set the limit of legacies at one-third. Later doctrine subjected gifts made during death-sickness to the same restriction. A particular decision to this effect is ascribed to Abān and later, fictitiously, to the Prophet.

It must be emphasised that one example like this cannot affect the fundamental validity of Schacht's thesis; but in disputing the particular conclusions he draws in this case it questions the degree to which he carries his thesis. Once the apocryphal nature of the great majority of alleged decisions of the Prophet is established, it is a perfectly acceptable premise that no Tradition can be simply taken at its face value. But this cannot reasonably be developed into the proposition that all Traditions should be regarded as fictitious until their authenticity is objectively established. Taking for granted the mechanics of "back projection" of doctrine and the development of fictitious *isnāds*, it would appear that the all-important criterion is presented by the actual subject matter of the report. Where the legal rule enunciated clearly represents an advanced stage in the development of doctrine, or where it concerns problems which cannot have faced Muslim society until well after the death of the Prophet, the presumption of falsehood is overwhelming. But where, on the contrary, the rule fits naturally into the circumstances of the Prophet's community at Medina, then it should be tentatively accepted as authentic until reason for the contrary is shown. Once again this has little or nothing to do with the question of the authenticity of the *isnād*. This may well be—and indeed usually is—spurious. So, too, the detailed circumstances surrounding the rule may be false or inaccurate. But these are simply embellishments to satisfy the demands of formality which were so important at this time.

Muslim jurisprudence, however, accepted as authentic the corpus of Traditions which the activities of the specialist scholars in the ninth century had produced, and we now return to the question of the effect this had on legal development.

Ash-Shāfiʿī's legal theory had established a compromise between the dictates of the divine will and the use of human reason in law. But his hopes that such mediation would resolve existing conflicts and introduce uniformity into jurisprudence were frustrated; in fact the varying reactions to his thesis of the authority of Traditions resulted in the formation of three further schools of law in addition to those which existed in his own time.

Those who were prepared to accept the precise terms

of ash-Shāfi'ī's doctrine on the role of Traditions were a minority and thus, despite the consistent repudiation of this possibility by ash-Shāfi'ī himself, the Shāfi'ī school of law was born. It represented the middle position between those whose attitude towards Traditions was more reserved and those whose enthusiastic support of them was carried to extremes.

From this latter group two more schools of law were formed, their common ground lying in their rejection of human reason in any form as a source of law and their insistence that each and every legal rule could find its requisite authority only in the divine revelation of the Qur'ān and the practice or example of the Prophet. Aḥmad ibn-Ḥanbal (d. 855), who is alleged never to have eaten water melon because he was not in possession of any Prophetic precedent on the subject, collected, in his work entitled the *Musnad*, more than 80,000 *ḥadīths*, and thus founded the Ḥanbalī school. Dāwūd ibn-Khalaf (d. 883), reacting strongly against the increasing subtlety of legal reasoning, expounded the principle that law should be based only upon the literal and evident (*ẓāhir*) meaning of the texts of the Qur'ān and the Traditions, and his acolytes thus became known as the Ẓāhirī school. One of their later outstanding adherents, Ibn-Ḥazm (d. 1064), denounced the use of analogical reasoning (*qiyās*) in law as a perversion and a heresy with such fervour that his voluminous writings were publicly burnt in Seville.

Within the established schools of law, the Mālikīs in Medina and the Ḥanafīs in Kūfa, the interests of past local tradition necessitated a cautious approach to ash-Shāfi'ī's thesis. Unwilling to undertake the complete revision of their existing *corpus juris*—as strict adherence to ash-Shāfi'ī's principles would have required—but at the same time forced to acknowledge the essential validity of those principles, they accepted the authority of Traditions in a qualified form, and on this basis found it possible to reconcile their existing law with the dictates of ash-Shāfiʿī's theory. The process of adjustment did not prove unduly difficult; for a great part of the doctrine of the early schools was already expressed in the form of Traditions.

A common feature of the jurisprudence of both schools was their reluctance to accept the binding nature of a single or isolated Tradition (*khabar al-wāḥid*) when this contradicted the established doctrine. The effect of such Traditions could be minimised by interpretation, however arbitrary and forced this sometimes might appear; the Ḥanafīs, for example, in order to preserve their rule that an adult woman had the capacity to conclude her own marriage, had to interpret the Tradition which stated: "If a woman marries herself without a guardian, her marriage is null and void", as referring to minor females only. More particularly, both schools recognised subsidiary, but additional, principles of jurisprudence whose authority could override that of an isolated Tradition; the Ḥanafīs maintained the validity of "preference" (*istiḥsān*) and the Mālikīs that of "the consensus (*ijmāʿ*) of Medina". These principles represent the survival of the distinctive characteristics of the early schools—the freedom of speculation in Kūfa and the reliance upon customary practice in Medina—and were actually invoked to deny the Tradition-based doctrine of *khiyār al-majlis*.[18]

By the end of the ninth century the sharp conflicts of principle which ash-Shāfiʿī's thesis had engendered had largely died away, and the place of the *sunna* or practice of the Prophet in Muslim jurisprudence was stabilised. On the one hand extremist support for the Traditions was tempered by the recognition that, in the elaboration of the law, it was necessary in practice to use human reason in the shape of analogical deduction (*qiyās*). (This at least, was the case with the Ḥanbalī school; the Ẓāhirīs adhered rigidly to their original principles, and as a result became extinct in the Middle Ages.) On the other hand the established schools, having succeeded in formally justifying their established doctrine, were now quite prepared to acknowledge, as a matter of principle, the authority of the Traditions.

This development, initiated by ash-Shāfiʿī, determined the whole future course of Islamic law. With the spread of the area of law covered by divine revelation came an increasing rigidity of doctrine; the scope for independent activity was progressively restricted as the particular terms of the law, through the Traditions, were identified with the command of God. The spring of juristic speculation, which had supplied the rapidly moving stream of Islamic jurisprudence in its early stages, gradually ceased to flow; the current slowed, until eventually and inevitably, it reached the point of stagnation.

Part Two

LEGAL DOCTRINE AND PRACTICE IN MEDIAEVAL ISLAM

CHAPTER 6

THE CLASSICAL THEORY OF LAW

WESTERN jurisprudence has provided a number of different answers to the question of the nature of law, variously finding its source to lie in the orders of a political superior, in the breasts of the judiciary, in the "silent, anonymous forces" of evolving society, or in the very nature of the universe itself. For Islam, however, this same question admits of only one answer which the religious faith supplies. Law is the command of God; and the acknowledged function of Muslim jurisprudence, from the beginning, was simply the discovery of the terms of that command. By the early tenth century the differences of principle which had arisen in the formative period concerning the precise scope of the divine will had been largely resolved, and the historical development described in Part I of this book had culminated in a generally accepted formula for the process of discovery which we may call the classical theory of law.

This theory, therefore, is not a speculative essay, in the manner of Western theories of jurisprudence, on the fundamental question of the origins of law. Since law can only be the pre-ordained system of God's commands or Sharīʿa, jurisprudence is the science of *fiqh*, or "understanding" and ascertaining that law; and the classical legal theory consists of the formulation and analysis of the principles by which such comprehension is to be achieved. Four such basic principles, which represent distinct but correlated manifestations of God's will and which are known as the "roots of jurisprudence" (*uṣūl al-fiqh*), are recognised by the classical theory: the word of God himself in the Qur'ān, the divinely inspired conduct or *sunna* of the Prophet, reasoning by analogy or *qiyās*, and consensus of opinion or *ijmā'*. But although these are the same *uṣūl* as were laid down by ash-Shāfi'ī, it will be seen that the composite structure of the classical legal theory is fundamentally different from ash-Shāfi'ī's scheme.

Appreciation of the terms of the Sharī'a is, of course, a process of human thought, whether this takes the form of the simple recognition of the manifest meaning of a Qur'ānic rule or lies in the derivation of a novel rule by analogy. Both the nature and the effect of this whole process of appreciation of the divine law, which is properly termed *ijtihād* (literally, the "effort" of one's own judgement) are regulated by the legal theory.

In the first place the course which *ijtihād* must follow is defined. The *mujtahid* (or person exercising *ijtihād*) should first seek the solution of legal problems in the specific terms of the Qur'ān and the *sunna*, applying thereto the accepted canons of interpretation and construction, including the doctrine of repeal or abrogation (*naskh*). Thus the classical theory adopts the doctrine of ash-Shāfi'ī by integrating the Qur'ān and the *sunna* as material sources of divine revelation. But the dominant position of the *sunna* has an even greater emphasis in the classical theory; for as well as explaining the Qur'ān the *sunna* may also repeal it. Where a problem is not specifically regulated by the Qur'ān or *sunna*, the method of analogical reasoning must then be used to extend the principles inherent in the divine revelation to cover new cases.

The second function of the legal theory is the evaluation of the results of such *ijtihād* in terms of the authority which is to be attributed to them as expressions of the divine will. A moment's reflection will bring to light the fundamental nature of the whole problem of the authority of the law in Islam. It was not merely a case of the values which were to be attached to the various possible interpretations of the Qur'ān and *sunna* and the results of juristic reasoning in general; there was also the primary question of the authority of the recognised sources of the divine will themselves. What, in fact, guaranteed the validity of the whole scheme of *uṣūl*? These questions find their answer in the concept of *ijmā'* or consensus.

Ijmā', in the classical theory, is the agreement of the qualified legal scholars in a given generation and such consensus of opinion is deemed infallible. Natural enough as a juristic principle, *ijmā'* is none the less the self-asserted hypothesis of Muslim jurisprudence. For although the validity of the principle is formally expressed in a Tradition from the Prophet which states: "My community will never agree upon an error", it is the *ijmā'* itself which guarantees the validity of the Tradition. *Ijmā'* is also the term used to denote the universal acceptance by all Muslims of the fundamental tenets of the faith, such as belief in the mission of Muḥammad and the divine nature of the Qur'ān. In this broadest sense, of course, *ijmā'* is not a criterion of authority at all but simply the collective expression of a common religious conviction. Here we are only concerned with *ijmā'* as a technical legal principle which operates, within the bounds established by basic religious dogma, to determine the precise significance of the terms of the divine will. And it is such *ijmā'* which, in the ultimate analysis, guarantees the authenticity of the Qur'ān and the various compilations of Traditions as records of divine revelation, the validity of the method of analogical reasoning (*qiyās*), and, in sum, the authority of the whole structure of the legal theory.

In the attempt to define the will of God, the *ijtihād* of individual scholars could result only in a tentative or probable conclusion termed *ẓann* (conjecture). This was so, strictly speaking, even where opinions were based upon an apparently unequivocal text of the Qur'ān or the *sunna*, and was *a fortiori* the case where principles of interpretation and construction or analogical reasoning were involved. Where, however, such conclusions were the subject of general agreement by the scholars, they then became incontrovertible and infallible expressions of God's law. *Ijmā'* thus guarantees the totality of the results of *ijtihād* legitimately exercised in accordance with the process laid down in the theory of *uṣūl*. Consensus of opinion produces certain knowledge (*'ilm*) of God's will, but at the same time, where no consensus is in fact achieved, variant opinions are recognised as equally valid attempts to define that will.

It is this function of *ijmā'* which constitutes the vital difference between the classical legal theory and ash-Shāfi'ī's thesis. Ash-Shāfi'ī had conceived of *ijmā'* as a material source of law of minor importance.[1] In the classical theory *ijmā'* does indeed operate as a material source of law in itself. For example, the basic doctrine of constitutional law, the elected office of Caliph, is not derived from any text of the Qur'ān or *sunna* or analogy thereon, but simply from the agreed practice of the early Muslim community. However, the dominant role of *ijmā'* in the classical theory is that of the paramount criterion of legal authority. The authority of ash-Shāfi'ī's theory had rested merely on its intrinsic merits and logical appeal. *Ijmā'* in the classical theory supplies the necessary ultimate test for the validity of juristic reasoning in general and in particular determines the measure of recognition and authority to be afforded to ash-Shāfi'ī's principles.

The formal operation of the classical theory of *uṣūl* may be shortly illustrated by the development of the doctrine of usury (*ribā*). A Tradition from the Prophet explains the general prohibition of *ribā* contained in the Qur'ān by declaring that, when certain commodities of the same species are bartered against each other, *ribā* exists if there is either inequality between the two amounts offered or a delay in delivery on one side. Six such commodities were specified in the Tradition—gold, silver, wheat, barley, dates, and raisins. By analogy, the so-called "*ribā* rules"—equality of offerings and immediate delivery—were applied to the barter of other commodities which were deemed to possess the same essential characteristics as those specified in the Tradition, on the ground that the same effective cause (*'illa*) which lay behind the original ruling was present also in these new cases. Divergence of opinion as to the nature of this effective cause produced variant doctrines in the different schools. In Shāfi'ī and Ḥanbalī law the *ribā* rules are applied to the barter of all foodstuffs, in Mālikī law only to foodstuffs which can be stored or preserved, while in Ḥanafī law they are extended to all fungible commodities normally sold by weight or measure. *Ijmā'* then confirms the area covered by general agreement—the *ribā* rules themselves and their application to all foodstuffs capable of being preserved—as a certain expression of God's will; beyond this point the possible extension of the *ribā* rules is a matter of conjecture, and the varying solutions of the different schools are ratified as equally probable interpretations of God's will.

Because it was not only differences of this type which were covered by the *ijmā'* but also more serious differences, such as the subsidiary principles of law adopted by the Ḥanafīs and Mālikīs to qualify the authority of Traditions and strict *qiyās*,[2] *ijmāʿ* represents, in a sense, the contradiction of ash-Shāfiʿī's thesis; for it tolerates those variations which it had been ash-Shāfiʿī's aim to eliminate. Yet this permissive and inclusive function of *ijmāʿ* is in fact limited to the ratification of the *status quo* at the time of its formation; from this stage onwards it becomes a purely prohibitive and exclusive principle. Once formed the *ijmāʿ* was infallible; to contradict it was heresy, and the possibility of its repeal by a similar *ijmāʿ* of a later generation, though admitted in theory, was thus highly unlikely in practice. Further discussion was precluded not only on those points which were the subject of a consensus, but also on those matters where the jurists had agreed to differ; for if the *ijmāʿ* covered two variant opinions, to adduce a third opinion was to contradict it. As the acknowledged sphere of the *ijmāʿ* in this broad sense spread, the use of independent judgement or *ijtihād*, which had been progressively restricted during the formative period by the emergence of such principles as the authority of Traditions and the strict regulation of methods of reasoning, eventually disappeared altogether. *Ijmāʿ* had thus set the final seal upon the process of increasing rigidity in the law.

Muslim jurisprudence of the early tenth century formally recognised that its creative force was now spent and exhausted in the doctrine known as "the closing of the door of *ijtihād*". The right of *ijtihād* was replaced by the duty of *taqlīd* or "imitation". Henceforth every jurist was an "imitator" (*muqallid*), bound to accept and follow the doctrine established by his predecessors. Certain modern writers[3] have suggested that this doctrine arose out of the peculiar circumstances of the Mongol invasions of the thirteenth century, when the treasured heritage of the Sharīʿa was thus embalmed and interred to preserve it from the ravaging hordes of Genghis Khan. But historically the phenomenon occurred some three centuries before this, and was probably the result not of external pressures but of internal causes. The point had been reached where the material sources of the divine will—their content now finally determined—had been fully exploited. An exaggerated respect for the personalities of former jurists induced the belief that the work of interpretation and expansion had been exhaustively accomplished by scholars of peerless ability whose efforts had fashioned the Sharī'a into its final and perfect form. This attitude was naturally closely linked with the enervating effect of the spread of the *ijmā'*. As a natural sequel to the classical theory it represents the *post facto* rationalisation of an existing state of affairs reached with the culmination of the quest to express the law in terms of the will of God. When the consensus of opinion in the tenth century asserted that the door of *ijtihād* was closed, Islamic jurisprudence had resigned itself to the inevitable outcome of its self-imposed terms of reference.

Thus circumscribed and fettered by the principle of *taqlīd*, jurisprudential activities were henceforth confined to the elaboration and detailed analysis of established rules. From the tenth century onwards the role of jurists was that of commentators upon the works of the past masters, and their energies were perforce expended in a scholasticism which on occasions attained a remarkable degree of casuistry. Serious consideration was given to such hypothetical cases as the problem of the precise moment at which succession opens to the estate of a person turned into stone by the devil. Extracting the last ounce of implication from original principles, the jurists ruled that melted butter, into which a mouse had fallen and drowned, could not be used as fuel for lamps because the air would be thus polluted by the impurity of the flesh of a dead animal. Similarly it was not permissible to ride a camel which had drunk wine because of possible contact with the forbidden substance through the sweat of the camel. A Mālikī scholar, Ibn-Rushd (d. 1126, grandfather of the philosopher Averroes), refers to this last rule as "the final word in godliness and the ultimate degree of piety", a phrase which in fact epitomises the purpose and attitude of the scholars. For although such extremes of pedantry were not normally indulged in the sphere of legal relationships strictly so called, jurisprudence as a whole was now dominated by a spirit of altruistic idealism.[4]

Islamic jurisprudence had in fact been essentially idealistic from the outset. Law had not grown out of the practice of the courts or the remedies therein available —as Roman law had developed from the *actio* or English Common law from the writ—but had originated as the academic formulation of a scheme alternative to that practice; its authority did not lie in the fact that it was observed but in the theoretical arguments of the scholars as to why it ought to be observed. Even so, the scholars in the original schools of law had paid considerable attention to actual legal practice, accepting it as authoritative unless an explicit principle of the religion was thereby infringed. But by the tenth century the growth and maturity of the theory of the four *uṣūl*, which dispelled outright any notion of an authority attaching to the activities of legal tribunals as a source of law, had produced an attitude of doctrinaire isolationism. Jurisprudence, divorced from actual legal practice, had become an introspective science, wherein law was studied and elaborated for its own sake.

One of the most obvious instances of this detached idealism of the doctrine—in the sense of its general neglect of the subject of legal remedies and its contentment to define substantive rights and duties without concerning itself with any procedural machinery for their enforcement—lies in the topic of constitutional law. Here the jurists propounded the doctrine of the election of the Caliph by the vote of representatives of the Muslim community, and defined the qualifications which aspirants to that office must possess. It was a scheme based upon the historical circumstances of the first four Caliphs, and was formulated largely in contradiction to the nature of Umayyad rule, of which one outstanding feature was the hereditary transmission of political power. But apart, perhaps, from the early years of the ʿAbbāsid dynasty, the scheme never again bore any resemblance to political reality. Such deviations from the ideal order of things might be lamented and condemned by the scholars, but the Sharīʿa itself was powerless to prevent them. Might, in fact, was right, and this was eventually recognised by the scholars in their denunciation of civil disobedience even when the political authority was in no sense properly constituted. Obviously the effective enforcement of the whole system of Sharīʿa law was entirely dependent upon the whim of the *de facto* ruler.

The ideal code of behaviour which is the Sharīʿa has in fact a much wider scope and purpose than a simple legal system in the Western sense of the term. Jurisprudence (*fiqh*) not only regulates in meticulous detail the ritual practices of the faith and matters which could be classified as medical hygiene or social etiquette—legal treatises, indeed, invariably deal with these topics first; it is also a composite science of law and morality, whose exponents (*fuqahā*', sing. *faqīh*) are the guardians of the Islamic conscience.

Hence all acts and relationships are measured by a scale of moral evaluation. On the positive side of a central category of acts which are permissible or indifferent (*mubāḥ*) are firstly acts which are recommended (*mandūb*)—where performance brings reward from

God but omission does not entail punishment—and secondly acts which are obligatory (*wājib*); on the negative side of the scale are firstly acts which are reprehensible (*makrūh*)—where omission brings reward but commission does not entail punishment—and secondly acts which are prohibited outright (*ḥarām*). Law and morality, however, are not fully merged and integrated within the Sharīʿa. For example, unilateral repudiation (*ṭalāq*) of a wife by the husband is morally reprehensible or *makrūh* but, even when pronounced in a particularly disapproved form called *bidʿa* ("innovation"), is none the less legally valid and effective. While our attention in this book is confined to law properly so called, the moral scale serves as a reminder of the essentially religious character of the Sharīʿa and of the fact that we are here dealing with but one part of a comprehensive guide to conduct, all of which is "law" in the Islamic sense and the ultimate purpose of which is to secure divine favour both in this world and in the hereafter.

From the tenth century onwards the effect of the doctrine of *taqlīd* was mirrored in the literature of the law. This consisted mainly of a succession of increasingly exhaustive commentaries upon the works of the first systematic exponents of the doctrine such as Mālik, ash-Shaybānī and ash-Shāfiʿī. Further glossaries were appended to these commentaries; different views and lines of development were collated and amalgamated, and concise abbreviated compendia were produced. Authors, almost without exception, betrayed a slavish adherence, not only to the substance but also to the form and arrangement of the doctrine as recorded in the earliest writings. By the fourteenth century various legal texts had appeared which came to acquire a particular reputation in the different schools and areas of Islam. Representing for each school the statement of the law ratified by the *ijmāʿ*, they retained their paramount authority as expressions of Sharīʿa law until the advent of legal modernism in the present century.

Classical jurisprudence had thus, by the principle of *ijmāʿ*, consecrated the whole body of doctrine enshrined in the authoritative texts as the complete expression of the divine command. Although historical research, as has been seen in Part I of this book, shows that the great bulk of the law had originated in customary practice and in scholars' reasoning, that its precise identification with the terms of the divine will was artificial, and that the classical theory of the four *uṣūl* was the culmination of a process of growth extending over two centuries, yet traditional Islamic belief holds that the four *uṣūl* had been exclusively operative from the beginning. The elaboration of the law is seen by Islamic orthodoxy as a process of scholastic endeavour completely independent of historical or sociological influences. Once discovered, therefore, the law could not be subject to historical exegesis, in the sense that its terms could be regarded as applicable only to the particular circumstances of society at a given point in time. Moreover the law was of necessity basically immutable; for Muḥammad was the last of the prophets, and after his death there could be no further communication of the divine will to man.

Law, therefore, does not grow out of, and is not moulded by, society as is the case with Western systems. Human thought, unaided, cannot discern the true values and standards of conduct; such knowledge can only be attained through divine revelation, and acts are good or evil exclusively because God has attributed this quality to them. In the Islamic concept, law precedes and moulds society; to its eternally valid dictates the structure of State and society must, ideally, conform.

CHAPTER 7

UNITY AND DIVERSITY IN SHARĪʿA LAW

A TREE, whose network of branches and twigs stems from the same trunk and roots; a sea, formed by the merging waters of different rivers; a variety of threads woven into a single garment; even the interlaced holes of a fishing net: these are some of the metaphors used by Muslim authors to explain the phenomenon of *ikhtilāf*, or diversity of doctrine, in Sharīʿa law. The various schools of law, in which such diversity of doctrine was crystallised, are seen as different but inseparable aspects of the same unity. According to an alleged dictum of the Prophet, there were no less than 360 such pathways to the eternal truth; but, leaving aside for the moment the minority groups or sects, four schools of law only have survived in Sunnite Islam since the fifteenth century—the Ḥanafīs, Mālikīs, Shāfiʿīs, and Ḥanbalis. This chapter will deal with the general topic of the relationship between these four schools, or *madhāhib* (sing. *madhhab*), which Islamic legal philosophy thus covers with the blanket authority of the *ijmāʿ*.

During the formative period of the law the schools were, as a natural result of their circumstances of origin, hostile and competing systems. The original schools of Medina and Kūfa, conscious of the fact that their law largely reflected local practice, had at first accepted differences of doctrine as natural and inevitable; but under the impetus of the ʿAbbāsid policy to create an order of State and society which would give full expression to the Islamic religious ethic, the two schools came to champion their respective systems as possessing a validity not confined to a particular locality but universal for Muslims. Conflict of juristic principles had then produced the opposing systems of the Shāfiʿīs and Ḥanbalīs, and until well into the second half of the ninth century the four schools adopted a polemical and intolerant attitude towards each other as they vied for recognition as the superior expression of God's law.

Legal practice, as may be gathered from al-Kindī's account of the early judges of Egypt, reflected and accentuated the controversies between the scholars. Some *qāḍīs* apparently evinced a regard for doctrines other than those of the school to which they belonged. For example, the Ḥanafī Ibrāhīm ibn-al-Jarrāḥ, *qāḍī* from A.D. 820–826, was in the habit of noting the variant views of Abū-Ḥanīfa, Mālik and others on the back of the case record and marking the one he preferred as an indication to his clerk that the decree was to be prepared on that basis. In general, however, the judiciary aligned themselves strictly with the tenets of a particular school, and in so doing lost their original character as representatives of a local legal tradition. Ḥanafī law was the system officially adopted by the central ʿAbbāsid government, and this naturally resulted in the widespread appointment of persons trained in that school to judicial office in the provinces. One Ismāʿīl ibn-al-Yasāʿ is on record as the first *qāḍī* to apply Ḥanafī law in Egypt. Although his ability as a judge commanded general respect, his application of unfamiliar and alien rules—particularly his policy of the annulment of charitable endowments, as advocated by Abū-Ḥanīfa—provoked sufficient resentment to cause his dismissal in A.D. 783.

Theological disputes served on occasions to underline the distinction between the schools and to cause outbreaks of bitter enmity and active hostility between them. During the course of the notorious inquisition (*miḥna*), inaugurated by the Caliph al-Ma'mūn in 833 to force persons of rank to make public profession of the doctrine of the createdness of the Qur'ān as expounded by the Muʿtazilite school of theology, the Ḥanafī *qāḍī* al-Layth, who himself espoused the Muʿtazilite creed, refused to allow Mālikī and Shāfiʿī scholars to hold audience in the mosque. Some years later after the end of the inquisition the Mālikī *qāḍī* al-Ḥārith retaliated by expelling the Ḥanafī teachers from the mosque, and is also said to have rejected in his court the evidence of witnesses who were known to have Ḥanafī affiliations.

That such rivalry between the schools could cause considerable frustration to litigants is shown by the case concerning the "House of the Elephant", which occupied the attention of various *qāḍīs* of Egypt over the span of more than a century. In its closing stages the case hinged on the question of whether or not the word "descendants" in a family settlement included the plaintiffs who were the issue of the settlor's daughter. Under Ḥanafī law, which recognises in many respects the importance of the cognate relationship, "descendants" would naturally include daughter's children, while the word would not be so construed under Mālikī law, where the agnate relationship is generally paramount. Thus the Mālikī *qāḍī* Hārūn dismissed the plaintiffs' claim in 835. Ten years later his Ḥanafī successor gave judgement for the plaintiffs, only to have his decision in turn reversed by the Mālikī al-Ḥārith in 859. Thereupon the plaintiffs appealed to the Caliph who, on the advice of a commission of Ḥanafī jurists appointed to review the case, ordered the reversal of al-Ḥārith's decision and entry of final judgement for the plaintiffs.

It was the development of jurisprudential theory in the late ninth century which was the chief contributive factor to a lessening of the tension between the different schools. With their general acceptance of a basic scheme of the *uṣūl* or sources of law and with the realisation of their identity of purpose which this produced, competitive hostility gradually gave way to a mutual tolerance, and ultimately the existing symbiosis of the different schools was recognised and ratified by the classical doctrine of *ijmāʿ*.

The Ḥanbalī school, however, for several centuries occupied a somewhat precarious position within this quartet of schools. As the supreme exponents of an anti-rationalist attitude in law the Ḥanbalīs had initially rejected the method of juristic reasoning by analogy and were regarded by the other schools as collectors of Traditions rather than lawyers proper; while on the theological plane fanatical Ḥanbalī elements violently opposed the tenets of the Ashʿarite creed, an attenuated form of rationalism accepted by the generality of Sunnite Islam, and during a series of revolts at Baghdad in the twelfth and thirteenth centuries aggressively persecuted particular scholars of the other three schools.[5] That the Ḥanbalīs were admitted within the ambit of the *ijmāʿ* at all is indicative both of the latitude of *ijmāʿ* as a principle of toleration and of the fact that the technical science of law was now largely divorced from strictly theological issues.

As has already been observed,[6] the emergence of a theory of *uṣūl* basically common to all the schools had little effect upon the existing diversity of substantive doctrine. For the Shāfiʿī and Ḥanbalī schools, indeed, legal theory preceded the elaboration of the law, and this basically accounts for the fact that their doctrine coincides more often than is the case with any other two schools. Even so, considerable variations arose between them, not only because the Ḥanbalīs rigidly adhered to the terms of Traditions of weak authority in cases where the Shāfi'īs resorted to analogical reasoning, but also because the Traditions themselves, embodying as they did the local practices and juristic speculations of the early schools, often allowed a choice between conflicting rules of apparently equal authority.

Ḥanafī and Mālikī law, on the other hand, were in existence before Shāfi'ī formulated his theory of *uṣūl*, and although much of their law was already formally expressed in terms of that theory, in particular as Traditions from the Prophet, there was a residuum of local doctrine which was not so expressed; this the Ḥanafīs and Mālikīs proceeded to rationalise, in the course of the ninth century, by modifying and supplementing ash-Shāfi'ī's theory in a variety of respects.

Most of these accretions represent qualifications of ash-Shāfi'ī's principal thesis—the paramount authority of Traditions from the Prophet—which, it will be recalled, had initially expressed the views of those who opposed the current doctrine of the Establishment in the early schools. Thus, one of the distinctive details of Ḥanafī legal theory is the maxim: "Addition constitutes abrogation", which means that where two texts of divine revelation (*naṣṣ*) deal with precisely the same point but one of them adds a novel element to the terms of the other, then the text which contains this addition or increase *prima facie* abrogates the other. The maxim was adopted to counteract the authority of two particular Traditions, one of which states that compelling legal proof is provided by the evidence of one witness and the oath of the plaintiff as to the truth of his claim, and the other that the penalty for fornication (*zinā'*) is one hundred lashes and one year's exile. Both exile as a penalty for fornication and the acceptance of the oath of the plaintiff supported by one witness as legal proof were current practices in the Umayyad period which had been rejected by the scholars of Kūfa. Their Hanafī successors, who, of course, accepted the principle of the authority of Prophetic precedents—as these two particular rules were now expressed to be—were forced to justify their established tradition to the contrary by the following argument. The Qur'ān itself mentions only the evidence of two witnesses as constituting legal proof, and only flogging as the penalty for fornication; hence the additional elements of the plaintiff's oath and banishment contained in the respective Traditions mean that each Tradition does not simply explain the Qur'ān but contradicts it, and therefore the normal rules of abrogation must apply; but since each Tradition is an individual report (*khabar al-wāḥid*) their authority is not in fact sufficient to abrogate the text of the Qur'ān, and therefore their terms are not binding.

The outstandingly distinctive feature, however, of Mālikī and Ḥanafī legal theory, as opposed to that of the Shāfiʿīs and Ḥanbalīs, is their recognition of supplementary sources of law. These represent the classical expression of precisely those elements in the legal method of the early schools which it was ash-Shāfiʿī's purpose to eliminate. Freedom and flexibility of legal reasoning is the keynote of the Ḥanafī principle of *istiḥsān*, or "juristic preference", and, to a lesser degree, of the Mālikī principle of *istiṣlāḥ*, or "consideration of the public interest"; while the concept of a local and limited consensus survives in the Mālikī principle of "the *ijmāʿ* of Medina", the authority of which was now formally substantiated on the ground that Medina was the home of the Prophet and therefore its agreed practice was simply the continuation of the Prophet's *sunna*. In their role of juristic criteria, alternative, and often superior, to the authority of Traditions or of strict reasoning by analogy, these principles are the very contradiction of the essence of ash-Shāfiʿī's thesis, which lay in his insistence that the authority of Traditions was paramount and that analogical reasoning was the exclusively valid method of legal reasoning. Although legal literature, from classical times onwards, naturally tended to minimise the importance of these supplementary principles, they in fact represent the real sources of the bulk of Ḥanafī and Mālikī law; their survival, under the umbrella of the *ijmāʿ*, shows how successfully the early schools had absorbed the shock of ash-Shāfiʿī's attack, and why they were able to preserve the distinctive characteristics which stemmed from their circumstances of origin.

Certain modern writers[7] have created the impression that *istiḥsān* and *istiṣlāḥ*, as principles peculiar to the Ḥanafīs and Mālikīs, are on the same level as the subsidiary principle of *istiṣḥāb* recognised by the Shāfiʿī school. *Istiṣḥāb*, however, is merely a natural principle of legal evidence—the presumption that a state of affairs known to exist in the past continues to exist until the contrary is established—and is, as such, endorsed by Islamic jurisprudence as a whole, although the Shāfiʿīs perhaps apply it more consistently than the other schools. Thus, a missing person (*mafqūd*) is presumed to be alive until the contrary is established, e.g. by a judicial decree of his putative death based on the fact that such a time has elapsed since his disappearance as completes his normal life span. Succession to the missing person's estate, therefore, opens at the time of the judicial decree, and the entitled heirs are determined accordingly. Only the Shāfiʿī school, however, recognises that this same principle governs the right of the missing person himself to succeed to the estate of a relative who dies during his absence; by *istiṣḥāb* it is presumed that the missing person survives any relative who dies prior to the decree of his putative death. But according to the other schools the missing person in this respect is to be accounted dead from the date of his disappearance; for them *istiṣḥāb* operates as a shield to protect the missing person's estate from the claims of his heirs, but not as a sword to support his own claims to the estates of others. It will be clear from this one example, therefore, that to regard the supplementary principles of the Mālikī and Ḥanafī schools as in any way parallel to the principle of *istiṣḥāb* is to misunderstand completely their function and significance.

Once the early hostility between the schools had disappeared and they had settled down to a state of peaceful co-existence, the development of doctrine naturally displayed traces of cross influences between them. But although this process of interaction often resulted in a superficial assimilation of the details of the law, it rarely affected the basic characteristics of the different systems.

In the laws of homicide, for example, all schools recognise the procedure of compurgation (*qasāma*). For the school of Medina this was a mode of proving the offence of homicide where the guilt of the accused could not be established either by his confession or by the normal standard of two acceptable eye-witnesses of the killing. Fifty accusatory oaths taken by the blood relatives (*ʿāqila*) of the victim established the responsibility of the accused provided there was some other indication of his guilt. According to Mālik himself such indication was provided by two circumstances only: a statement by a dying person charging the accused with his death, or one eye-witness of the killing. This second case Mālik specifically calls "suspicion" (*lawth*). Ash-Shāfiʿī, however, broadly defined "suspicion" as any circumstances raising a *prima facie* case against the accused, and later Mālikī law was influenced by this view to the extent that it specified several additional situations which constituted sufficient "suspicion" to support the compurgation procedure, including, e.g., the accused being discovered near the body with blood-stains on him. But even so Shāfi'ī and Mālikī law never reached complete agreement, for the Mālikīs included the naming of his killer by the dying victim as one of the categories of "suspicion", which the Shāfi'īs did not admit, and excluded proof of existing enmity between the accused and the victim, which the Shāfi'īs admitted.[8] Ḥanafī law, it may be noted, took no part in this development but preserved the particular tradition of the school of Kūfa, under which compurgation was an essentially defensive procedure, fifty oaths being taken by the inhabitants of a neighbourhood in which a corpse had been discovered to repudiate the charge that one of their community had perpetrated the killing.

An example of interaction in the realm of family law is provided by the doctrine of *kafā'a*, or marriage equality.[9] This had originated in Kūfa, and, though unknown to early Medinan law, was later adopted into the Mālikī system. Here, however, it never assumed so elaborate a form as it did in Ḥanafī law. The Ḥanafīs, for example, hold that the trade or occupation of the husband is an important element in determining whether he is the equal of his spouse, and recognise for this purpose a detailed hierarchy of the professions; the Mālikīs, on the other hand, do not consider this a material factor at all. Nor does the doctrine have the same significance within the general scheme of Mālikī family law as it has for the Ḥanafīs, where it is primarily designed to protect the interests of the marriage guardian; for he is allowed to obtain, on grounds of non-equality, the annulment of a marriage contracted by his adult ward without his consent or intervention. In Mālikī law a marriage can be validly contracted only by the bride's guardian and a petition for annulment on grounds of non-equality is accordingly restricted to cases where the husband has fraudulently misrepresented his status.

For Islamic legal history the most important result of

this whole complex process of development of legal theory and the adjustment of the substantive doctrine thereto was the loss of conscious knowledge of the real origins of the law. The Ḥanafī and Mālikī schools both attempted to consolidate their traditions by ascribing doctrines as they had finally emerged in the classical period to their early representatives. Mālik and Abū-Ḥanīfa particularly thus came to enjoy an undeserved authority as originators of the doctrine.[10] Again, differences between the two schools, which had stemmed from their originally local character, were perpetuated in the guise of legitimate results of the jurisprudential process prescribed by the theory of the four *uṣūl*, and this was so whether the initial cause of diversity had lain in the actual custom of the locality, or in juristic speculation (*ra'y*), or in some other factor. The schools of Medina and Kūfa, as we have seen,[11] had differed as to the measure of support due from a husband to his irrevocably divorced wife during her "waiting period" (*ʿidda*); in Kūfa the husband was bound to provide full maintenance, while in Medina the wife, unless she was pregnant, had the bare right to lodging in the husband's home. Mālikī and Ḥanafī jurists of the classical era retained the respective doctrines of their predecessors, but now explained them in terms of what had become the generally accepted criterion governing a wife's right to support, namely that maintenance was the consideration provided by the husband for the control (*iḥtibās*) he had over his wife. Both schools recognised that the *ʿidda* period was imposed in the interests of the husband inasmuch as it was designed to determine the paternity of any child born to the divorced wife; but while the Ḥanafīs considered that this in itself amounted to sufficient control of the wife's activities by the husband to make her maintenance incumbent upon him, the Mālikīs argued that this was only so where the wife in fact proved to be pregnant as a result of the former marriage. Obviously the original cause of the divergence—the existence of variant texts of the Qur'ān on this subject—had long since faded into oblivion.

It is often asserted that the differences of doctrine among the Sunnite schools are of relative insignificance compared with their essential agreement, and that their respective systems have the same fundamental structure and principal institutions of law, and diverge only on subsidiary particulars.

This, admittedly, is the nature of the bulk of the variations. All schools agree, for example, on the basic notion of legitimacy as being dependent upon conception, and not merely birth, during the lawful wedlock of the parents, and all recognise six months as the minimum period of gestation so that there is no presumption of legitimacy in favour of a child born within the first six months of a marriage. They differ only, in this context, as to whether the six-month period begins to run from the contract of marriage itself or from the actual consummation thereof. Again, the fundamental rules governing the care and custody of children (*ḥaḍāna*) are common to all the schools. Following the divorce or estrangement of parents, custody of their young children belongs to the mother; but she loses the right if she remarries or if the children are wholly removed from the father's influence and control, in which case custody passes to the child's maternal grandmother or other relatives, in accordance with a generally agreed scheme of priorities. Differences between the schools are here largely confined to the question of the duration of such care and custody, which is held to terminate in the case of girls at the age of seven (Shāfi'īs), or at nine, or at puberty (Ḥanafīs), or on their starting married life (Mālikīs). Such details of the law, it may be remarked, are often the subject of as much variance between the individual scholars within a school as they are between the schools themselves.

There are, however, many issues which provide a clear-cut distinction between one school and another and which can hardly be classified as subsidiary points of detail. Divorce is one example. While all schools recognise that a marriage may be terminated extra-judicially, either by unilateral repudiation by the husband or by mutual consent, they differ radically as to the grounds upon which it may be terminated by a judicial decree. In Ḥanafī law the only ground for a wife's petition is the incapacity of the husband to consummate the marriage because of sexual impotence. Mālikī law, however, allows a wife to rest her petition on the husband's desertion, failure to maintain her, cruelty, sexual impotence (even where this occurs after the consummation of the marriage), or the fact that he is afflicted with some incurable or chronic disease which makes marital relations harmful to the wife. The distinction, therefore, is between a system which recognises only judicial annulment on the ground of an original defect in the marriage and one which recognises judicial dissolution for a wide variety of marital "offences" committed by the husband.

Succession provides a further example of differences which can scarcely be brought under the head of legal *trivia*. For all schools the golden rule of intestate succession is the distribution of the fixed shares (*farā'iḍ*) to the Qur'ānic heirs and the residue of the estate to the nearest agnate relatives (*ʿaṣaba*). But in the absence of any agnate relative the Mālikīs hold that the Public Treasury is a residuary heir, while in the other three schools the Treasury succeeds only by escheat. Three principal effects flow from this distinction. Firstly, the whole doctrine of *radd*, or proportionate return of the residue to the Qur'ānic heirs in the absence of any agnate relative, has no place in the Mālikī system. Secondly, cognate relatives (*dhawū 'l-arḥām*) such as the children of the deceased's daughter or sister, succeed in Ḥanafī, Shāfi'ī, and Ḥanbalī law in the absence of any Qur'ānic heir or *'aṣaba* relative, but never succeed in Mālikī law, where they are excluded by the ever present Public Treasury. Finally, since the restriction of the power of testamentary disposition to one-third of the estate is designed to protect the interests of the legal heirs, a person who has no surviving relatives may, in the majority view, dispose of the whole of his estate by will, while in Mālikī law he remains subject to the one-third limitation.

The cumulative effect, therefore, of the results of the rule that the Public Treasury is an heir gives the Mālikī system of inheritance a distinctive character of its own. It is often the case that a series of variations between the schools can be traced back to a single basic conflict of principle; and to regard them as piecemeal variations on isolated topics is to lose sight of the essential unity and cohesion of each of the separate systems.

In fact, the divergence between the schools often goes much deeper than mere variations of substantive doctrine, and strikes to the very roots of their juristic method and outlook. A distinction is popularly drawn between the Ḥanafīs as being the exponents of *ra'y* and the Mālikīs as being the exponents of *ḥadīth*. There is little truth in this distinction if the terms are taken to indicate a conflict between those who employed human reason in law and those who observed the divinely inspired precedents of the Prophet; for during the formative period of the law the two schools adopted essentially the same position in this regard. The labels were probably attached to the two schools because of the supplementary principles of jurisprudence they recognised; for the "consensus of Medina" of the

Mālikīs was regarded in classical times as the perpetuation of the *sunna* of the Prophet—and the terms *sunna* and *ḥadīth* were in fact now used synonymously—while the Ḥanafī "preference" (*istiḥsān*) was identified, at least by their opponents, with unfettered and arbitrary opinion. Regarded in this light, then, the distinction does reflect that fundamental difference of character between the two schools which their supplementary sources of law in fact express—the conservative attachment to tradition of Mālikī law and the freedom of juristic speculation which dominated Ḥanafī jurisprudence. Many aspects of family law—for example, the paramount importance of *patria potestas* in Mālikī law—show the distinction to lie between a school whose object was to preserve an established tradition and one whose task it was to create a tradition of its own.

A further difference of attitude between the Ḥanafī and Mālikī schools concerns the scope of law and the role of the courts who apply it. In many respects the Mālikī system represents a moralistic approach to legal problems in contrast to a formalistic attitude adopted by the Ḥanafīs; for while the Mālikīs place great emphasis upon the intention of a person as affecting the validity of his conduct, the Ḥanafīs mainly confine their attention to the external conduct itself.

Thus, where a person on his death-bed acknowledges himself to be in debt, the Mālikīs hold that the acknowledgement is subject to the scrutiny of the court, and will be valid and effective only where the court is satisfied that the acknowledgement was true in fact and that the acknowledgor did not thereby intend to benefit the acknowledgee to the detriment of his legal heirs. In Ḥanafī law, on the other hand, there is no enquiry into the intention of the acknowledgor as such: basically the acknowledgement is valid if made in favour of a person who is not his heir, and invalid if made in favour of an heir. Again, a bar to marriage exists between a husband and his former wife whom he repudiated in a triple form which can only be removed by the marriage of the woman to a third party, the consummation of this intervening union and, of course, its subsequent termination. Mālikī law maintains that the intention of the parties to the intervening marriage is of paramount importance, and that, if the court finds that the purpose of such a marriage was simply to enable the wife subsequently to remarry her former husband, it will not have this effect. Ḥanafī law, on the contrary, deems any enquiry into the intention of the parties to be outside the province of the courts, and the marriage will always be effective in removing the bar, unless, at least, this was its expressly declared purpose. As we shall see later,[12] the technical formalism of Ḥanafī law is particularly evident in its endorsement of the system of legal stratagems (*ḥiyal*).

Traditions are often the expression of ethical norms rather than of strictly legal rules, and the moralistic approach to law is at its most extreme among those who regard the Traditions as the supreme guide to conduct.[13] Not surprisingly, therefore, it is the Ḥanbalīs who go further than any other school in attempting to integrate the twin strands of law and morality in the Sharīʿa. In Ḥanbalī law a loan with interest is *ipso facto* a complete nullity simply because *ribā* is forbidden. Mālikī and Shāfiʿī law also hold a loan with interest to be void, but on the more technically legal ground that the contract is vitiated in its essence—i.e. in the mutual agreement of the parties to enter into a transaction not recognised by the law. Ḥanafī law, on the other hand, applies its popular doctrine of severance, removes the offending terms relating to interest, and regards the transaction which remains as a valid gratuitous loan. These different attitudes naturally govern the question of whether and when the lender or borrower may recover sums actually paid.

Such considerations as these reveal the true extent of the divergence between the different schools; they appear as essentially distinct systems whose individual characteristics were fashioned by their circumstances of origin. An objective assessment of the nature of *ikhtilāf*, in all its various manifestations, thus penetrates the veil of the classical legal theory and is the clue to the historical growth of Sharīʿa law in the first three centuries of Islam.

Although the relationship between the schools in legal practice will be more conveniently discussed later,[14] it may be remarked here that, geographically, the division between them in mediaeval times was well defined, inasmuch as the courts in different regions of Islam had gradually come to apply the doctrine of one particular school. Various factors had conditioned the physical distribution of schools. A school would spread because of the influence of the various centres of scholarship, or because it had been officially imposed upon a population by the political authority—it will be recalled that the litigants in the "House of the Elephant" case had themselves no choice as to the school applicable to their suit;[15] or a school might spread because it was adopted by a population concurrently with its conversion to Islam through contact with missionaries or merchants travelling along the recognised trade routes. Thus, broadly speaking, Ḥanafī law came to predominate in the Middle East and the Indian sub-continent, Mālikī law in North, West, and Central Africa, and Shāfiʿī law in East Africa, Southern Arabia, and South East Asia. The Ḥanbalī school never succeeded in gaining any real territorial dominion until its tenets were adopted by the Wahhābī movement in the eighteenth century, so that today the Ḥanbalī school is the official law of Saudi Arabia.

Yet, however distinct the four schools might appear from the standpoint of both their doctrine and the conduct of legal practice generally, they were fused and blended together by Islamic legal philosophy as inseparable manifestations of the same single essence. This theory of the mutual orthodoxy of the schools, which, on an objectively historical view, rationalises and minimises the existing differences between them in the light of the common theory of the sources of law, finds a classical exposition in ash-Sha'rānī's *Mīzān*, or "The Balance", written about 1530. Differences between the schools, he asserts, are simply the results of the legitimate exercise of independent judgement (*ijtihād*) in the absence of any explicit guidance from divine revelation. God permitted a wide scope in the elaboration and interpretation of his basic precepts, and variations in doctrine can all be explained in terms of one standard, that of the comparative severity or leniency of interpretation. Ash-Sha'rānī accordingly prefers to speak of "latitude of interpretation" (*tawsi'a*) rather than of "divergence" or *ikhtilāf*. A closely parallel attitude was adopted towards the two schools of early Talmudic law, which were both recognised as the words of the living God. Talmudic law thus, it has been said, "announces a philosophy of bold and candid pluralism. Since human judgements at their best are destined to be incomplete and partial, two or more entirely disparate judgements of the same transaction may be equally rational and equally estimable."[16] Islamic jurisprudence succinctly expresses the very same notion in the alleged words of the Prophet: "Difference of opinion among my community is a sign of the bounty of God".

CHAPTER 8

SECTARIAN LEGAL SYSTEMS IN ISLAM

ON the supreme constitutional issue of the nature and incidents of political sovereignty in the Islamic theocratic state the four Sunnite schools of law speak with one voice. Their doctrine of the Caliphate, of which the central feature is that the office belongs to a member of the tribe of Quraysh upon election by the qualified representatives of the community, is based upon their recognition of the authority of the Medinan, Umayyad and ʿAbbāsid Caliphs. Two minority groups in Islam, however, do not so ratify and support the actual historical devolution of power. Emerging as distinct political factions during the civil war between Muʿāwiya and ʿAlī (A.D. 656–661), they both refused to accept the claims of the victorious Muʿāwiya and the succeeding Umayyad dynasty to leadership. But this was the limit of their agreement. For while the supporters of ʿAlī (*shīʿat ʿAlī*) inaugurated the Shīʿite movement and held that political sovereignty belonged, after ʿAlī, to the issue of his marriage with the daughter and sole surviving child of the Prophet, Fāṭima, the second group, the "seceders" or Khārijites, demonstrated their hostility to both sides in the civil war by assassinating ʿAlī and attempting to assassinate Muʿāwiya. Rejecting equally descent from Quraysh or from the Prophet as essential attributes for leadership, the Khārijites held that the sole requisites were piety in the faith of Islam and personal capability. Moreover, the two factions were radically divided from each other and from the majority on the question of the nature of political authority itself. The Shīʿites ultimately came to maintain that leadership was a matter of divine right, the ruler deriving his authority from the hereditary transmission of divine inspiration along the line of the Prophet's descendants. The Khārijites, on the other hand, held that the ruler was to be elected—and, if necessary, deposed—by the votes of the entire community. Schism in Islam thus took the form of two extremist factions ranged on opposite sides of the intermediate position adopted by the majority group of the Sunnites, for the Shīʿites represented a rigidly authoritarian concept of political power and the Khārijites advocated a more liberal and democratic system. As communities spiritually, if not always physically, separated from the Sunnites, the Shīʿites and Khārijites naturally formulated their own systems of religious law; and the purpose of this chapter is to ascertain how far, if at all, the particular constitutional principles of the two sects affected the general nature and substance of their law so as to distinguish it from that of Sunnite Islam.

No geographical or intellectual barriers isolated the sects from the Sunnites during the eighth and ninth centuries, and the evolution of their legal systems coincided and merged with the general process of historical development described in Part I of this book. Legal scholars of Khārijite or Shīʿite persuasion were inspired by the same purpose as the Sunnite jurists; the raw material of their jurisprudence, the local popular and administrative practice, was the same; they shared the same general method of juristic speculation, were subject to the same influences, and evinced the same trend to ascribe their doctrines to their own representative authorities in previous generations; and thus, not surprisingly, their law emerged in the ninth century having the same broad pattern, recognising the same principal institutions and expressed in the same literary form as Sunnite law.

In fact, the sectarian legal systems, far from being wholly independent growths, often directly borrowed rules developed in the Sunnite schools. This has been convincingly demonstrated by Schacht.[17] Nevertheless it is difficult to agree with the same eminent authority that the Khārijite and Shīʿite systems "do not differ from the doctrines of the . . . Sunnite schools of law more widely than these last differ from one another".[18] For while this is generally true of Khārijite law, Shīʿite law in its final form possesses certain distinctive characteristics which stand in sharp contrast to the principles recognised by the Sunnite systems as a whole.

Considering first jurisprudential theory, the schemes of *uṣūl*, which were propounded by the sects, represent, just as much as the Sunnite scheme, a systematically idealised rather than a historically factual account of the sources of law. It goes without saying that both the Shīʿites and the Khārijites regard the Qur'ān and the *sunna* or practice of the Prophet as the basic material of divine revelation, although their respective versions of the *sunna* differ, sometimes on points of considerable substance, from that accepted by the generality of Sunnite jurists. As distinct from the standard corpus of Traditions recognised as authoritative by the Sunnites, the sects came to possess their own collections which satisfied their own standards of authenticity, one of the most important probative criteria for the Shīʿites being the transmission of a Tradition by one or other of their recognised leaders, or Imāms. Beyond this point, however, Shīʿite legal theory develops a unique character: for while the Khārijites agree with the Sunnites that the principles embodied in the divine revelation are to be extended, and new problems solved, by juristic reasoning—even if the forms which this might assume are less rigidly defined—the majority of the Shīʿites reject this role of human reason and maintain that the further elaboration of the law is the sole prerogative of their divinely inspired Imām.

Here it becomes necessary to indicate briefly the composite structure of the Shīʿite movement. Controversy at various points in history as to who among the descendants of the Prophet was the rightful Imām split the Shīʿite community into a variety of branches, distinguished not only by the person of the Imāms to whom they acknowledged allegiance but also by their doctrines concerning the nature of his office. From a legal standpoint the three most important branches of the Shīʿites are the small minority of the Zaydites, the Ismāʿīlites and the overwhelmingly most numerous group of the Ithnā-ʿasharites or Imāmites. For the Zaydites the authority of the Imām is that of a human being; he is elected by the community on the basis of his personal abilities and has no closer link with God than that of being generally "guided upon the right path". The Ismāʿīlites and the Ithnā-ʿasharites, on the other hand, hold that the Imām, although he may be formally designated by his predecessor, is in fact appointed by God and possesses something of the divine essence; but while the Ismāʿīlite Imāms have continued in unbroken line from the time of ʿAlī down to the present day, the Ithnā-ʿasharites ("Twelvers") are so called because they recognise only twelve Imāms, the last of whom retired from this world in 874 and is destined to reappear in the fulness of time.[19] Since these three groups all possess their own distinct legal systems, the term "Shīʿite law" can only be used by way of the broadest generalisation and is often, without further qualification, as meaningless as the term "Sunnite law".

Except in the case of the Zaydites, however, the doctrine of the Imamate dominates Shīʿite jurisprudence to the degree that it produces a concept of law, and the relationship of the political authority therewith, fundamentally different from that obtaining among the Sunnites. Such administrative powers as belong to the Sunnite Caliph must always be exercised within the limits set by the law, for the Caliph is as much bound by its terms as the rest of his subjects. On the other hand legal sovereignty, in the real sense of the term, vests in the Shīʿite Imām, who speaks with the supreme authority of the divine Lawgiver himself. Politically the difference is between a constitutional and an absolute form of government;[20] legally it is between a system which is basically immutable and represents the attempt by human reason to discern the divine command and one which purports to be the direct and living expression of that command.

It follows that consensus (*ijmāʿ*), whether as a spontaneous source of law or as a criterion regulating the authority of human reasoning, has no place in such a scheme of jurisprudence, where the authority of the Imām supersedes that of agreed practice and his infallibility is diametrically opposed to the concept of probable rules of law (*ẓann*) and equally authoritative variants (*ikhtilāf*). For the Khārijites and Zaydites, on the other hand, both of whom accepted the necessity for human reason in law, consensus plays much the same role as it does for the Sunnites, though it is naturally only the opinions of their own scholars which are relevant in the formation of such a consensus. Here, however, the Khārijite recognition of the consensus of the early community at Medina prior to their own "secession" serves to accentuate a further distinctive and important feature of Shīʿite jurisprudence. No authority whatsoever, in their view, can attach to the practices of the early Muslim community because it was not then properly constituted; in particular the election of the first three Caliphs—one manifestation of the *ijmā'* of the Medinan community—had contradicted outright the first principle of the Shī'ite creed that 'Alī was the legitimate successor to the Prophet.

On a purely theoretical plane, then, such coincidence as exists between Sunnite and Shī'ite jurisprudence is overshadowed and outweighed by the doctrine of the Imāmate. Yet in practice the potentially legislative role of the Imām has been a reality only for the Ismā'īlites. As far as the Ithnā-'asharites are concerned, it has represented, since 874, an ultimate ideal which awaits the return of the hidden Imām for its implementation. During the protracted interregnum the exposition of the law has been the task of qualified scholars (*mujtahids*), and however much they may have been regarded as the agents of the Imām and working under his influence, their use of human reason (*'aql*) to determine the law has been accepted as necessary and legitimate. Inevitably, therefore, the concept of probable rules of law (*ẓann*) and the authoritative criterion of consensus have been recognised by the Ithnā-'asharites, and their system is certainly not without its variant scholastic opinions. Furthermore the actual historical evolution of law in the various Shī'ite groups has closely followed that in Sunnite Islam; for although Shī'ite jurisprudence knows no doctrine of "imitation" or *taqlīd*, Imāms or their representative scholars have seldom seen fit to depart from the traditional law as expressed in authoritative manuals belonging to the early mediaeval period. Similarly Khārijite law, which continued in theory to be capable of development by the exercise of independent judgement (*ijtihād*), in fact remained as stable over the centuries as its Sunnite counterpart.

Passing now to the sphere of substantive legal doctrine, Khārijite law knows a limited number of rules, all of a subsidiary nature, which have no parallel in the Sunnite schools. A mother's right of custody of her male children, for example, terminates in Khārijite law when the child is two years old—a rule which incidentally coincides with that of the Ithnā-'asharites. But the great bulk of Khārijite law—and certainly all its basic tenets—can find adequate authority among the Sunnite jurists. Thus, custody of girls belongs to the mother until the age of seven, when the child may opt to live with either parent; this is normal Shāfi'ī doctrine. A wife is entitled to be maintained on a scale determined by exclusive reference to the husband's means; this, again, is the Shāfi'ī view as opposed to the other Sunnite schools, who take into account the wife's own circumstances and background. Arrears of maintenance cannot be claimed by a wife unless the amount of maintenance was fixed by a previous court order or agreement between the spouses; this is substantially Ḥanafī law, while the other Sunnite schools hold arrears of maintenance to be a recoverable debt notwithstanding the absence of an agreement or judicial maintenance order. Cruelty is a ground for a wife's petition for dissolution of her marriage—as it is for the Mālikīs but not for the three other schools. Khārijite law is not, of course, simply a haphazard amalgam of Sunnite principles; it is a cohesive system with its own spirit and character. But the variations between Khārijite law and one particular Sunnite school or another, while they may be of considerable practical consequence, have no peculiar Khārijite stamp or sectarian significance.

Far different is the case with the Shī'ites. Confining our attention to the majority group of the Ithnā-'asharites, their doctrine assumes in several fundamental respects a unique character sharply opposed to that of the Sunnite (and the Khārijite) systems as a whole. A brief review of three outstanding features of

Ithnā-ʿasharite law will illustrate the nature and extent of the divergence.

Sexual intercourse in Sunnite Islam (and in the Khārijite, Zaydite, and Ismāʿīlite sects) is legal and permissible on two grounds only—the dominion that a master possesses over his slave-girl or a valid contract of marriage (*nikāḥ*). Ithnā-ʿasharite law, however, recognises a third, and totally different, permissible form of sexual relationship known as *mutʿa*.

While *nikāḥ* is, in essence and intention, a life-long union, *mutʿa* is a temporary relationship contracted for a specific period and in consideration of a specific remuneration (*ujra*) payable to the woman. The normal impediments to a *nikāḥ* marriage arising out of the blood, affinity, or foster relationship of the parties apply equally to *mutʿa*, as also does the bar created by difference of religion; a man may therefore contract *mutʿa* with either a Muslim woman or one from the "people of the book" (Jewish, Christian, etc.), but a Muslim woman only with a Muslim. On the other hand, as opposed to the permissible maximum of four wives, there is no limit to the number of women with whom a man may conclude *mutʿa* contracts. Furthermore, none of the principal rights and duties which stem from the permanent bond created by *nikāḥ* applies to a *mutʿa* contract. No right of maintenance belongs to the woman and no corresponding duty of obedience falls upon her, and there are no rights of mutual inheritance between the partners. Nor can there be a divorce in the technical sense, either by the husband pronouncing a formal repudiation or by the wife petitioning the court for dissolution. The contract may, however, be terminated prematurely either by mutual agreement or by one party unilaterally. Where the man prematurely terminates the union he is said to "make a gift of the remaining period" to the woman and has no right to recover any proportionate sum of the remuneration (*ujra*). Conversely, the woman is bound to return a proportionate part of the *ujra* if she fails to fulfil her obligations for the specified period.

Mutʿa, then, is not simply a *nikāḥ* with an accompanying condition of a time-limit, but is a distinct and individual legal institution. If *nikāḥ* is classified, however artificially, by Muslim jurisprudence as a type of sale (*bayʿ*), which results in the transfer of an absolute proprietary interest, *mutʿa* falls under the head of hire or lease (*ijāra*), as being the transfer of the *usus* only for a limited period. Such a concept of marriage is utterly alien to general Muslim jurisprudence, and however proper the motive for the conclusion of a *mutʿa* may be —as where, for example, a term of 99 years is stipulated —the resulting relationship is, outside Ithnā-ʿasharite jurisdiction, not only void in civil law but amounts to the criminal act of fornication (*zināʾ*) and will, in strict theory, be sanctioned by the severe penalties prescribed therefor.

Ṭalāq (divorce by repudiation) provides our second example of a major clash between Ithnā-ʿasharite and Sunnite law. Here there is no dispute as to the basic right of a husband unilaterally to repudiate his wife at will; but in the regulation of the incidents governing the exercise of this right, Ithnā-ʿasharite law is restrictive to a degree that betrays an essentially different attitude from that adopted by the Sunnites to this form of divorce.

In the first place, no formalities are attached by Sunnite law to the manner in which a repudiation may be pronounced: it may be effected orally or in writing; any words indicative of repudiation may be used, and witnesses are not necessary for its validity (as distinct from its proof). Ithnā-ʿasharite law, on the other hand, postulates a strict adherence to form: the pronouncement must be made orally, using the precise term *ṭalāq* or some form thereof, in the presence of two witnesses. Furthermore, there must be proof of a definite intention to repudiate, while for the Sunnites generally repudiations pronounced as a jest or threat, and for the Ḥanafīs in particular repudiations uttered under duress or by a husband in a state of intoxication, are valid and effective.

Secondly, *ṭalāq* is classified by the Sunnites, according to the circumstances in which it is pronounced, as either "approved" (*ṭalāq as-sunna*) or "disapproved" (*ṭalāq al-bid'a*). *Ṭalāq as-sunna* may take the form either of a single repudiation, which is revocable by the husband until the expiry of the wife's *'idda* period, or of one repudiation followed by two further confirmatory repudiations in successive months, when divorce becomes irrevocable on the third pronouncement. *Ṭalāq al-bid'a*, on the other hand, primarily designates forms of repudiation which are immediately irrevocable, such as where a single repudiation is expressly declared to be final or where three repudiations are pronounced at the same time. But in order to qualify as "approved" a repudiation must also be made in a wife's period of "purity" (*ṭuhr*, *sc.* when she is not menstruating) during which she has had no sexual relations with her husband, and failure to observe these attendant conditions will render the repudiation "disapproved". In Sunnite Islam the distinction between these two forms of *ṭalāq* is a purely moral one, for both types are equally valid and effective in law. Ithnā-'asharite law, however, does not recognise the "disapproved" forms of *ṭalāq* at all, but insists upon strict adherence to the "approved" forms under pain of nullity. In sum, therefore, the Ithnā-'asharite doctrines clearly manifest a desire to confine the husband's exercise of his power to repudiate within rigidly defined limits—a policy of which there is little evidence in the generally lax and permissive nature of Sunnite law.

It is the Ithnā-ʿasharite law of inheritance, however, which stands out in boldest relief as the supremely distinctive feature of their whole system. Entitlement to succeed on intestacy rests, for the Sunnites, on three distinct grounds which produce three separate groups of legal heirs—the Qur'ānic sharers, the male agnate relatives (*ʿaṣaba*) of the deceased, and, failing these two primary groups, female and cognate relatives. Ithnā-ʿasharite law, on the other hand, recognises one basis of entitlement only, that of "relationship" (*qarāba*) simply, and accordingly divides all relatives (with the exception of the spouse relict who always takes his or her Qur'ānic share) into three classes. These, in order of priority, are (a) the lineal descendants and parents of the deceased, (b) brothers, sisters and their issue and grandparents of the deceased, and (c) uncles and aunts and their issue. Entitlement, therefore, depends solely upon the position of the claimant heir within this scheme; and while the Qur'ānic heirs, when entitled, will take their allotted share, and the basic rule applies that a male relative generally takes twice the share of a female relative of corresponding order and degree, the system differs vitally from Sunnite law in that it affords no distinctive place to the male agnate relatives. Jaʿfar aṣ-Ṣādiq, the sixth Shīʿite Imām (d. 765), is alleged to have peremptorily dismissed their claims with the remark: "Dust in the jaws of the ʿ*aṣaba*"; and those female and cognate relatives who only succeed in the last resort in Sunnite law are integrated within the general framework of the Shīʿite classes of heirs.

The paternal grandfather of the deceased, for example, occupies a favoured position in the Sunnite scheme in the absence of the deceased's father. Ranking as a substitute heir for the latter, he will take a Qur'ānic share of one-sixth in the presence of any child of the deceased, while by virtue of his agnate relationship he will be entitled, in addition, to any residue where the only surviving child of the deceased is a daughter, will take twice as much as the deceased's mother, when in competition with her alone or in company with the spouse relict, and finally will totally exclude any children of the deceased's daughter. In the Ithnā-ʿasharite system the presence of any one of the relatives mentioned—child, grandchild or mother of the propositus —precludes the paternal grandfather from any rights of succession at all.

Brothers and sisters of the deceased are equally excluded from succession in Ithnā-ʿasharite law by either of the deceased's parents or any lineal descendant. In Sunnite law, on the other hand, they are excluded only by the deceased's father or male agnatic descendant. Germane or consanguine brothers and sisters take as residuary heirs when in competition with the deceased's daughter; in competition with the mother, sisters, in the absence of brothers, take a collective Qur'ānic share of two-thirds of the estate, and brothers, with or without sisters, inherit as residuaries—two or more of them restricting the mother to her minimum share of one-sixth; while any brother or sister will totally exclude the issue of the deceased's daughter. Here, perhaps, the real nature and significance of the divergence between the two systems is at its most apparent. It is not only that females and cognate relatives generally enjoy a more privileged position in Shīʿite law, but rather that Sunnite law, in recognising the claims of agnate collaterals, embodies a much broader concept of the family group than Shīʿite law, which rests firmly upon the predominance of the narrower tie of relationship existing between a mother and father and their issue.

It may now be appreciated that the Ithnā-ʿasharite doctrines on the three topics we have discussed are of so pronouncedly individual a character that they cannot be regarded in the same light as the variations among the Sunnite schools or explained in terms of the same causes.

Political considerations, it has often been suggested, adequately account for the special features of Ithnā-ʿasharite law. Denying the authority of the first three Caliphs of Medina, the Ithnā-ʿasharites maintained the validity of *mutʿa* "for no better reason than that its prohibition had been attributed to ʿUmar".[21] Similarly, their rejection of the "disapproved" forms of repudiation of a wife is explicable on the ground that these were innovations practised by the Muslim community during the same period of its government by usurpers, and as such were devoid of authority. Finally the Ithnā-ʿasharite scheme of inheritance is even more obviously allied with their political tenets; for the principles that cognate relationship is as strong a ground for succession as the agnate tie, and that the claims of collaterals are subordinate to those of all lineal descendants, appear indispensable to a faction whose hierarchy of leaders traces its descent from the Prophet's daughter Fāṭima and claims to have inherited through her something of Muḥammad's own divinely given qualities.

ʿAlī holds the position of first Imām because, in Shīʿite belief, the Prophet so appointed him. Even so, the desire that the principles of relationship (*qarāba*) should show ʿAlī to be closer in line of succession than the Prophet's uncle ʿAbbās (and the dynasty to which he gave his name) produces a striking anomaly in the Ithnā-ʿasharite law. Where the claimants to an estate are relatives in the third class of heirs—uncles and aunts of the deceased and their issue—the normal rule of priority in degree is that any uncle will totally exclude the issue of uncles, i.e. cousins of the deceased. Ithnā-'asharite law, however, maintains that where the only competing heirs are a consanguine paternal uncle and a germane paternal uncle's son, the latter excludes the former. 'Abbās was the consanguine paternal uncle of the Prophet, 'Alī his germane paternal uncle's son.

Yet to ascribe the Ithnā-'asharite variations to purely political factors is not wholly convincing. If they recognised *mut'a* solely because 'Umar forbade it, they would have rejected, equally flatly, any ruling ascribed to the first three Caliphs or any practice followed by the early Medinan community, and this they did not do: rather, they did not accept 'Umar's prohibition of an institution whose validity they recognised on other grounds. Furthermore, as we have pointed out, their rejection of the "disapproved" forms of repudiation was merely one aspect, albeit an important one, of their fundamentally distinct attitude to this form of divorce as a whole. Similarly the differences in their law of inheritance go far beyond those that would be required by bare political motives. The hypothetical competition between 'Alī and 'Abbās for succession to the Prophet is a case in point; this is indeed a superficial modification dictated by political tenets, but the basic principles to which it forms an exception are themselves quite distinct from Sunnite law. For these reasons the Ithnā-'asharite doctrines would appear to have some deeper significance than that of mere championship of the cause of 'Alī and his descendants against the acknowledged rulers of the Sunnites.

Ithnā-'asharite jurists themselves consistently claim that their system is a closer expression and a more faithful representation of the spirit of the Qur'ānic laws than its Sunnite counterpart. *Mut'a* is recognised because it is explicitly endorsed by the Qur'ān in their interpretation thereof. Repudiation is only effective when pronounced in the "approved" forms because these were the only forms expressly recognised by the Qur'ān and the authentic precedents of the Prophet. Their scheme of succession is the development of the necessary implications underlying the Qur'ānic rules on the subject, which stress the rights of female relatives and nowhere indicate the pre-eminence of the agnate relationship as such. These views of the Ithnā-'asharite scholars, then, reveal a vitally different approach to the question of the juristic interpretation of the Qur'ān. Existing customary law is, for the Sunnites, impliedly endorsed by the Qur'ān unless it is expressly rejected; hence the fusion in their scheme of inheritance between the old agnate heirs of the customary law (*'aṣaba*) and the new heirs specified by the Qur'ān. For the Ithnā-'asharites, on the contrary, existing customary law is impliedly rejected by the Qur'ān unless it is expressly endorsed; and the express Qur'ānic norms are no more subject to modification by practices arising after their revelation (the "disapproved" forms of repudiation) than they are by pre-existing custom (the rights of the *'aṣaba*). In short, the Sunnites view the Qur'ānic regulations as piecemeal reforms to be superimposed upon the existing law, while the Ithnā-'asharites regard them as providing an outright break with past practice and laying down the first principles for the elaboration of an entirely novel system.

Are the distinctive doctrines of the Ithnā-'asharites, then, the result of political factors, or do they stem from a particular method of juristic interpretation of the Qur'ān, as they themselves assert? Formulated in extreme terms, the problem would thus appear to be whether the law of the Ithnā-'asharites precedes and supports their political doctrine or whether their political doctrine precedes and determines the form of their law. In fact, however, the problem and the apparent conflict only exist if the term "political" is given the narrow connotation, such as it would normally have in Western terminology, of the bare form and incidents of temporal authority in the state. Now in an Islamic context, political, religious, and legal factors are inextricably merged in the notion of the theocratic state; and if we give the term "political" this comprehensive meaning, the Ithnā-ʿasharite doctrine regarding leadership in Islam and their juristic approach to the interpretation of the Qur'ān appear as complementary and interdependent aspects of the same political creed. Sunnite political theory represents an amalgam of Islamic principles and pre-Islamic practice—rule by the traditional tribal aristocracy subject to the dictates of the religious law. Ithnā-ʿasharite political theory, on the other hand, renounces any connection with pre-Islamic practice and sees the sole source of authority to lie in the founder-Prophet and his attributes as a religious leader. The respective attitudes adopted by the two groups towards the relationship between the Qur'ānic laws and pre-existing custom are not only directly parallel with their distinct political concepts but are a necessary and integral part of them. Juristically as well as politically, Islam meant a re-orientation and modification of existing practice for the Sunnites, while for the Ithnā-ʿasharites it marked a completely new point of departure.

Ithnā-ʿasharite law, therefore, cannot properly be regarded as a system adopted from the Sunnites and superficially modified to accord with political tenets. It appears as a natural manifestation and product of their own version of the nature of Islam, inseparably connected with the whole body of dogma and beliefs which constitute their religious faith. Just as this explains the fundamental divergences of Ithnā-ʿasharite law, it equally accounts for the general similarity of Khārijite law with the Sunnite system, for the approximation of Ismāʿīlite law to the Ithnā-ʿasharite position, and for the fact that Zaydite law represents a fusion of Sunnite and Shīʿite principles. Yet, whatever the extent of their coincidence with, or divergence from, Sunnite doctrines, the sectarian legal systems are, in the ultimate analysis, quite distinct from each other and from those of Sunnite Islam; for they derive their authority exclusively from those individual politico-religious beliefs by virtue of which the several sects and the Sunnites mutually regard each other as heretical.

CHAPTER 9

ISLAMIC GOVERNMENT AND SHARĪʿA LAW

SHARĪʿA law had come into being as a doctrinal system independent of and essentially opposed to current legal practice. But the scholars, at least in the early period, had in no way opposed the existing constitution or its legal and administrative machinery as such. Primarily concerned to regulate the relationship of the individual Muslim with his God, the jurists had formulated standards of conduct which represented a system of private, and not of public, law, and which they conceived it to be the duty of the established political power to ratify and enforce. Having traced the growth of the doctrine itself to its maturity of expression in the mediaeval texts, we now proceed to consider how far the *de facto* authority of Islamic government supported the religious authority of Sharīʿa doctrine by securing its effective application in the legal tribunals.

Organisation of the Islamic state under the Umayyads was not based upon any firm separation of the executive and the judicial functions. Supreme power in both these respects vested in the Caliph, and through the delegation of his authority a great variety of subordinate officials possessed judicial competence within the territorial or functional limits of their administrative duties. Provincial governors, army commanders, masters of the treasury, market-inspectors, and even officials in charge of the water supply all possessed powers of jurisdiction within their own spheres of activity, while the police (*shurṭa*) provide perhaps the best example of the integration of the different aspects of authority inasmuch as the investigation of crimes, the arrest, trial and punishment of criminals all fell within the scope of their office.

Settlement of disputes of a private nature, however, was a specific duty delegated to the *qāḍī* or judge. Increasing importance and prestige were attached to this office; the *qāḍīs* came to have a general judicial competence which cut through the subsidiary administrative divisions of the state, and by the end of the Umayyad period they had become the central organ for the administration of law. At the same time the *qāḍīs* were in no sense an independent judiciary since their judgements were subject to review by the political superior who had appointed them, and upon his support they were entirely dependent for the enforcement of their decisions.

With the accession to power of the ʿAbbāsid dynasty and its declared policy of implementing the system of religious law currently being worked out by the scholar-jurists, the status of the judiciary was greatly enhanced. Henceforth the *qāḍīs* became inseparably linked with Sharīʿa law which it was their bounden duty to apply. Organised as a profession under the central authority of a chief *qāḍī* (*qāḍī al-quḍāt*), they were no longer the spokesmen of a law which represented the command of the provincial or district governor but now owed allegiance exclusively to God's law. But this did not mean that the future course of the Islamic ship of state was to be steered by the Sharīʿa courts. The ʿAbbāsid rulers maintained a firm grip on the helm, and the Sharīʿa courts never attained that position of supreme judicial authority independent of political control, which would have provided the only sure foundation and real guarantee for the ideal of the *Civitas Dei*.

Although they may have been formally appointed by the chief *qāḍī*, the judiciary held office only during the pleasure of the political authority, as indeed did the chief *qāḍī* himself, and their character of political subordinates was responsible for a serious limitation on their powers of jurisdiction which existed from the outset. This was the inability of the *qāḍīs* to deal effectively with claims against high and powerful officials of state. Such inability was simply the result of the failure of the political authority to recognise the decisions of the *qāḍīs* in these cases and to enforce them by the machinery at his command. Although executive authorities may have been understandably reluctant to submit to the jurisdiction of an official whom they considered certainly no higher in the political hierarchy than themselves, they could have been forced to do so. But when the sovereign chose not to do this but to sit himself as a court, known as the court of *Maẓālim* (Complaints), to hear cases of this type, he demonstrated the subordinate position that had been assigned to the *qāḍīs* in the direction of the affairs of state. *Maẓālim* jurisdiction, particularly as it involved dealing with complaints against the behaviour or the judgements of the *qāḍīs* themselves, underlined the fact that supreme judicial power was vested in the political sovereign, and that the jurisdiction and authority of Sharī'a courts were subject to such limits as he saw fit to define.

The 'Abbāsids may have held themselves out as servants of the Sharī'a law; they may have represented their policies as based on its dictates; but they were not prepared to allow independence to the courts whose sole duty it was to apply it. While the annalists are at pains to record instances of Caliphs and governors personally submitting to the decisions of their *qāḍīs*, their more usual theme is that of peremptory directives issued by the ruler to the judiciary, of the reversal of their decisions and the arbitrary dismissal of those who had incurred the displeasure of their master.

This situation naturally provoked a deep resentment on the part of the legal scholars (*fuqahā'*), and was, in part at any rate, the reason why so many of them showed an extreme reluctance to accept appointment as *qāḍīs*. One of the more graphic anecdotes illustrating their attitude in this regard concerns the appointment of 'Abd-Allāh ibn-Farūk as *qāḍī* of Qairawān in 787. This scholar, because of his refusal to accept the office, found himself in chains and about to be precipitated from the roof of the mosque by the governor's guards. He succumbed but was none the less reduced to a state hysteria by the arrival of his first litigants.[22] The protests of the jurists, however, were directed against the vulnerability of the decisions given by the *qāḍīs*, not against the extent of their jurisdiction. However much they deplored interference by the political authority in the activities of Sharī'a tribunals, they did not contest his right to impose initial restrictions upon their sphere of jurisdiction. Indeed, the Sharī'a courts cannot have been intended, even by the scholars themselves, to provide the exclusive organ of jurisdiction in the Islamic state, as consideration of two aspects of the nature of the doctrine which the courts were bound to apply will make plain.

In the first place the essential function of the doctrine was the portrayal of the ideal relationship between man and his Creator. Although this naturally involved the precise formulation of the individual's rights and duties towards his fellow beings, the regulation of the position of the individual *vis-à-vis* the temporal authorities in the state lay largely outside the scholars' self-imposed terms of reference. Accordingly the early doctrine contained no system of constitutional law, nor did it make any attempt to regulate those matters which make up the field of public law. Criminal law, for example, did not exist in the technical sense of a comprehensive scheme of offences against the public order. Homicide was regulated in meticulous detail, but was treated as a private and not as a public offence. For the rest the doctrine was largely confined to the exposition of six specific offences—illicit sexual relations, slanderous allegations of unchastity, theft, wine-drinking, armed robbery, and apostasy—in which the notion of man's obligations towards God predominated and which, because God himself had "defined" the punishments therefor, were known as the *ḥadd* (pl. *ḥudūd*) offences.

Similarly in fiscal law, scholars were primarily concerned with those limited aspects of public finance which were deemed to constitute a man's obligations towards God—e.g. *zakāt* tax or "legal alms". In both these spheres of the law the scholars, at least in the early period, made no claim of comprehensiveness for the doctrine. Provided the religious duties were not contravened the sovereign had the right, and the duty, to take such measures against criminals or pursue such fiscal policies as the interests of the state required. But these were activities strictly outside the purview of the Sharīʿa and jurisdiction over them was, by necessary implication, outside the competence of the *qāḍīs'* courts.

The second factor which seriously impaired the efficiency of the Sharīʿa courts was the system of procedure and evidence by which they were bound. On the basis of the initial presumption attached by the law to the facts in issue (e.g. the presumption of innocence in a criminal case or the presumption of freedom from debt in a civil suit) the parties to litigation were allotted the roles of *muddaʿī* ("claimer", plaintiff) and *muddaʿā ʿalayhi* ("claimed against", defendant) respectively, the former being the party whose assertion ran counter to this presumption, the latter the party whose assertion was supported by it. Upon the *muddaʿī* fell the burden of proof, and this burden could shift many times in the course of the same suit—as when, for example, the original *muddaʿā ʿalayhi* in an action for debt became the *muddaʿī* by pleading payment, a counterclaim, or set-off. But whether on an intermediate or the ultimate issue the burden of proof was always the same; the *muddaʿī* had to produce two male adult Muslims to testify orally to their direct knowledge of the truth of his claim. Written evidence was not acceptable and any form of circumstantial evidence was totally inadmissible. Some limited exceptions to this normal standard were recognised—in certain cases one witness might be sufficient if the *muddaʿī* also took the oath confirming his claim and the testimony of women might be acceptable (though two women were usually required to take the place of one man)—but in all cases the witness had to possess the highest quality of moral and religious probity (*ʿadāla*). Some indication of the stringency of law and practice in this regard is afforded by one *qāḍī's* rejection of the testimony of a trusted and personal friend because he had, on one occasion, been smitten with passion for a slave girl and had purchased her for a sum far in excess of her real value. Where the *muddaʿī* failed to discharge this rigid burden of proof, the *muddaʿā ʿalayhi* was offered the oath of denial. Properly sworn on the Qur'ān such an oath secured judgement in his favour; if he failed to take it, judgement would be given for the *muddaʿī*, provided, in some circumstances, he himself took the oath. Oral testimony (*shahāda*) thus provided the one form of legal proof admissible in Sharīʿa doctrine. Duly produced it was conclusive, in the sense that the court was bound to decide according to its terms, and there was thus no question of assessing the weight of evidence or deciding an issue on the balance of probabilities. No cross-examination of witnesses on the facts was allowed, and the only recourse for the opponent was to impugn their character of moral and religious probity. The same procedure and the same standard of proof applied in both civil and criminal cases, the only difference of substance being that a formal admission or confession (*iqrār*) was binding in a civil suit but revocable in a criminal case.

Based on the assumption that a witness of hitherto blameless character would always tell the truth and that even the most hardened criminals would hesitate to swear a false oath of their innocence, the doctrine displayed an altruistic reliance upon the force of religious belief which often proved out of touch with the practical circumstances of litigation. This sphere of the law particularly reflects the fundamentally academic and idealistic approach adopted by the early scholars, who saw themselves in the role of spiritual advisers to the conscience of Islam rather than authoritarian directors of its practical affairs. It was this attitude in fact which lay at the root of the abhorrence which many scholars demonstrated towards the office of *qāḍī* and which explains why the famous jurist of Qairawān, Saḥnūn, after his investiture as *qāḍī* in 848, and despite the fact that he had been guaranteed complete independence in his office, nevertheless had "such intense grief on his face that none dared to congratulate him. He rode straight home to his daughter Khadīja, and said to her: 'Today your father is slaughtered without a knife'." [23]

The rigidly formalistic and mechanical nature of Sharī'a procedure left little or no scope for the exercise of any discretion by the *qāḍī* in controlling proceedings before him. The rules of evidence aimed at the establishment of the truth of claims with a high degree of certainty, a policy which found perhaps its most striking expression in the rule that proof of the offence of fornication (*zinā*ʾ) could be established only by the testimony of four upright male eye-witnesses to the very act of carnal conjunction. But the postulation of the rigid standards of evidence in all cases could obviously occasion considerable injustice; and it was largely because of the often impractical burden of proof imposed upon a plaintiff, and the corresponding ease with which unscrupulous defendants might avoid a civil or criminal liability which reason declared to exist, that the Sharīʿa courts proved, at least in certain spheres of the law, an unsatisfactory organ for the administration of justice.

Effective organisation of the affairs of state, therefore, necessitated the recognition of jurisdictions other than that of the *qāḍī*. Although the scope itself of Sharīʿa doctrine meant that certain types of case fell altogether outside the province of the Sharīʿa courts—litigation on fiscal matters, for example, was normally brought before the Master of the Treasury—it was the system of procedure and evidence to which the Sharīʿa courts were tied which was chiefly responsible for the curtailment of their jurisdiction. Indeed, there existed an official, known as the *ṣāḥib ar-radd*, whose specific function it was to hear cases rejected by the *qāḍī* because the evidence proffered by the plaintiff, however intrinsically compelling, did not fulfil the precise standards exacted by the Sharīʿa.

Criminal law was the obvious sphere where political interests could not tolerate the cumbersome nature of Sharīʿa procedure. Jurisdiction here mainly belonged to the police, the delegate who exercised it being alternatively called the *wālī al-jarāʾim* (official in charge of crimes). These courts considered circumstantial evidence, heard the testimony of witnesses of dubious character, put them on oath and cross-examined them; they imprisoned suspects, convicted on the basis of known character and previous offences, might make the accused swear the oath by a local saint instead of on the Qur'ān, and in general could take such measures to discover guilt, including the extortion of confessions, as they saw fit. Nominally respecting the substance of the religious law, these courts could apply the *ḥadd* or "fixed" punishments but were not bound to do so where the Sharī'a standards of proof were not fulfilled; so that to their flexibility of procedure was added a wide discretion in the determination of penalties which gave a highly arbitrary flavour to their administration of criminal justice.

Land law was a further matter of particular concern to government, inasmuch as the important land-owners had received their land by way of concessions from the sovereign to secure their political allegiance. For this reason the political authority himself chose to exercise jurisdiction in this sphere, on the basis of a discretionary system of procedure, and indeed of substantive law, the delegate he might appoint for the purpose being usually known as "the one in charge of complaints" (*Ṣāḥib al-Maẓālim*). *Maẓālim* jurisdiction thus came to have an area of operation much wider than the enquiry into complaints against officials of the state. Its limits were such as the sovereign cared to define and were often extended so as to constitute serious competition for the Sharī'a tribunals, as is shown by the comprehensive powers of jurisdiction assumed under the Mamlūk sovereigns of Egypt by the Court Chamberlain (*ḥājib*), whose court decided cases of personal law normally justiciable by the *qāḍīs*.

Islamic legal practice, therefore, was based on a dual system of courts, and although all functions in the Islamic state were theoretically religious in nature, the distinction between the *Maẓālim* and Sharī'a jurisdictions came very close to the notion of a division between secular and religious courts. For whereas the *qāḍī* was regarded as the representative of God's law, the *Ṣāḥib al-Maẓālim* was regarded as the representative of the ruler's law. A detail from the legal practice in Egypt in the early ninth century would appear to indicate this aspect of the distinction: when a *Ṣāḥib al-Maẓālim* was appointed during the temporary absence of a *qāḍī*, he held his court in a private building, not in the mosque, which was the normal seat of the *qāḍī's* court.

Legal scholarship from the eleventh century onwards[24] evolved a doctrine of public law which rationalised the place which the Sharīʿa had in fact come to occupy in the organisation of the Islamic state. Basically common to all the Sunnite schools, the doctrine laid down the conditions for the office of Caliph—the two major requirements being extreme piety of character and the ability to ascertain and understand the terms of God's law (*ijtihād*)—and recognised that a ruler so qualified had the power to take such steps as he saw fit to implement and supplement the principles established by the religious law. This system of government was known as "government in accordance with the revealed law" (*siyāsa sharʿiyya*), but it is obvious that the term "*sharʿiyya*"[25] here has a far wider connotation than the technical system of law which is expounded in the manuals of the jurists and which we consistently refer to in this book as Sharīʿa law. To the public lawyers the concept of the sovereign being bound to rule according to the Sharīʿa meant that he was bound to give effect to the general purposes of God for Islamic society. While legal doctrine had explained these purposes in terms of the rights and duties of individuals and had established certain inviolable standards of conduct, the wider and supreme duty of the sovereign was the protection of the public interest; and in pursuance of it he was afforded an overriding personal discretion to determine, according to time and circumstances, how the purposes of God for the Islamic community might best be effected.

According to the treatises on public law, the court of the *qāḍī* forms the normal organ for the administration of law and "the pivot of the judicial system".[26] The duty of *qaḍā'* (acting as *qāḍī*) is one of supreme religious merit and a vital function of state, and any unwillingness on the part of scholars to undertake it is strongly condemned. At the same time doctrine recognised the limitations imposed upon the *qāḍī's* jurisdiction by the nature of Sharī'a law when it allowed him to abstain from giving judgement in cases where the evidence adduced did not meet the rigid Sharī'a standards—although the view is often expressed that the *qāḍī* should temper the dictates of the doctrine in the light of practical necessity, by admitting, for example, the testimony of witnesses who are not strictly men of probity.

Above the *qāḍīs* in the hierarchy of judicial authority are the *Maẓālim* courts, whose pronouncements are the direct expression of the supreme judicial and executive powers combined in the sovereign and whose jurisdiction is superior particularly because of their recognised competence to formulate principles of substantive law additional and supplementary to the scheme of strict Sharī'a doctrine. One example of such activity, quoted as a precedent by the author al-Māwardī, is a decision of the Caliph 'Alī introducing a rule of contributory negligence in accidental homicide. Where three children were playing a game of horses and riders and child A pinched "horse" B, causing him to dislodge "rider" C who died from the fall, 'Alī decided that each of the three participants in the game should bear the responsibility for one-third of the compensation or blood-money (*diya*) due. Although early decisions such as this in fact became an integral part of the Sharī'a law itself, the doctrine of public law set no limit upon the future exercise of this power by the sovereign—beyond the natural one that an express prohibition of the Sharī'a should not thereby be violated. This attribute of *Maẓālim* jurisdiction naturally had a vital significance in view of the fact that Sharī'a doctrine had become set in a rigid mould, and it provided, in the view of the public lawyers at least, an instrument for the potential development of law in Islam along lines remarkably parallel to the way in which Equity freed the English legal system from the strictures of the common law.

Apart from the "official in charge of crimes" (*wālī al-jarā'im*), who is perhaps best regarded as exercising a species of *Maẓālim* jurisdiction in the particular domain of criminal law, the doctrine of public law acknowledges the validity of certain other jurisdictions, ranked as inferior, because of their restricted competence, to the *qāḍīs'* courts. But the majority of these are essentially administrative offices and often purely ancillary to the *qāḍī's* jurisdiction, such as the assessment of damage to property or of the compensation due in cases of physical injury. Undoubtedly the most typically Islamic of these subsidiary functions described by the texts is that of an official called the *muḥtasib*, who is charged with the general supervision of the religious and moral welfare of the local population and whose duties range from the enforcement of the ritual prayers and fast to the proper segregation of the sexes in public places. He has the particular power to deal summarily with petty offences committed in the market place, such as the hoarding of foodstuffs or the fraudulent concealment of defects in merchandise; but this limited jurisdiction is merely an incidental part of his primary role and, as it has been expressed, while the *Maẓālim* courts act where the *qāḍī* is powerless, the *muḥtasib* acts in those cases which are beneath the *qāḍī's* dignity.[27]

In thus describing a broad scheme of judicial administration the writers on public law were simply commenting upon the existing state of affairs known to them and were not propounding a system of universal application or exclusive validity; for they recognised that the distribution of judicial powers was ultimately the sole prerogative of the political sovereign and that the extent of his "governmental" regulations must necessarily be determined by particular circumstances of time and place. Historically the scope of the several offices has varied considerably in different periods and areas of Islam. Ibn-Taymiyya, for example, writing in the fourteenth century, states that the military authority in contemporary Egypt and Syria had jurisdiction in most criminal cases and in certain civil suits, but had no judicial competence at all in the Maghrib where its function was simply to enforce the decisions of the *qāḍīs'* courts. Sometimes indeed the *qāḍīs* themselves exercised Sharī'a and *Maẓālim* jurisdictions concurrently, but as a general rule their province was that of private law—family law, inheritance, civil transactions and injuries, and *waqf* endowments.

It is the criminal law, perhaps, which provides the outstanding instance of the wide discretionary powers granted to the sovereign under the doctrine of *siyāsa shar'iyya.* As far as concerns procedure, he may order the use of such methods as he sees fit to discover where guilt lies; for, as one author states, "were we simply to subject each suspect to the oath and then free him, in spite of our knowledge of his notoriety in crime, saying: 'We cannot convict him without two upright witnesses', that would be contrary to *siyāsa shar'iyya*".[28] As for substantive law, the sovereign is completely free, outside the *ḥadd* offences, to determine what behaviour constitutes an offence and what punishment is to be applied in each case. Such discretionary punishment is known as *taʿzīr* or "deterrence", since its purpose is to "deter" the offender himself or others from similar conduct. Most jurists, however, adhere to the view that *taʿzīr* punishment should be restricted to flogging or imprisonment and should never exceed the prescribed *ḥadd* punishments of this nature—i.e. one hundred lashes or one year's imprisonment; but for the Mālikīs the principle that the punishment should fit the nature of the crime and the character of the offender is of absolute application and may, in suitable cases, necessitate the death penalty. Finally, since the broad purpose of *taʿzīr* punishment is the prevention of any conduct prejudicial to the good order of the state, the sovereign may intervene under this head in cases of a strictly civil nature; in particular he may punish at his discretion persons who have committed homicides or assaults when they have been pardoned by the victim or his representatives.

Doctrine had granted the ruler such wide discretionary powers on the assumption that he would be ideally qualified for office. But it is precisely here that the idealistic nature of the doctrine is at its most apparent; for there existed no constitutional machinery, and in particular no independent judiciary, to guarantee that the ruler would be so qualified and that those powers would not be abused. Although the doctrine expressed to perfection the concept of a state founded upon the rule of God's law, it never seriously challenged the ruler's autocratic power to control the practical implementation of that law; and it finally reached the point of abject surrender and recognition of its total impotence by acknowledging the principle that obedience was due to the political power whatever its nature, and that even the most impious and tyrannical regime was preferable to civil strife. The order of allegiance expressed in the Qur'ānic verse: "Obey God, his Apostle and those at the head of affairs" had been reversed, and the only limits upon the *de facto* power of the ruler were those that he found in his own conscience.

Enough has now been said to indicate that Sharīʿa law, however strong its religious force as providing an ideal and comprehensive code of conduct for the individual, can form only a part of the Islamic legal system. The doctrine of *siyāsa sharʿiyya*, based on a realistic assessment of the nature of Sharīʿa law and the historical process by which it had been absorbed into the structure of the state, admitted the necessity for, and the validity of, extra-Sharīʿa jurisdictions, which cannot therefore be regarded, in themselves, as deviations from any ideal standard. Islamic government has never meant, in theory or in practice, the exclusive jurisdiction of Sharīʿa tribunals.

CHAPTER 10

ISLAMIC SOCIETY AND SHARĪʿA LAW

ISLAMIC ideology required that those standards of conduct which had evolved out of the past experiences and the present needs of society should, upon acceptance of the faith, be abandoned and superseded by the religious law as it had crystallised in the classical doctrine of the tenth century. It is the purpose of this present chapter to consider the results of the basic tension which was thus created, for the world-wide community of Islam, between Sharīʿa doctrine and established custom in the two major spheres of private law—the law of the family and the law of civil transactions.

Family law, as far as the Arab populations of Islam were concerned, was generally administered in accordance with strict Sharīʿa doctrine. As a system which was based upon the customs of those localities where the law had originated, such as the Hijaz and Iraq, and which had successfully absorbed, within this framework, the reforms introduced by the Prophet, it was largely in accord with the innate temper of Arab society and supportable by it. For other peoples, however, the reception of Sharīʿa law posed serious problems, for its basic concepts were often wholly alien to the traditional structure of their societies.

Among some communities the force of indigenous custom was strong enough to deny the Sharīʿa any influence at all in the regulation of their family relationships. However sincere their profession and practice of the faith may have been, they accepted Islam as a religion but not as a way of life, and consequently remained, from the standpoint of strict orthodoxy, only superficially Islamicised. Here we are not referring to the situation where social practice itself was contrary to the law as it would have been applied had the jurisdiction of the courts been invoked—Islamic, no less and no more than any other, society knew such a state of affairs—but our concern lies with those Muslim communities whose only official tribunals applied a law other than Sharīʿa law. The Berber peoples of North Africa, for example, have been governed down to the present day by a customary law which is rigidly patriarchal in its terms. In the region of Kabylie in Algeria marriage is a form of purchase wherein the husband pays the dower to the bride's father, and upon repudiation of his wife, which is always irrevocable, a husband may claim compensation, which usually approximates to the sum he has paid as dower, either from the wife's father or from the next husband she marries.[29] Berber customary law of this nature, one of the consistent features of which is the denial of rights of inheritance to women, is applied to almost half of the Muslim population of Morocco in all civil matters. At the opposite geographical fringe of the Muslim world an entirely different system of customary law, but one which is equally at variance with Sharīʿa doctrine, prevails among the matriarchal societies of the Menangkabau region of Sumatra.[30] Similarly, outside the ritual practices and duties, Sharīʿa law is scarcely applied at all among the Yoruba in Western Nigeria.[31]

For other Muslim communities custom gave way to the dictates of the Sharīʿa in some legal spheres, but continued to apply in others. In the Indian sub-continent, for example, the Ismāʿīlite Khojas, the Bohoras and the Cutchi Memons continued, after their conversion to Islam from Hinduism, to be governed by the Hindu law of testate and intestate succession, and thus retained the power, in outright contravention of Sharīʿa principles, to will away the whole of their estate. In Java, inheritance continued to be regulated by the customary matriarchal law and was not a matter for the religious courts, which, however, possessed a general competence to deal with matters of family law. Nor was it only in the outlying provinces of Islam, nor among those peoples whose conversion to the faith took place at a relatively late date, that Sharīʿa law failed to supersede existing custom. Certain Arab tribes of the Yemen never relinquished their established customary law under which, *inter alia*, women did not enjoy any proprietary rights.[32]

Although the total or partial exclusion of the Sharīʿa by customary law thus brought about, at times, a sharp demarcation between the spheres of influence of the two systems, at other times Sharīʿa principles and elements of the customary law merged to form a composite legal system administered by a single jurisdiction. This phenomenon particularly followed the spread of Islam into the sub-Saharan African territories, where history produced gradations of fusion, which ranged from a tentative and piecemeal application of Sharīʿa norms by the established customary courts to a restricted recognition of elements of the customary law by Sharīʿa tribunals.

Legal practice in Northern Nigeria after the Fulani conquests of the early nineteenth century provides some telling examples of the concessions which Sharīʿa law had inevitably to make to custom, even when a conscientious attempt was made to apply the Sharīʿa in its entirety.[33] Here the courts of the *qāḍīs* (or *Alkalai* in the Hausa language) recognise the right of a wife to obtain dissolution of her marriage by returning to the husband the dower she received from him. Although this may be represented as the form of divorce known to Sharīʿa law as *khulʿ* (release of the wife in consideration of a payment made by her) it is in fact an application of the customary rule which allowed divorce on return of bride-wealth; for in Sharīʿa law *khulʿ* can never be so enforced by the wife unilaterally, but is a normal contract to which the husband's free consent is indispensable. Again, it is on the basis of the customary practice that the courts normally remove male children from the custody of their divorced mother when they are two years old; for the normal Mālikī law, to which the *Alkalai's* courts are in principle bound, allows the mother's custody to continue until the boy reaches puberty. Such mergers of Sharīʿa and customary law were not confined to African territories, as one final example must suffice to show. In Java, the customary regime of common ownership of acquisitions by husband and wife gained recognition in the Sharīʿa courts by the fiction that a commercial partnership (*shirka*) existed between the spouses,[34] a device which allowed the courts to apply, *inter alia*, the customary rule that a wife was entitled on divorce to claim from the husband one-third of their joint earnings.[35]

Turning now to the subject of civil transactions, the doctrine expounded by the classical jurists was of a highly idealistic character; for the two prohibitions of *ribā* and *gharar* or uncertainty had been developed to a degree of systematic rigour which eliminated any form of speculative risk in contracts, and which postulated standards totally unrealistic in the light of the practical demands of commercial dealings. Here, then, the conflict between the dictates of the Sharīʿa and the needs of society was particularly acute; it affected the Arab communities of early Islam no less than subsequent converts, and it eventually produced a situation wholly different from that which obtained in the domain of family law. For there the concessions which were made in favour of local custom always appeared as deviations from the one theoretically valid law, and, however integral a part of the law administered by Sharīʿa courts custom may have become, the doctrine of the texts remained unchanged as setting a standard superior to, and quite distinct from, the adulterated legal practice. In the field of civil transactions, on the other hand, the doctrine merged with the legal practice and was gradually modified to satisfy economic needs, as a brief survey of the three principal features of legal development in this regard will make clear.

In the first place the letter of the existing law was utilised and manipulated to create a system of "devices" (*ḥiyal*, sing. *ḥīla*), designed to achieve purposes fundamentally contrary to the spirit of the Sharīʿa. Thus, despite the prohibition of *ribā*, a loan with interest could be effected in a way in which the mutual obligations arising thereunder would be enforced by a Sharīʿa court. This was by the simple expedient of a double sale. *L*, the lender, would purchase an object from *B*, the borrower, for an agreed price of £*X*, payable immediately in cash. *B* would then contract to re-purchase this same object from *L* for a price of £*X* + *Y* (*Y* representing the agreed rate of interest) payable by a future specified date. Again, a Ḥanafī vendor of land could defeat the right of pre-emption belonging to the owner of adjoining property, and avoid the ouster of the original purchaser, by making a prior gift to this purchaser of a strip of land one inch wide along the neighbour's border. This destroyed the basis of the neighbour's pre-emptive power since, as distinct from sale, no right of pre-emption arose on transfer by way of gift. Finally, a formal acknowledgement (*iqrār*) of debt would often be in itself sufficient to create an enforceable obligation, however contrary to the principles of the Sharīʿa the transaction from which it in fact arose might be; for doctrine held that a debt, duly acknowledged, was binding without any enquiry into the circumstances of its origin, and was effective subject only to proof of its non-existence or illegality by those who might assert it; and proof of such a negative, difficult by any standards, was to all intents and purposes impossible under the rigid rules of Sharī'a evidence.

Although such *ḥiyal* are often referred to as "legal fictions" they bear little resemblance, in form or substance, to the fictions known to English legal history. When English courts accepted the fact that an imaginary occupier of land, Richard Roe by name, had ousted an equally imaginary lessee John Doe, they did so as a procedural basis for the trial of the issue between competing claimants to the title of freehold land. In the Islamic *ḥiyal*, however, the act or transaction of which the Sharī'a court took cognisance was a real not a fictitious one, and its purpose was not to facilitate the application of the law but to circumvent its substantive provisions. Legal devices commonly erupt at a stage of immaturity in the growth of legal systems, and often prove as harmless and as transient a blemish as the pimples of adolescence. But there was an indication of a more serious malady in the acceptance by Muslim jurists of the shallow stratagems of the *ḥiyal*, and in their condonations of acts which were transparently illegal by the religious standards of which they professed to be the guardians; for this may well appear as a betrayal of their trust where any claim that the letter of the law was being observed was little short of blatant hypocrisy. At best the system of the *ḥiyal* may be regarded as a reluctant concession wrung from jurists who were tied to a fixed and rigid law, and who saw this as the only method by which the doctrine could retain some semblance of control over actual practice.

Muslim jurisprudence, however, by no means unanimously accepted the validity of *ḥiyal*. The Ḥanafī school, largely because of the formalism which was one of its distinctive characteristics,[36] was able to endorse them, and all the major treatises written in support of *ḥiyal* are the work of Ḥanafī lawyers. Later Shāfi'ī scholars, radically diverging from the views of the founder of their school, also recognised *ḥiyal*, but the Mālikī school, with its concern for the real intention behind overt acts, consistently repudiated them. Mālikī jurisprudence, indeed, went so far as to formulate a principle, known as "the stopping of the means" (*sadd adh-dharā'i'*), which was specifically designed to prevent the use of legal means to achieve an illegal end. Yet it was the Ḥanbalīs, as may be expected from their extreme moralistic approach to law, who were perhaps the most hostile opponents of the *ḥiyal*, and a lengthy treatise denouncing and condemning their employment flowed from the pen of the Ḥanbalī scholar Ibn-Taymiyya.

The second method by which doctrine accommodated itself to economic pressures was the formulation of novel rules by way of a supplement to the classical law. Some of these accretions were of a subsidiary nature and an inevitable result of the changing circumstances of society. In the early days, for example, the different rooms (*bayt*) within a house (*dār*) were constructed to a standard pattern. Accordingly, inspection of one room was deemed in law to be inspection of the whole house by a prospective purchaser, who could not subsequently, if dissatisfied, claim recision of the sale on the ground of a lack of proper inspection. But when architecture adopted a more adventurous and less repetitive style, it became the rule that only inspection of every room constituted a proper inspection of the whole house. Other innovations of the doctrine, however, were nothing less than complete legal institutions. And although these were designed to permit results unattainable under the form of the earlier doctrine they cannot in any way properly be regarded as a species of *ḥiyal*, for they represent direct and forthright modifications of the classical law and not the veiling of an illegal activity behind a façade of existing legal machinery.

Thus, while strict classical doctrine required that a transfer of ownership by way of sale (*bayʿ*) should be absolute and unconditional, later jurists admitted a form of sale in which the vendor retained a right of redemption. Known as *bayʿ biʾl-wafāʾ*, this institution could meet a variety of needs: it could provide the basis for what was in fact a long-term lease of certain types of agricultural land (against the strict terms of classical doctrine) where the purchaser might pay the price by instalments, or it could serve to effect a mortgage with interest, the vendor remaining in occupation of the property sold prior to its redemption and paying an agreed rent therefor to the purchaser. Again, the strict rule of the inalienability of landed property constituted as a *waqf* settlement proved burdensome in practice, when funds for the proper upkeep or exploitation of the property were not available. Jurisprudence in Morocco catered for this situation by recognising the validity of "the sale of the air" (*bayʿ al-hawāʾ*) above the property concerned. Although he had thus not, in theory, purchased the property itself, the purchaser—and subsequent transferees of the same *superficies*—could in fact enjoy and develop the property with security. The same institution was also used to qualify the strict rule which prohibited the alienation of the immoveable property of minor wards by their legal guardians.

Development of the law along these lines was essentially the work of the *muftī* or jurisconsult who gave his formal opinion (*fatwā*) upon the legal issues involved in a factual situation. Such *responsa* formed the vital link between the academic theories of pure scholarship and the influences of practical life, and through them the dictates of the doctrine were gradually adapted to the changing needs of Muslim society. But however fundamental the modifications so introduced may have been, the *muftīs* regarded themselves as bound by the existing doctrine and claimed only to be developing, by dint of necessity, its inherent principles. This is the light in which it is necessary to interpret certain statements which apparently contradict outright the theory of "imitation" or *taqlīd*, such as that of the great Egyptian Mālikī jurist and *muftī* of the fourteenth century, al-Qarāfī: "All categories of law based upon customs change if the customs upon which they are based change".[37] *Fatwās* were not, of course, confined to civil transactions but embraced the whole field of Sharīʿa law, and compilations of them came to have an authority as works of legal reference complementary to that of the standard Sharīʿa manuals. Perhaps the most famous and most comprehensive of these collections is that made in India during the seventeenth century and known as the *Fatāwā ʿĀlamgīriyya*.

While the first two methods of legal development discussed were essentially creations of the doctrine, the initiative in the third and final aspect of development was taken by the *qāḍīs*' tribunals. Limited in point of geographical extent to north-west Africa, that part of the Muslim world which the Arabs know as "the Island of the West" (*Jazīrat al-Maghrib*), this was a process whereby certain customary contracts succeeded in becoming an integral part of the *corpus juris* applied by the Mālikī Sharīʿa courts.[38]

It will be evident from the classical doctrine of the sources of law, as we have described it, that custom *per se* had no binding force in Islamic legal theory. Within the framework of the recognised *uṣūl*, however, *ʿurf* (literally "what is known" about a thing, and therefore, loosely "custom") operated as a principle of subsidiary value. Thus a contract of sale should ideally be concluded by oral offer and acceptance. But most jurists accepted as valid the customary form of sale known as *muʿāṭāt* (offer), where there was an oral declaration on one side only and some action indicative of acceptance on the other. "A sale is effected", stated Mālik himself, "by what the people believe to be a sale." To take a further example from the sphere of family law, it was widespread practice to divide the dower payable to the wife in a marriage contract into two parts, one payable promptly and the other deferred until, usually, the termination of the marriage. In the absence of a stipulation in the contract itself determining the respective proportions of prompt and deferred dower, the allotment would usually be decided in the basis of local custom—which represents an application of the legal maxim: "Custom ranks as a stipulation".

In addition to this limited recognition of custom or *ʿurf*, Mālikī legal writings laid considerable stress upon the notion of the public interest (*maṣlaḥa*) and on the maxim that "Necessity makes prohibited things permissible". And although the purist would regard the scope of these principles as finally determined by the terms of the substantive doctrine enshrined in the texts, their combined influence resulted in the judiciary adopting a tolerant and permissive attitude towards customary practices. Continually confronted with claims arising out of transactions which offended the strict doctrine, a *qāḍī* would eventually recognise the binding nature of the transaction, and his decision, finding favour with other and succeeding *qāḍīs*, soon became established practice. In so acting the courts were not according any intrinsic force to custom as such, but were accepting the external facts of that custom on the broad ground of public necessity.[39]

Perhaps the most outstanding example of this process is afforded by the agricultural contract of *khamessa*, under which the tenant retains a quota part of four-fifths of the produce of the land which he occupies and works, the remaining fifth representing the rental required by the land-owner. Such a type of land tenure contravenes two cardinal principles of strict Sharīʿa doctrine—namely that rental should not consist of foodstuffs and that its precise value should be known and determined. But the existence of this contract in north-west Africa was widespread, indeed an economic necessity in a society which possessed little floating capital, and from mediaeval times onwards it was universally recognised by the Sharīʿa courts in this area.

To appreciate the significant place which this phenomenon of Maghribi legal practice occupies in the historical development of Islamic law as a whole it is necessary to consider in general terms the relationship between doctrine and practice, between jurists and judges, to which the nature of Sharīʿa law gave rise.

Divergence of opinion was widespread, even among the jurists of the same school. Within each school doctrine graded the relative authority of conflicting views on the basis of the support they commanded among its representative scholars, and opinions were accordingly broadly classified as either "dominant" (*mashhūr*), "preferable" in certain circumstances (*rājiḥ*) or "weak" (*ḍaʿīf*). In a given area the practice (*ʿamal*) of the Sharīʿa courts naturally tended to apply consistently one opinion among the several possible variants. Thus, on a matter of personal status, the Moroccan courts had consistently applied the view of Mālik that the validity or otherwise of the transactions undertaken by a mentally defective person depended solely upon whether he had, or had not, been formally placed under interdiction, however much to his personal advantage or disadvantage the transaction might be. But during the nineteenth century the practice changed and became settled in favour of the precisely contrary opinion of Mālik's pupil, Ibn-al-Qāsim. Theory, of course, required that in cases of conflict the *qāḍī* should normally follow the dominant doctrine of his school. But in the interests of justice it was often a "preferable" or even a "weak" opinion which found favour with the courts, while in the Maghrib, as we have just seen, the *qāḍīs* recognised transactions for which the texts supplied no real authority at all.

For those whose concern lay with the practical administration of the law, the practice of the courts naturally supplanted the doctrine of the texts as the focal point of attention, and this attitude received a particular impetus in the Maghrib from the activities of a class of persons who were known as *'udūl*. The *'udūl* had originated, as early as the eighth century, as a body of "professional" witnesses, whose moral probity (*'adāla*) had been established after a process of screening (*tazkiya*) by the courts, and whose services in witnessing contracts relieved the parties concerned of undue embarrassment or delay should the necessity of litigation arise. It gradually became the procedure of the *'udūl*, as business flourished, to make a note, at first by way of a simple *aide-mémoire*, of the terms of the contracts they witnessed, and eventually they assumed the function of public notaries, the deeds they drew up being known as *wathā'iq*. These documents in fact came to be accepted as evidence by the courts, and thus provide an outstanding example of a legal institution created by practice against the strict terms of the doctrine; but their particular importance for our present purposes lies in the fact that their terms were always drafted in accordance with the established practice of the courts, regardless of whether this agreed with the doctrine of the texts or not. Thus the *'udūl* were a potent instrument in strengthening the notion of the authority of the *'amal*.

As a result of this development there eventually emerged in north-west Africa a relationship between doctrine and practice unique in the legal world of Islam; for the Mālikī jurists recognised the practice of the courts as the supreme criterion of legal authority. In the words of the author of the seventeenth-century *Al-'Amal al-Fāsī* (The Practice of Fez): "In principle the judgements of *qāḍīs* of our time which are based upon an isolated opinion ought to be rescinded immediately. The *'amal*, however, must prevail over the 'preferable opinion'. It cannot be neglected." Maghribi jurisprudence, therefore, diverges radically from the classical Islamic concept of law. It appears as the single instance of a "realist" form of Islamic jurisprudence which follows the decisions of the courts rather than precedes them, and which, in the ultimate analysis, is concerned not with the law as it ought to be, but with the law as it is actually administered.

Briefly to summarise the results of this and the previous chapter, legal development in mediaeval Islam may be assessed in terms of the extent to which actual legal practice diverged from the classical doctrine of the Sharī'a texts. In the field of family law the dichotomy between this doctrine and the practice was clearly defined. Because family law was regarded as a particularly vital and integral part of the scheme of religious duties, the classical doctrine of the Arab authorities remained inviolate as expressing the only standards of conduct which were valid in the eyes of God; and such deviations from this norm, as legal practice in certain areas condoned, were never recognised as legitimate expressions of Islamic law. In the other spheres of law, however, no such firm line could be drawn to separate doctrine from practice. The public law doctrine of *siyāsa shar'iyya* recognised that in the domain of public, and particularly criminal, law political interests necessitated additional jurisdictions supplementary to that of the Sharī'a courts; while in the field of civil transactions forces inherent in Islamic society had brought about considerable modifications of the strict classical doctrine. In both these respects it was the *muftīs* or jurisconsults who were primarily responsible for the synthesis of doctrine and practice; for not only did they adapt the civil law by their *fatwās*, but they also often sat as advisory counsellors ratifying the activities of the *Maẓālim* tribunals.

In the light of these developments the classical doctrine begins to fall into historical perspective as a stage in the evolution of law in Islam. The classical Sharī'a texts were always accorded a supreme respect and veneration as the portrayal of a pure religious ideal, which is why developments in the doctrine often assumed the aspect of reluctant concessions to the practice by way of *exceptio utilitatis*; but from a realistic standpoint the classical doctrine never formed a complete or exclusively authoritative expression of Islamic law.

Part Three

ISLAMIC LAW IN MODERN TIMES

CHAPTER II

FOREIGN INFLUENCES: THE RECEPTION OF EUROPEAN LAWS

FROM the nineteenth century onwards there grew up an increasingly intimate contact between Islamic and Western civilisation, and legal development was henceforth conditioned, almost exclusively, by the novel influences to which Islam thus became subject. During the Middle Ages the structure of Muslim states and society had remained basically static, and for this reason Sharīʿa law had proved able to accommodate itself successfully to such internal requirements as the passage of time had produced. But the pressures which now arose from without confronted Islam with an entirely different situation. Politically, socially, and economically, Western civilisation was based on concepts and institutions fundamentally alien to Islamic tradition and to the Islamic law which expressed that tradition. Because of the essential rigidity of the Sharīʿa and the dominance of the theory of *taqlīd* (or strict adherence to established doctrine), an apparently irreconcilable conflict was now produced between the traditional law and the needs of Muslim society, in so far as it aspired to organise itself by Western standards and values. Accordingly there seemed, initially at any rate, no alternative but to abandon the Sharīʿa and replace it with laws of Western inspiration in those spheres where Islam felt a particular urgency to adapt itself to modern conditions. Any understanding, therefore, of the nature of modern Islamic legal practice first requires an appreciation of the extent to which, and the manner in which, laws of European origin came to be adopted in the various territories of Islam.

In the relationships between Muslim and Western states it was naturally the fields of public law (constitutional and criminal law) and of civil and commercial transactions which proved particularly prominent. And it was precisely here that the deficiencies of the traditional Islamic system, from the standpoint of modern conditions, were most apparent. Sufficient has been said of the law of civil obligations generally to indicate its total inadequacy to cater for modern systems of trade and economic development, at least as long as the only permissible methods of adaptation of the classical law were of the nature discussed in the previous chapter. Equally insupportable to the modernist view was the traditional form of criminal jurisdiction, not only because such potential penalties as amputation of the hand for theft and stoning to death for adultery were offensive to humanitarian principles; nor because the notion of homicide as a civil injury, acceptable though it might be to a tribal society, was no longer suited to a state organised on a modern basis; but more particularly because modern ideas of government could not tolerate the wide arbitrary powers vested in the political sovereign under the Sharīʿa doctrine of "deterrence" or *taʿzīr* (page 132 f. above).

European law—criminal and commercial—had a foothold in the nineteenth-century Ottoman empire through the system of Capitulations, by which the Western powers ensured that their citizens resident in the Middle East would be governed by their own laws. This brought about a growing familiarity with European laws particularly when, as in the realm of commercial transactions, they were applied in mixed cases involving Europeans and Muslim traders. Naturally, therefore, it was to the laws applied under the Capitulatory system that Middle Eastern authorities turned when the desire for efficiency and progress appeared to necessitate the superseding of their traditional law. At the same time the adoption of these European laws as a territorial system meant that foreign powers might acquiesce in the abolition of Capitulations, which became increasingly irksome as a growing emphasis was placed on national sovereignty.

As a result of these considerations a large-scale reception of European law was effected in the Ottoman empire by the *Tanẓimat* reforms of the period 1839–1876. The Commercial Code promulgated in 1850 was in part a direct translation of the French Commercial Code, and included provisions for the payment of interest. Under the Penal Code of 1858, which was a translation of the French Penal Code, the traditional *ḥadd* or defined punishments of Sharī'a law were all abolished except that of the death penalty for apostasy. There followed a Code of Commercial Procedure in 1861 and a Code of Maritime Commerce in 1863, both of which, again, were basically French law. To apply these Codes a new system of secular, or *Niẓamiyya*, courts was established, and it was because all civil jurisdiction (excepting cases of personal status) now fell within the competence of these courts that the basic law of obligations was also codified, between 1869 and 1876, in the compilation known as the *Majalla* or *Mejelle*. For, although the substance of this Code owed nothing to European sources, but was derived entirely from Ḥanafī law, the secular courts could not be expected properly to ascertain that law from its traditional form of expression in the authoritative manuals. Codification, of course, was also intended to achieve uniformity in the application of the law, a consideration of some moment in view of the widespread divergencies of juristic opinion recorded in the Sharīʿa texts.

Egypt, from 1875 onwards, went even further than the Ottoman authorities in the adoption of French law, for apart from promulgating Penal, Commercial and Maritime Codes and setting up a system of secular courts to apply them, she also enacted Civil Codes which were basically modelled on French law and contained only a few provisions drawn from the Sharīʿa.[1]

As a result of these initial steps taken during the Ottoman period, laws of European origin today form a vital and integral part of the legal systems of most Middle Eastern countries. Criminal law and procedure are almost completely Westernised, though the last few decades have witnessed a movement away from the French Codes towards other sources. In 1926 Turkey promulgated a Criminal Code based on Italian law, and her Code of Criminal Procedure which followed two years later was of Germanic inspiration. Italian law was also directly adopted by Egypt in her Criminal Code of 1937, is the predominant influence in the current Lebanese Criminal Code, and has been amalgamated with French law in the Criminal Code now operative in Libya. As for the law of civil transactions and obligations, this has become increasingly Westernised, throughout the Middle East generally, during the present century. Today the Ottoman *Majalla* is applicable only in Jordan; it was superseded in Turkey by the adoption of the Swiss Civil Code in 1927, and in Lebanon by the Law of Obligations and Contracts of 1932 which rested squarely on French law, while Syria and Libya have recently promulgated Civil Codes derived from the Civil Code which came into effect in Egypt in 1949.

This last Code, however, represents a definite departure from the previous practice of indiscriminate adoption of European law, and may be regarded as an attempted compromise between the traditional Islamic and modern Western systems: for great emphasis was laid by the framers of the Code—in particular by its chief designer, ʿAbd-ar-Razzāq as-Sanhūrī—on the fact that its provisions were an amalgam of existing Egyptian law, elements drawn from other contemporary Codes and, last but not least, principles of the Sharīʿa itself. As far as the actual terms of the Code itself are concerned, the debt owed to traditional Sharīʿa law was slight, for more than three-quarters of the Code was derived directly from the previous Egyptian Codes of 1875 and 1883.[2] At the same time the insistence of the authors of the Code upon its composite nature and their assertion that the rules of foreign origin had been selected on the basis of their general consonance with Sharīʿa doctrine evinced a distinctly novel attitude towards the reception of foreign law. There was a tendency to regard the provisions of the Code as wholly divorced from their actual sources, and it might not be too fanciful to see here the embryonic beginnings of a process of the Islamicisation of foreign elements such as had taken place in the first two centuries of Islam. Moreover, since Article I of the Code provides that, in matters not specifically regulated by the Code, the courts should follow "customary law, the principles of Islamic law, or the principles of natural justice", it obviously opens the door to a wider reference to Sharīʿa law. It is true that such reference was not likely to have any important concrete results as long as the notion of Sharīʿa law as a fixed and rigid system expressed in the mediaeval texts prevailed. But recent developments in Sharīʿa family law, as we shall see, have largely dispelled this notion; and in the light of these developments the recognition of Sharī'a principles as a formative instrument of civil law may well come to assume an altogether deeper significance.

From the latter part of the nineteenth century onwards, then, the pure Sharī'a in its traditional form was generally confined in the Middle East to the realm of family law, which term should be taken henceforth to include the laws of succession, the system of *waqf* settlements and, in most cases, the law of gift. Only the Arabian Peninsula remained generally immune to the influence of European laws. Here, in Saudi Arabia, the Yemen, the Aden Protectorate and the Hadramaut and the various principalities of the Persian Gulf, traditional Islamic law has remained the fundamental law up to the present day and, with the introduction of but a few superficial modifications, still governs every aspect of legal relationships.

Outside the area of the Middle East the infiltration of Western law into the Islamic world was closely connected with the policies of occupying imperial and colonial powers. Since the completion of the French conquest in 1850, the Muslim population of Algeria has been subject to exactly the same Codes of criminal and civil law as have been currently in force in France, and Sharī'a law has been restricted to matters of personal status. Dutch public and penal laws were similarly imported into Indonesia from the nineteenth century onwards, while custom (*adat*) continued to govern the general field of private law—for in this area of Islam, as we have noted, the Sharī'a had never won more than a limited recognition, despite the efforts of the Dutch to impose it as the proper law of the Muslim populations.[3]

British policy in India, by contrast, had initially aimed at the preservation of the existing legal system, which was the traditional Ḥanafī law sponsored by the

Moghul Emperors and administered by the *Kazis* (*qāḍīs*). After the reorganisation of the courts by Warren Hastings in 1772, English law was specifically applied by the courts in the Presidencies, but elsewhere Islamic criminal law was applied by Muslim judges, and in civil matters Sharī'a law was applied to Muslims (as Hindu law was to Hindus) in accordance with the advice of native law officers, or *maulvis*, attached to the courts. In 1862, however, the Indian Penal Code—a codification, for export, of English criminal law—and the Code of Criminal Procedure came into force to supersede what remained of the Islamic criminal law. Civil law, meanwhile, had become increasingly anglicised by virtue of the principle adopted by the courts of deciding cases according to "justice, equity, and good conscience"; for British judges, and Indian judges trained in English law, inevitably resorted to the introduction of English rules as a result of both their desire for uniformity in the law applicable to a very mixed population and the general difficulty they experienced in properly ascertaining the terms of Islamic law from the authoritative Arabic texts. Indeed, "justice, equity, and good conscience" was in practice synonymous with English law. Codification of considerable portions of the civil law on an English basis naturally ensued, and from the latter part of the nineteenth century Islamic law has been confined in the Indian sub-continent, as elsewhere, to the domain of family law.

Substantially the same position came to prevail in the Sudan about this time under the Anglo-Egyptian condominium. In 1899 a Penal Code was promulgated which was based on the Indian Penal Code but which was adapted to its Sudanese environment by the retention, *inter alia*, of the Islamic institution of blood-money (*diya*), payable in cases of accidental homicide among communities still organised on a tribal basis. Civil law, on the other hand, was not codified—except in regard to particular aspects such as bankruptcy, bills of exchange and limited liability companies—but, as in India, became anglicised through the principle of "justice, equity, and good conscience", so that the courts of the Sudan are today guided, but not bound, by the English common law. The jurisdiction of Sharīʿa courts was eventually defined by the Sudan Mohammedan Law Courts Ordinance of 1902, which declared them competent to entertain, in the case of Muslim litigants, "any question regarding marriage, divorce, guardianship of minors or family relationship . . . wakf, gift, succession, wills, interdiction or guardianship of the interdicted or lost person".[4]

By way of contrast with the areas so far discussed, the Muslim territories of Morocco, Tunisia and Northern Nigeria preserved their traditional systems of Islamic law virtually intact until very recent times. This was so not only because of the innate conservatism of these peoples or because their close contact with Western civilisation came at a comparatively late date, but also because the Protectorate forms of colonial rule (established by France for Tunisia in 1881 and for Morocco in 1912, and by Great Britain for Northern Nigeria in 1912) tended to perpetuate the *status quo*.

In Morocco and Tunisia the competence of the *qāḍīs'* courts was restricted, at the time of French occupation, to matters of family law, while most of the civil and all the criminal jurisdiction were in the hands of other tribunals—those of the *Qā'ids* and the *Wuzarā'* in Tunisia and those of the *Qā'ids* and *Pashas* in Morocco. This dichotomy, of course, represented to a large degree the distinction between religious and secular courts, but it was in effect nothing more than the traditional Islamic distinction between Sharīʿa and *Maẓālim* jurisdictions. In any event the law applied by the "secular" or *Maẓālim* tribunals for long remained essentially Islamic, though due account was taken of those peculiar developments of the traditional Sharī'a which had occurred in Morocco through the phenomenon of *'amal* (page 145 above). A Code of Obligations and Contracts was indeed enacted in Tunisia in 1906, but this rested squarely on Islamic sources, and was designed simply to achieve uniformity and certainty in the application of the law.[5] Only in the last few years has French law been directly adopted in these countries, for example in the Criminal Code promulgated in Morocco in 1954, which incidentally retained the Islamic offence of *ẓinā'* (fornication) and attached thereto a maximum penalty of six months' imprisonment, and in the Codes of Commerce (1960), Civil and Commercial Procedure (1960), and Maritime Commerce (1962) enacted in Tunisia.

In Northern Nigeria traditional Mālikī law was applied by the courts of the *Alkalai* and the *Maẓālim* courts of the Emirs in all civil and criminal matters, excepting the sphere of land tenure where customary law prevailed, at the time the Protectorate was established. Under the British policy of non-interference in matters of religion and the preservation of "native law and custom" this supremacy of Sharī'a law was consolidated, except that the courts were not permitted to impose sentences upon convicted criminals which were, in the words of Lord Lugard, "repugnant to natural justice and humanity". This formula covered the Sharī'a punishments of amputation of the hand for theft and lapidation for adultery which had, however, rarely been applied in practice. But the *ḥadd* or defined penalties of flogging for fornication, wine-drinking, and slanderous allegations of unchastity continued to be exacted, although the traditional manner of their application makes it evident that they constitute a form of public shame and religious penance rather than a physical ordeal; for the one who administers the lashes must hold the whip between his fingers, must keep a stone or similar object under the arm he is using and must not raise his wrist above the level of his elbow.

Yet the jurisdiction of the courts which applied Mālikī criminal law in the case of Muslim offenders was not exclusive in Northern Nigeria, where there also existed British courts bound by the English law of the Nigerian Criminal Code. A variety of circumstances might determine whether the statutory or the Islamic law was to apply—such as whether the Emir's court within whose Emirate a capital offence was committed had competence, under the Native Courts Ordinance, to deal with such offences or not—and in cases of homicide the question of which system was to apply could, for the accused, be a matter of life or death. Mālikī law regards as deliberate homicide, for which the heirs of the victim may demand the death of the offender, death caused by any conduct intrinsically likely to kill, even where there is no intention to kill or seriously injure, as well as death caused by any hostile act, whether intrinsically likely to kill or not; and since Mālikī law recognises no general defence of provocation, the death penalty is obviously applicable thereunder for offences which would only amount to manslaughter under the Criminal Code. This divergence between the two systems assumed prominence because a conflict of judicial opinion arose, from 1947 onwards, as to whether or not the Supreme Court could, on appeal, interfere with a death sentence properly imposed by a native court for deliberate homicide when the act or omission concerned amounted only to manslaughter under the Criminal Code. Not, in fact, until 1957 could it be regarded as in any way settled law that a native court must not impose a punishment in excess of the maximum punishment permitted under the Criminal Code for the same act or omission.[6]

The same considerations, however, which had led to the adoption of modern Criminal Codes almost everywhere else in the Muslim world, applied also to Northern Nigeria, and the need for reform was felt more urgently as independence approached. Accordingly, a new Penal Code was promulgated in 1959 and followed by a Code of Criminal Procedure in 1960. Based on the Sudanese Criminal Code, and hence tracing its descent from the Indian Penal Code drafted by Lord Macaulay in 1837, the new Code retains traditional Islamic doctrine in one respect; for the *ḥadd* (or defined) lashings may be imposed upon Muslims guilty of the offences of *ẓinā'* (fornication), false accusation of unchastity, or wine-drinking, in addition to the sentences prescribed therefor by the Code. Unlike the Sudanese Code, however, the Nigerian Code does not retain the institution of blood-money (*diya*) in its traditional form. In certain cases compensation may be exacted from offenders in addition to, or in substitution for, any punishment prescribed; but a conviction on the basis of the incidents of criminal liability as established by the Code is an essential prerequisite, and so it is obvious that such compensation cannot take the place of the blood-money payable in cases of purely accidental homicide.[7] It is finally noteworthy that the Penal Code is to be administered through the existing court system, a policy which naturally involves considerable re-orientation of the traditional training of Muslim judges (*Alkalai*).

Introduction of Western Laws had not been achieved without initial difficulties in many Muslim countries. In Turkey, for example, prisons were built for communal confinement and the inmates were not obliged to work. Because the Italian Criminal Code, which Turkey adopted in 1926, contained provisions for solitary confinement and penal servitude, its full application was impractical until new prisons suitable for these purposes had been constructed. Again, under traditional Islamic law as applied in Turkey, recalcitrant debtors had been imprisoned. When such sanction was abolished with the introduction in 1927 of a Civil Code and Code of Obligations based on Swiss legislation, relieved debtors concealed their assets from their creditors to such an extent that the government had perforce swiftly to introduce criminal sanctions.[8] In other countries problems have arisen from the existence side by side of Western and Islamic laws and the interaction between them. An interesting example is provided by a recent Sudanese case[9] concerned with the interpretation of a clause in the Rent Restriction Ordinance, which allows a landlord to recover possession of a controlled house as a residence for "himself". Here a Muslim landlord with three wives argued: first, that it is an accepted principle of English Common law that husband and wife are one and therefore the use of a house by his wife was a use by "himself"; second, that each of several Muslim co-wives is entitled to a separate house as part of her right of impartial treatment established by the Sharīʿa; and third, that he, as a Muslim husband, was bound to treat his wives equally. Accordingly he claimed recovery under the Ordinance of three houses on these grounds and was successful before the Court of Appeal.

Such minor problems, however, do not seriously qualify the fact that Western laws have been successfully assimilated in the various regions of Islam and that, while they may have been imposed initially from above, they are today in broad harmony with the temper of Muslim populations. Opposition to the introduction of secular laws was indeed voiced by the scholars of the religious law, but was never strong enough to constitute a formidable obstacle. In general the attitude was taken that it was better to let the Sharīʿa pass peacefully away from the field of legal practice intact rather than attempt such radical surgery of its principles as modern conditions required. At the same time Islamic legal tradition had always recognised the right of the ruler, through his *Maẓālim* jurisdiction, to supplement strict Sharīʿa doctrine in the fields of public law and general civil law, and the adoption of Western Codes in these spheres could appear as no more than a necessary extension of his admitted powers. From this standpoint the representation of the new Criminal Codes in the Middle East as an exercise of the sovereign's prerogative of *siyāsa* regulations and in particular his power of "deterrence" (*taʿzīr*) was not, perhaps, a purely formal and superficial attempt to justify them.

Family law, on the other hand, had always been the stronghold of the Sharīʿa, and the reception of secular and Western laws in other spheres created a sharp dichotomy between the two systems which resulted in a growing emphasis upon the religious and Islamic significance of the Sharīʿa and a strengthening of its influence in those matters which remained under its sway. One important example of this tendency to consolidate the position of the Sharīʿa in its traditional preserves was the Indian *Shariat Act*, 1937, which asserted the Sharīʿa to be the fundamental law of all Muslims in India in regard to their personal status (including succession, gifts and *waqf*), and aimed at obliterating customary practices contrary to the Sharīʿa which prevailed among certain communities. Yet Western standards and institutions had created an impetus for reform in the field of family law also, and this at first seemed to have brought about the same apparent impasse between the needs of society and an allegedly immutable law as had caused the adoption of Western civil and criminal codes. Turkey indeed saw as the only solution the total abandonment of the Sharīʿa and the adoption of Swiss family law in 1927. But, fortunately for the future of Islamic law, no other Muslim country has as yet followed this example. With the determination to preserve the influence of the religious law means have been sought, and found, whereby traditional Sharīʿa doctrine could be adapted to the circumstances of modern life. Only Afghanistan, the various states of the Arabian Peninsula, Northern Nigeria and other "colonial territories" like Zanzibar have to date taken little or no part in this development, although current indications are that the time of their doing so will not be long delayed. Our future concern, therefore, will lie mainly with Islamic family law and the striking phenomenon of its recent evolution among the majority of Muslim peoples.

CHAPTER 12

ADMINISTRATION OF SHARĪʿA LAW IN CONTEMPORARY ISLAM

For the administration of Sharīʿa family law classical Muslim tradition recognised one judicial organ only: the court of a single *qāḍī*. No hierarchy of Sharīʿa courts existed and no system of appeal as such, although dissatisfied litigants could always seek the intervention of the political authority through his *Maẓālim* jurisdiction. Nowhere in modern Islam, however, does this rudimentary organisation still prevail. Systems of appeal have been introduced almost everywhere, even in the most conservative areas such as Northern Nigeria, where one of the most recent developments in this regard was the establishment of a Muslim Court of Appeal in 1956, and in Saudi Arabia and Afghanistan, where a kind of judicial hierarchy now exists with a plurality of judges in important cases. Egypt and Tunisia, in 1955 and 1956 respectively, abolished the Sharīʿa courts entirely and Sharīʿa family law, along with the civil and the criminal law, is now administered by a unified system of national courts. In Algeria the *qāḍīs*' courts act only as courts of the first instance and appeals lie to judges sitting in the ordinary civil courts, while in India Sharīʿa law has been administered for almost two centuries through the ordinary civil courts from which a final appeal lay, prior to independence and partition, to the Judicial Committee of the Privy Council. Moreover, the systems of procedure and evidence applicable even in the *qāḍīs*' courts have been greatly modernised during the present century in all but the most traditional Muslim countries.

Substantive law, in many legal systems, is merged inextricably with the structure and procedure of the courts through which it is applied. Islamic substantive doctrine, however, because of the circumstances of its historical origin, has an existence quite independent of the machinery of legal administration. Theoretically, therefore, the modern reorganisation of the traditional Sharī'a courts and their procedure was a separate and distinct issue, unconnected with the nature of the law they were to apply. Nevertheless, as a result simply of the circumstances surrounding the administration of Sharī'a law in recent times, considerable modifications have been woven into its traditional fabric. Direct reform of the substance of the Sharī'a by political authorities has also, as we shall see in the following two chapters, been successfully accomplished. Our purpose in this chapter, however, is to consider only those developments which fall essentially under the head of the administration of the law and in particular to contrast the widely different positions which obtain in this regard in the Indian sub-continent on the one hand and the Middle East on the other.

In the Indian sub-continent the administration of Sharī'a law by British or anglicised courts, subject to the supreme authority of the decisions of the Privy Council, led to a remarkable fusion of the two systems. This is aptly termed Anglo-Muhammadan law, because, through the introduction of English legal principles and concepts, the law applied by the Indian courts came to diverge in many particulars from traditional Sharī'a law. But this was not the result of any deliberate attempt to reform Islamic law as such; on the contrary, the conscientious endeavour of the courts to apply Islamic law, as they understood it, is beyond question. It was simply that the judiciary did not possess, in the nature of things, the same knowledge of strict Sharīʿa doctrine or the same attitude towards its paramount and exclusive authority as, say, the *qāḍīs* of the Arab countries, and as a consequence two principal features of judicial activity in this part of the Muslim world may be discerned.

Firstly, because it was not in the character of the courts fully to appreciate or accept the doctrine of strict adherence to established authorities, they did not hesitate to formulate novel principles by way of supplement to the traditional law when this seemed necessary on general grounds of justice and equity. A widow, for example, was given a privileged position in regard to her claim for unpaid dower against her deceased husband's estate; for by the rule of Anglo-Muhammadan law known generally, albeit inaccurately, as "the widow's lien", she is allowed to retain possession of her husband's estate, when such possession has been lawfully and peaceably acquired, until her dower debt is satisfied.[10] Although this may be regarded as a particular implementation of the principle of "self-help" recognised by the Sharīʿa, under traditional law the widow in such circumstances normally ranks as an ordinary unsecured creditor. Again, the traditional law of gift (which remained firmly within the province of the Sharīʿa in the Indian sub-continent) is centred upon the strict principle that a gift is only effective when the thing given has been actually delivered to the donee. The rigid application of this rule was deemed harsh and inequitable under modern conditions and it was tempered by considerable development of the doctrine of constructive delivery which found only scant recognition in traditional law. Particularly prominent, in this context, was the Ḥanafī rule that a gift of an undivided share in property (*mushāʿ*) was not effective unless the share to be transferred was first divided off from the rest of the property and duly delivered. This rule applied in all cases except where the property concerned was "indivisible", which term was traditionally interpreted as meaning property whose division necessarily entailed the loss of its normal usufruct. Judicial decisions in India, however, confined the necessity for division in gifts of *mushāʿ* within the strictest limits, first by introducing a number of specific exceptions to the Ḥanafī rule, such as the gift of a share in freehold property in a commercial town or of shares in a Land Company, and secondly by adopting a modified interpretation of "indivisible" property as referring to property which could be used to better advantage in an undivided state. In these, as in other similar developments of Anglo-Muhammadan law, it is clear that the courts regarded traditional Sharīʿa law, no less than the English common law, as subject to modification by the superior standards of equitable jurisdiction. Indeed, it is interesting to note how many of the most important Indian decisions of this nature belong to the period of the late nineteenth century, just after the supremacy of Equity in the English legal system had been finally established by the Judicature Acts of 1873 and 1875.

The second major development in the Indian subcontinent was the complete eclipse of traditional Sharīʿa doctrine in certain respects and its replacement by the precepts of English law. This, again, was not a process of wilful substitution. As had happened in the civil law, the courts often experienced extreme difficulty in ascertaining the correct Sharīʿa principles applicable, and in such circumstances naturally resorted to English law as the most convenient and equitable expedient. Perhaps the outstanding example of this is supplied by the principles which today govern the administration of a deceased's estate in India and Pakistan. Under the Ḥanafī law as found in authoritative texts the various rules of administration stem from the basic doctrine of the fictitious survival of the deceased, who remains, in contemplation of law, the owner of the estate until his obligations have been discharged. This doctrine is, of course, particularly vital in the case of insolvent estates where there is no devolution of ownership to the heirs at death and where the other major Sharī'a principle—that there is no inheritance until after the payment of debts—has its full effect. Judicial decisions in India, however, betrayed a total ignorance of the doctrine of the deceased's fictitious survival. Solvent or insolvent, the deceased's estate was held to devolve upon his heirs, as it did upon the old English heir-at-law, in accordance with their shares in the inheritance at the moment of death. The ownership of the heirs was, of course, subject to their personal liability to pay the deceased's debts in proportion to their shares in the estate. But under English law a debtor is generally competent to deal with his property and pass a good title to a *bona fide* transferee for value. Accordingly, because the heir was owner of his inheritance, it was held that he could pass a valid title to his share of the inheritance before the debts of the deceased had been paid; and the failure to apply the doctrine of the deceased's fictitious survival thus also completely destroyed the real significance of the Sharī'a principle that there can be no inheritance until after the payment of debts.[11]

In some cases judicial decisions in India have been based upon an imperfect and partial appreciation only of the terms of traditional Sharī'a law, and principles and institutions of the Sharī'a have been interpreted in the light of English legal concepts.

Gifts of property for a limited period, in particular for the lifetime of the donee, provide one example of the way in which the preoccupation of the Indian courts with English legal notions hampered the true comprehension of the Sharī'a. These gifts were regarded essentially as the "life-estate" of English law, which is technically the transfer of the ownership, or *corpus*, of property for a limited period with restrictions attached to its use or alienation; and, as such, gifts for the lifetime of the donee were properly declared by the Indian High Courts to be invalid under Ḥanafī law. For Ḥanafī law insists that a gratuitous transfer of the *corpus* of property (*hiba*) should be absolute and unqualified: any purported limitations as to time or use are regarded as void conditions; but, while the conditions fail, the gift itself remains valid and the donee therefore acquires an absolute estate. However, while the Indian courts had correctly ascertained the Ḥanafī law of *hiba*, they had in fact concerned themselves with one aspect only of the Ḥanafī law of gift. Apart from a transfer of the *corpus* (*ʿayn*), Ḥanafī law also recognises the gratuitous transfer of the *usus* (*manfaʿa*) of the property only. Such a transaction is termed *ʿāriyya*, and may be validly accompanied by conditions limiting the period or the mode of enjoyment of the property. Limited interests, therefore, but certainly not the English life-estate, may be effectively created under Sharīʿa law by a transfer of the *usus*, and this was finally recognised by their Lordships of the Privy Council in *Sardar Nawazish Ali Khan's Case* (1948), where it was held that it was a matter for construction by the court as to whether the gift was intended as a transfer of the *corpus* or the *usus*, and that, if the latter was the case, any limitations imposed upon the duration of the donee's interest were valid and effective. But it should be noted that under strict Ḥanafī law an *ʿāriyya* is revocable at any time by the donor.

Undoubtedly the most notorious misinterpretation of Ḥanafī law, however, occurred in regard to the law of *waqf* endowments. In the celebrated case of *Abul Fata v. Russomoy* (1894) an Indian High Court declared invalid a *waqf* of which the income was to go to the issue of the settlors, generation following generation until their extinction, and after them to widows, orphans, beggars and the poor. On appeal their Lordships of the Privy Council upheld this decision on the ground of the well-known principle of English Equity that the ultimate gift to the poor was so remote as to be illusory. The poor, it was said, had been put into the settlement "merely to give it a colour of piety, and so to legalise arrangements meant to serve for the aggrandisement of a family". This, therefore, was not a charitable settlement in any substantial sense and must fail.

English and Islamic concepts of charity, however, differ radically in this context. "An approach to God" (*qurba*), is the essence of a *waqf*, and such *qurba* is deemed to lie, by the consensus of Muslim jurists, in the very act of the settlor relinquishing his ownership of the property. The *corpus* of the property having been thus immobilised (for it is deemed, in Ḥanafī law, to belong only to God), Sharīʿa law is no longer concerned to ensure that the income or usufruct of the property is devoted to a "charitable" purpose. Certainly the settlor's own family may be validly designated as beneficiaries in the unanimous opinion of all the schools of Sharīʿa law, while in the view of the Ḥanafī jurist Abū-Yūsuf, which had previously been applied in India, the settlor could reserve for himself the exclusive right to the income of the *waqf* during his lifetime. Many jurists, indeed, opined that no specific mention of such ultimate beneficiaries as the poor or the sick was necessary for the validity of the *waqf*; and those who did require such a designation sought only thereby to ensure the permanent nature of the settlement and not to indicate that such "charitable" institutions were in any way a more fitting purpose for a *waqf* than its enjoyment by the settlor's own family.

Contrary as the decision in *Abul Fata* v. *Russomoy*

thus was to all the accepted authorities of the Sharīʿa, there is no doubt that the Privy Council was here endeavouring to apply Islamic law—and indeed they expressly stated this to be the case. But, in the first place, they preferred to follow the trend of recent decisions in the Indian High Courts rather than the opinions of such scholars as Ameer Ali as to the terms of the law enshrined in the authoritative manuals; and in the second place their Lordships appeared to be in some uncertainty as to the principles upon which Sharīʿa law was to be properly ascertained. Three years later, in *Aga Mahomed* v. *Koolsom Bee Bee* (1897), it was correctly stated in accordance with the traditional doctrine of *taqlīd* (adherence to established authority) that "it would be wrong for the court . . . to put their own construction on the Koran in opposition to the express ruling of commentators of such . . . high authority" (the Ḥanafī text of the *Hedaya*). In *Abul Fata* v. *Russomoy*, however, their Lordships felt able to ignore the authoritative Ḥanafī texts and place their own interpretation on certain alleged dicta of the Prophet, stating in reference to them that "it would be doing wrong to the great lawgiver to suppose that he is thereby commending gifts for which the donor exercises no self-denial . . . and which do not seek the benefit of others beyond the use of empty words . . .". In short, therefore, it would seem that once again British judges had failed to appreciate the real significance of the doctrine of *taqlīd*, but had assumed that traditional Sharīʿa law was just as much subject as the English common law to modification by those equitable principles which had found acceptance in the courts.

In this case, however, such influence did not prove, as it had done on so many other occasions, acceptable to the Muslim community in India, and the Legislature eventually overruled the Privy Council by the *Mussal-*

man Waqf Validating Act, 1913, which substantially restored the traditional Ḥanafī doctrine of family settlements under the *waqf* system. It is finally noteworthy, however, that British courts applying Islamic law in Aden, Zanzibar, and Kenya continued to regard the decision of the Privy Council in *Abul Fata's* case as binding upon them, and this has in turn necessitated the promulgation of legislation on the pattern of the *Waqf Validating Act* in each of these territories. Furthermore, even after the passing of such legislation, the unwillingness of the East African courts to abandon English notions of charity has resulted in a series of cases, the last a decision of the Privy Council of December 1962, in which the relevant legislation has been so strictly interpreted that its aims have been partly frustrated.[12]

Anglo-Muhammadan law, then, is an expression of Islamic law unique not only in form—for it is genuinely applied as a case-law system through a hierarchy of courts which observes the doctrine of binding precedent—but also in substance, inasmuch as it has absorbed English influences, particularly those of Equity, in as generally facile a manner as nascent Islamic law had absorbed Roman influences in the earliest historical period. French influence in Algeria, it may be observed, resulted in a broadly parallel, though less extreme, situation because of the strict control the French judiciary exercised, through the system of appeal, over the *qāḍīs'* courts. For example, the French courts insisted upon the consent of an adult girl to her marriage, on the formal ground that this was necessary in Ḥanafī if not in Mālikī law, while in the matter of the custody of minor children they largely rejected the rigid rules of custody under Sharīʿa law and regarded the interests of the minor as the paramount and overriding consideration in all cases. These and other similar principles reflecting French influence became an integral part of Sharī'a law as applied in Algeria.

Turning now to the Middle East, we find a very different state of affairs prevailed. Sharī'a courts were dominated by the doctrine of *taqlīd* to an extent which precluded them from administering the law in any way other than in strict accordance with the terms of the mediaeval texts. For this reason changes could only be effected through the intervention of the political authority, and this in fact occurred when the political authority proceeded to exercise its power, which it claimed under the principle of *siyāsa*, to determine the manner in which Sharī'a law should be administered.

The doctrine of *siyāsa*, it will be recalled, is the fundamental doctrine of Islamic public law which defines the position of the political authority *vis-à-vis* the Sharī'a, and which grants him the right to take such administrative steps as he deems to be in the public interest, provided no substantive principle of the Sharī'a is thereby blatantly infringed. One important aspect of this prerogative of the sovereign is his power to define the jurisdiction of his courts, in the sense that he may set limits to the sphere of their competence. It was on this ground, of course, that the public lawyers had recognised the validity of the "extra-Sharī'a" tribunals of mediaeval times, which had exercised jurisdiction in matters withdrawn from the competence of the Sharī'a courts. On this broad ground also, the entirely new court system through which Sharī'a law is currently administered in Egypt and Tunisia can hardly be condemned, from the standpoint of legal theory, as "un-Islamic", especially since the office of *qāḍī*, albeit for centuries the traditional organ of Sharī'a jurisdiction, was nevertheless an office created by the Umayyad administration and did not stem from any postulates of the divine revelation. Particular emphasis, however, is laid by the texts of public law on the right of the sovereign to enforce new rules of procedure and evidence, and it is this limb of the *siyāsa* doctrine which concerns us here. For Middle Eastern political authorities, by a series of regulations normally termed *qānūn*, restricted the competence of the *qāḍīs'* courts to cases which fulfilled certain procedural and evidential conditions. Although these were administrative measures which theoretically left the substantive Sharīʻa doctrine unimpaired, they had a far-reaching effect upon the nature of Sharīʻa jurisdiction as the following outline of the principal instances of their use will show.

Traditional Sharīʻa law, as we have noted, attached no value to written evidence, despite an explicit injunction of the Qur'ān that transactions should be recorded in writing. Abuses arising from the reliance of the courts on oral testimony resulted in *siyāsa* regulations in the Middle East which prevented the courts from entertaining certain types of claim that were not based on documentary evidence. Thus the Egyptian *Code of Organisation and Procedure for Sharīʻa Courts* of 1897 provided that "no claim of marriage, divorce, or acknowledgement thereof shall be heard after the death of either party unless it is supported by documents free from suspicion of forgery . . .". This simple requirement of documentary evidence was later extended to the necessity, in certain prescribed transactions, for documentary evidence of a specific kind—i.e. the certificate of a duly authorised official. And when the Jordanian *Law of Family Rights*, 1951, precluded the courts from entertaining any plea of repudiation (*ṭalāq*) from a husband (raised by him, for example, as a defence to his wife's claim for maintenance) unless such repudiation had been properly registered before the *qāḍī*, a step had been taken in the direction of making divorce by repudiation a judicial proceeding. Here the opportunity might conveniently be taken to depart from our preoccupation with the major blocs of Muslim populations and to observe that registration of repudiation has always been a legal requirement, from the time of their conversion, for the two-million-strong Muslim community in Yugoslavia and, since 1937, for the fifty thousand Muslims in Dutch Guiana.

The same procedural device was also employed in Egypt to counteract the effects, which proved unacceptable to modern opinion, of the excessive periods of gestation recognised by Sharīʿa doctrine. Ḥanafī law presumes that a maximum period of two years may elapse between the conception of a child and its birth, while the other schools recognise even longer periods; four years is the term of Shāfiʿī and Ḥanbalī law, while there is considerable Mālikī authority for a term of seven years. Such rules were not entirely due to the ignorance of the mediaeval jurists on matters of embryology, although belief in the phenomenon of "the sleeping foetus" may well have contributed to their acceptance. It goes without saying that the jurists were well aware of the normal period of gestation, which formed the basis of many legal rules, and most Ithnā-ʿasharī jurists in fact adopted a maximum period of nine lunar months. It was, however, the particular effects of illegitimacy which probably induced the jurists to adopt an attitude of excessive caution. There was the desire to avoid attributing the status of illegitimacy to children born to widowed or divorced women after the normal period of gestation had elapsed since the termination of their marriage; for the illegitimate child had no claims whatsoever, particularly as regards maintenance, upon its father. Again, for the Mālikīs at any rate, the birth of a child out of wedlock and outside the recognised periods of gestation after the termination of a marriage was *prima facie* evidence of fornication, which might entail the *ḥadd* penalty of lapidation, on the part of the mother; and the jurists had consistently demonstrated an unwillingness that these severe *ḥadd* penalties should be applied except where there was proof positive of guilt. In short, humanitarian principles seem to have influenced the jurists to accept the possibility of protracted periods of gestation. As the question was bound up with the criminal law, their general attitude was that legitimacy should always be presumed unless circumstances made its non-existence certain beyond any shadow of doubt.

Such considerations, however, had largely lost their force in modern Egypt, where fornication was no longer a criminal offence and where provision had been made for the support of illegitimate children by their fathers. On the other hand there was growing concern for the abuses to which, in the light of modern medical opinion, the traditional law gave rise. Since the *ʿidda* or "waiting period" of divorced women lasted as long as they were pregnant, divorcees could claim, on the assertion that their *ʿidda* period was not yet completed, maintenance from their ex-husbands for a period of two years. Moreover they would have the right to share in his estate if he died within this period, at least where the divorce was not of the final and irrevocable variety. Finally, children born to divorced or widowed women within two years of the termination of their marriage possessed rights of maintenance against the former husband and the right (indefeasible under the Sharīʿa law of succession) to take a major share in his estate.

Legal presumptions regarding gestation are, of course, a matter of evidence and as such a proper subject for administrative regulations. Accordingly the Egyptian government felt able to tackle the problem by the device of restricting the competence of the

Sharīʿa tribunals. Article 17 of Law No. 25 of 1929 thus provided that "No claim of maintenance shall be heard in respect of an *ʿidda* period in excess of one year from the date of divorce. Nor shall any disputed claim of inheritance on the grounds of marriage be heard regarding a divorced woman whose husband died more than a year after the date of the divorce." Similarly, under Article 15, "no disputed claim of paternity shall be heard regarding . . . the child of a divorced or widowed woman who gave birth to him more than a year after her divorce or widowhood". Sharīʿa courts, in other words, were not allowed to entertain claims in these respects unless the factual situation involved was in accordance with modern medical opinion on matters of gestation, the period of 365 days being deemed sufficient to cover all exceptional cases.

Also incorporated in Article 15 of the Egyptian Law of 1929 was a further provision which negated another aspect of the traditional law of legitimacy, and which again was a matter of evidence. Under Ḥanafī doctrine the presumption that a child born to a married woman after six months of marriage was the legitimate child of her husband could be rebutted neither by proof that the marriage had never been consummated nor by proof that there was no physical access between the spouses at any possible time of conception. Traditional law knew only one method by which a husband might disown a child born to his wife. This was the highly formalised procedure of *liʿān*, which owes its existence to the fact that a husband's disclaimer of the paternity of a child born to his wife amounts to charging her with the crime of adultery and makes him liable, in the event of his being unable to establish the offence by the requisite four witnesses, to the penalty of eighty lashes for an unproved assertion of unchastity (*qadhf*). A husband who sought to disown his wife's child, therefore, was obliged to swear four solemn oaths (taking the place of the four witnesses) that the child concerned was not his, and then to call down upon himself the curse of God (taking the place of the penalty for *qadhf*) if he had falsely sworn. The wife, failing her confession of adultery, could then avoid the penalty for adultery by swearing four oaths of her innocence in rebuttal and finally calling upon herself the curse of God if she was in fact guilty. As a result of this procedure (termed *li'ān* from the Arabic *la'ana* "to curse"), which also effected a divorce between the couple and created a permanent bar to their re-marriage, paternity of the child concerned was no longer attributed to the husband.

Li'ān was obviously an institution wholly out of line with modern notions of procedure and evidence and the natural substitute for it—proof of non-access—was introduced in Egypt in 1929 by the same device of restricting the competence of the Sharī'a tribunals. Accordingly, the courts were forbidden to entertain disputed claims of paternity where it could be established either that the marriage had not been consummated at all or that the child concerned had been born to the wife more than one year after the last physical access between herself and the husband.

Modifications of the traditional Ḥanafī law of legitimacy were also introduced in the Indian sub-continent, but stand in sharp contrast to the Egyptian reforms in regard to both their juristic basis and, to a large degree, their substance. For here judicial decisions recognised that the Sharī'a had been superseded by the Indian *Evidence Act* of 1872, the substance of which was, naturally enough, English law. Under Section 112 of the Act, a child born during the continuance of a valid marriage or within 280 days of its dissolution will be presumed to be the legitimate child of the husband unless non-access at any possible time of conception can be proved. Thus, as distinct from normal Sharīʿa law and the present position in Egypt, the presumption of legitimacy operates in favour of a child born during the first six months of a marriage, while the legitimacy or otherwise of children born more than 280 days after the termination of a marriage will presumably be determined by the normal principles of the English law of evidence.

Although administrative regulations in the Middle East were essentially matters of adjectival law, in one instance they were clearly directed against substantive Sharīʿa doctrine. This was in relation to the topic of child-marriage. In the Egyptian *Code of Procedure for Sharīʿa Courts* enacted in 1931 a number of previous provisions on this subject were consolidated with the following effect. No disputed claim of marriage was to be entertained by the courts unless such marriage could be established by an official certificate, and under the existing law the competent officials were forbidden to conclude a marriage or to issue such a certificate where the bride was less than sixteen or the bridegroom less than eighteen years of age at the time of the contract. Nor was *any* claim of marriage, even where it was not disputed, to be heard if either of the spouses was less than the ages prescribed at the time of the claim. These provisions clearly affected the substantive rights of marriage guardians, recognised by all schools of Sharīʿa law, to contract in marriage their minor wards of whatever age, inasmuch as no judicial relief would be forthcoming in the case of marriages so contracted. But in theory the substantive Sharīʿa law remained untouched, and a marriage concluded between minors was still perfectly valid. The indirect procedural method appeared the only way open to the Egyptian reformers at this stage, in the face of the established doctrine of *taqlīd*, to restrict the practice of child marriage.

A somewhat similar situation came to exist in Algeria

under French influence, where administrative regulations required a formal deed of marriage to be drawn up by the *qāḍīs*, who were ordered by the Procureur-Général to refuse such a document if the bride was under the age of fifteen. In India, however, developments in this regard were again of a totally different nature. Marriage of girls below the age of fourteen and boys below the age of sixteen was prohibited under pain of penalties by the *Child Marriage Restraint Act* of 1929. At the same time marriages concluded in defiance of the provisions of the Act were valid, and some relief was granted to girls contracted in marriage during minority by an extension of their so-called "option of puberty". Under traditional Ḥanafī law a minor girl contracted in marriage by any guardian other than her father or paternal grandfather may repudiate the marriage, provided it has not been consummated with her consent, upon her attainment of puberty. Under the *Dissolution of Muslim Marriages Act*, 1939, this right of repudiation may also be exercised where the girl concerned has been married by her father or paternal grandfather.

The role played in the modern evolution of Middle Eastern Sharīʿa law by the method of restricting the competence of the courts should not be exaggerated. As a means of remedying purely procedural defects in the law it appears to be perfectly consistent with Islamic tradition; but when specifically directed against the terms of the substantive law it becomes of questionable validity. Practically effective though the denial of judicial relief may be, it is a harsh method of reform when the act or relationship concerned is admittedly valid, and a method which, if pursued to its logical conclusion, could wrest all semblance of authority from the Sharīʿa. Certainly its most extreme advocates could never contemplate its employment against the two firmly entrenched rights of the husband upon which the attention of the reformers came to be focussed—his rights of polygamy and unilateral repudiation. To many, indeed, the particular manner in which the jurisdiction of the courts had been confined seemed an altogether illegitimate exercise of the sovereign's admitted power. For this right, they argued, existed in order that the sovereign might distribute different classes of case as between one court and another, and could not be properly employed so as to deny certain types of claim, tenable under the substantive law, any enforcement at all. Practical and theoretical considerations of this nature, therefore, make the limitations of this method of reform readily apparent.

Nevertheless, as opposed to the position in the Indian sub-continent, where judicial activities had modified the substance itself of the Sharī'a, Islamic law in the Middle East had begun to take on a new look without any direct interference in its substantive provisions. The developments which we have briefly discussed in both these areas, however, may be conveniently termed "administrative" to distinguish them from outright reforms of the substantive law introduced under the aegis of the political authority, which will form the subject matter of the following two chapters. This distinction, however, is primarily an analytical rather than an historical one in regard to the Middle East as a whole, inasmuch as it was by no means always the case that the administrative aspects of development preceded direct substantive reform. Finally, in regard to the method of reform of the substantive law, it will be seen that an equally striking divergence exists in this respect also between the Indian sub-continent and the Middle East. In India, Sharī'a family law was directly superseded in particular and limited spheres by statute law on the English pattern, examples of which have already been noted. In the Near and Middle East, on the other hand, the Sharīʿa was systematically codified, a process more in accord with the temper of Arab jurisprudence but naturally owing much to recent French influence, while great pains were taken to represent the reforms embodied in the Codes as legitimate applications of established Sharīʿa principles. In short, modern trends in the family law of both areas have perpetuated their own particular legal traditions.

CHAPTER 13

TAQLĪD AND LEGAL REFORM

IJMĀʿ or consensus had in theory established that the family law expounded in the mediaeval legal manuals was the final and exclusively authoritative expression of the Sharīʿa, and under the ensuing doctrine of *taqlīd* the basic principles of the texts, although they might be extended to cover new cases, were themselves inviolate and immutable. Diversity of doctrine, however, abounded both within and between the several schools of Sunnite law, and *ijmāʿ* had ratified these variations as equally valid and legitimate interpretations of the Sharīʿa. It is the principle that *taqlīd* allows a choice from among these variant views recorded in the authoritative texts which has permitted extensive modification of the law as traditionally applied in Middle Eastern countries and which, as exploited by modern reformers, has lent an added significance to the alleged statement of the Prophet that "Difference of opinion among my people is a sign of the bounty of God".

Islam had already experienced a considerable breakdown of the barriers that geographical division had erected between the different schools of law in mediaeval times. Official sponsorship of the Ḥanafī doctrine by the central Ottoman government had resulted in the establishment of Ḥanafī courts in provinces of the empire, where the population belonged to another school. Thus Shāfiʿī and Mālikī litigants in Egypt, and Mālikī litigants in Tunisia and the Sudan were, of necessity, often subject to the application of Ḥanafī law. However, the apparent conflict of allegiance which this situation might seem to create for the individual conscience was not in reality a serious one, for it was primarily in regard to matters of cult and ritual practices that Muslim populations identified themselves with a particular school or rite, and on technically legal issues they were prepared to accept the jurisdiction of tribunals applying the tenets of some other school. At any rate the influence of Ḥanafī law in the territories mentioned survived the dismemberment of the Ottoman empire. Ḥanafī courts continued to operate in Egypt; two chief *qāḍīs*, one Ḥanafī and one Mālikī, sat in Tunisia, while judicial practice in the Sudan gradually created a fusion of the Mālikī and Ḥanafī systems.

In theory the right of a Muslim to be governed by the law of his school, at least in matters of personal status, is beyond dispute. With the growing intercourse between Muslim peoples in modern times this principle has naturally assumed a greater importance and courts owing allegiance to one school have not proved averse to applying another school, as the personal law of the litigants involved, on the advice of scholars learned in its tenets. Furthermore, traditional doctrine allows a Muslim to change his school at will, as an Indian court recognised in the Bombay case of *Muhammad Ibrahim* v. *Gulam Ahmad* (1864). Here, the marriage of a girl who had been brought up as a Shāfiʿī and who had married without her father's consent, was held to be valid on the girl's assertion that she had become a Ḥanafī and had married as such. Ḥanafī law, it will be recalled, is the only system which permits an adult girl to conclude her own marriage contract without the intervention of her guardian. Until recently, legal practice in Zanzibar provided an interesting, although from a purist standpoint a wholly illegitimate, extension of this right of a Muslim litigant to opt out of an inconvenient rule obtaining in his own school. For here

'Ibāḍī law (the 'Ibāḍites being the surviving branch of the original Khārijite sect) allowed a wife to obtain dissolution of her marriage on the ground of the husband's cruelty. Shāfi'ī law, on the other hand, recognises a temporary form of judicial separation as the only remedy available to a wife in such circumstances; but Shāfi'ī wives used to be able to obtain a dissolution of their marriage on grounds of cruelty by the simple expedient of presenting their petition to the 'Ibāḍī *qāḍī*. To confine ourselves, however, to the four Sunnite schools, modern conditions had thus brought about a growing awareness of the existence of their variant doctrines and a recognition by the Sharī'a courts of their mutual orthodoxy.

It is against this broad background of a developing contact and comity between the several schools in legal practice that the modernist legislative activities in the Ḥanafī Middle East should be viewed. In 1915 the principle that the Sharī'a courts might be ordered to apply, in all relevant cases, an opinion other than that of the school to which they were traditionally bound was recognised by Section 53 of the Sudanese *Mohamedan Law Courts Organization and Procedure Regulations*, which empowered the Grand *Qāḍī* to direct, by the issue of judicial circulars or memoranda, the application of rules other than the authoritative Ḥanafī doctrine. It was, however, Ottoman legislation of 1915 and 1917 which took the lead in this process of reform and set the example which was later followed by the rest of the Middle Eastern Arab countries generally. Family law, or substantial parts of it, was codified on the juristic basis that the sovereign, as part of his acknowledged *siyāsa* powers, had the right to define the jurisdiction of the courts, in the sense that he might order them to apply one among several existing variant opinions. These codifications also contained regulations of the type we have already discussed, which set procedural limits upon the competence of the courts; but the vast bulk of their substance consisted of those rules which had been selected from the whole corpus of traditional Sharīʿa doctrine as most suitable for application in modern times. This, then, is the second, but by far the more important aspect of legal reform under the authority of the doctrine of *siyāsa* regulations. *Takhayyur* is the general Arabic term for the process of selection; and if we omit the case of a restricted choice from among Ḥanafī variants only, such as had taken place in the Ottoman *Majalla*, it will be seen that the exercise of *takhayyur* falls under three distinct heads which may generally be regarded as chronological stages in the development of the principle.

The first and natural step was to consider the dominant doctrine of one of the three other Sunnite schools as a possible alternative to the existing Ḥanafī law. Divorce, and in particular a wife's petition for dissolution of her marriage, is perhaps the outstanding example of a topic where reform was felt to be a matter of particular urgency in Ḥanafī countries and where it could be effectively achieved by the method of "selection". A Ḥanafī wife could obtain a judicial annulment of her marriage if the husband had proved totally incapable of consummating it, and she could obtain dissolution on the grounds of putative widowhood if her husband had become a missing person and ninety years had elapsed since the date of his birth. But beyond this she had no means of freeing herself from a prejudicial union, apart from negotiating a divorce by mutual agreement; whereas the other schools, and in particular the Mālikīs (who were the most liberal in this regard), allowed a wife to ground a petition on the husband's cruelty, his refusal or inability to maintain her, his desertion, or his affliction with some serious ailment which made the continuance of the marital relationship harmful to the wife.

Accordingly, the first great monument of reform in the traditional family law—the *Ottoman Law of Family Rights*, 1917—provided for judicial dissolution of marriage in the case of wives whose husbands were suffering from some serious disease or had deserted them without providing for their maintenance. In the first case Mālikī authority was the basis of the provisions, while in the second case Ḥanbalī doctrine had been adopted. Egypt, however, proceeded to effect a more complete adoption of Mālikī doctrine in laws of divorce promulgated in 1920 and 1929. This legislation contained provisions for divorce in the case of failure to maintain by husbands who were not absent (the wider Mālikī as opposed to the Ḥanbalī rules) and included as a separate and additional ground for judicial dissolution desertion by the husband for a continuous period of one year, even though there might be property of the husband available to provide maintenance for the wife.

But although predominantly of Mālikī inspiration, the Egyptian legislation did involve certain modifications of strict Mālikī doctrine. In the first place the fact that a husband has a reasonable excuse for his absence (e.g. business commitments) is a good defence, under the Egyptian law, to a wife's petition based on desertion. This is, indeed, normal Ḥanbalī doctrine, but Mālikī law holds the reasons for the husband's absence to be irrelevant; and it may be observed that the Sudan had followed the Mālikī law more closely in this regard when a Judicial Circular of 1916 allowed divorce to wives whose husbands had been absent, for whatever cause, for a year or more, provided only that the wife asserted that she was afraid of falling into immoral conduct as a result of being left alone. A second departure of the Egyptian legislation from strict Mālikī law occurs in regard to a wife's petition alleging cruelty against the husband. Where a wife proves cruelty in the required fashion the court will grant a decree of dissolution forthwith; but where cruelty cannot be so established and yet discord obviously exists, arbitrators will be appointed from the families of both the spouses. Failing the success of attempts at reconciliation, the arbitrators will decree a divorce for the wife if they find that the fault for the discord lies chiefly with the husband, and up to this point the procedure under the Egyptian Law is in accord with Mālikī doctrine. But where the arbitrators find that the blame for the discord rests clearly with the wife they are empowered by Mālikī law to enforce the form of divorce known as *khul'*, by which the wife is obliged to pay a consideration—usually the dower or part thereof—for her release. Under the Egyptian Law, however, the arbitrators do not have this power; and although the Mālikī jurist Ibn-Rushd might be quoted in support of such a view, this was presumably because the purpose of the reformers was to grant relief to ill-used wives and not husbands, whose right of repudiation (*ṭalāq*) provided the obvious remedy in such circumstances.

Substantially similar reforms of the law of divorce as applied in the Indian sub-continent were effected by the *Dissolution of Muslim Marriages Act*, 1939. This Act, however, cannot be regarded, in the same way as the Egyptian legislation and similar laws subsequently promulgated in other Middle Eastern countries, as a conscientious substitution of Mālikī or other doctrines for the traditional Ḥanafī law. Certainly the Indian reformers claimed to be adopting Mālikī rules, and in one respect at least the Act is perhaps more obviously Mālikī in its terms than its Egyptian counterpart; for it specifically states that a wife may obtain dissolution on grounds of cruelty where she is one of several co-wives and is not treated impartially with the rest—behaviour which the Mālikī texts always recognise as constituting legal cruelty (*ḍarar*). Certain provisions of the Act, however, salutary though they may be in a modern setting, contradict all traditional doctrine outright, such as the rule that "renunciation of Islam by a married Muslim woman . . . shall not by itself operate to dissolve her marriage". Other provisions represent considerable modifications of basic Mālikī principles—the requirements, for example, that a husband should have failed to provide maintenance for a period of two years, and that his desertion, or failure to perform his marital obligations, should have run for a continuous period of three years before a wife's petition on these grounds can be successful. More particularly, however, the Act wholly ignores the special procedures of Mālikī law by which a wife may be granted relief on these various grounds. Not only is there no provision for arbitrators in cases of alleged cruelty, but the Act also adopts as the general mode of dissolution a judicial decree of *faskh* (literally "recission") in place of the judicial repudiation or *ṭalāq* prescribed by Mālikī law and adopted in the Egyptian legislation. The distinction between these two types of legal machinery has a particular significance in cases of divorce for the husband's failure to maintain. Under the *Dissolution of Muslim Marriages Act* a decree of *faskh* on this ground operates as a final dissolution of the marriage, whereas the judicial repudiation of Mālikī and Egyptian law is a revocable repudiation—i.e. one which will only become final on the expiry of the divorced wife's *'idda* period and which will cease to be effective if the husband proves himself, during the period of *'idda*, able and willing to maintain his wife. On the question of the standard or level of maintenance to which a wife is entitled Egypt had already adopted Shāfi'ī doctrine, which fixes the standard by exclusive reference to the financial position of the husband. Hence a husband who demonstrates his ability to provide the bare necessities of life will be able to effect revocation of a judicial repudiation pronounced for failure to maintain under the Egyptian Law.

A second example of the selection by Middle Eastern countries of the principles of another school—in this case the Ḥanbalīs—concerns the right of a husband and wife to regulate the incidents of their marital relationship by the stipulation of conditions in the marriage contract itself. Adoption of Ḥanbalī rules is, in fact, a notable feature of modernist legislation in the Middle East, and it is somewhat of a paradox that the tenets of a school which was traditionally renowned for its strictness and rigidity, and which in history had never commanded a wide allegiance, should now be considered suitable to govern the lives of a great number of Ḥanafī Muslims. However, with regard to conditions in marriage contracts, Ḥanafī, Mālikī, and Shāfiʿī doctrine stems naturally from the basic theory of contracts as a whole which obtains in these schools, namely that the effects of a given contractual relationship have been precisely determined by the law, in terms of the rights and obligations which arise, and are not susceptible to variation at the will of the parties. Conditions, accordingly, are only valid and enforceable in so far as they serve to consolidate the prescribed effects of the contract.

As applied to contracts of marriage this principle means that any conditions deemed contrary to the essence of marriage, such as the stipulation of a time limit, render the whole contract a complete nullity; while any condition which seeks to modify or contradict the established rights of the parties—the rights of the wife to dower and maintenance, for example, or the rights of the husband to the general obedience of his wife, to take three additional wives, and to exercise repudiation (*ṭalāq*) at will—is itself void and regarded as non-existent while the contract remains valid. Only conditions which reinforce the rigid scheme of the marital relationship are valid, such as stipulations for a specific amount of dower. Ḥanbalī law, on the contrary, goes a considerable way towards endorsing the principle of individual freedom to regulate contractual relationships. This was largely the result of the peculiar characteristics of original Ḥanbalī jurisprudence. Because their early scholars considered the accepted texts of divine revelation to be the only valid sources of law, an overriding emphasis was placed upon the obvious implications of the Qur'ānic injunction: "Muslims must abide by their stipulations". According to Ḥanbalī law, therefore, any agreement entered into by husband and wife as part of their marriage contract is valid and enforceable unless it involves something expressly prohibited by the law or is manifestly contrary to the institution of marriage. While this formula precludes such stipulations as the introduction of a time limit, it permits, as opposed to the doctrine of the other schools, stipulations which modify the normal rights and duties of the spouses, and in particular those which represent safeguards for the wife's position. For it is not expressly forbidden and not contrary to the institution of marriage that a husband should have only one wife, or that the wife should not be obliged to live anywhere against her will, or that she should be free to engage in social or professional activities. Accordingly, conditions to this effect are valid and enforceable in Ḥanbalī law.

Since the primary purpose of the Middle Eastern reformers was the amelioration of the position of women under the law, the appeal of this Ḥanbalī doctrine was undeniable and it has been adopted, to varying degrees, in most Arab countries. In the *Ottoman Law of Family Rights*, 1917, it was only stipulations against a second marriage by the husband which were declared valid on this basis, and the same is true of the Moroccan *Code of Personal Status*, 1958. Proposals were put forward in Egypt in 1926 to apply the Ḥanbalī doctrine on a broader basis—to provide a means of restricting not only the husband's right of polygamy but also his general dominion over his wife—but were not enacted as law. However, under the Jordanian *Law of Family Rights* of 1951, any "stipulation of benefit to one of the parties" was declared valid, while the Syrian *Law of Personal Status* of 1953 specifically included stipulations which restricted "the liberty of the husband in those matters permitted to him by the law". And a similar position now obtains, apparently, under the most recent Code of Personal Status to appear in the Middle East—that promulgated in Iraq on December 30th, 1959—although the vague phrasing of the relevant section gives the courts considerable scope for interpretation.[13] In all these cases, following normal Ḥanbalī doctrine, conditions securing some benefit for the wife are legally effective not in the sense that their observance will be enforced upon the husband by means of a prohibitive injunction, but in the sense that their infringement by him constitutes a sufficiently serious breach of the contract to release the wife from her own obligations thereunder and entitles her to claim a dissolution of the marriage.

Courts in the Indian sub-continent, it may finally be remarked, have recognised the validity of agreements in Muslim marriage contracts provided they are "reasonable and not contrary to the provisions or policy of the law", which apparently would include most conditions denying the husband the right to exercise his traditional powers.[14] But this situation arose from the natural tendency of jurists and judges who were conscious of the principles of English law to give effect to such agreements and quietly to disregard the strict dictates of Ḥanafī law; it was certainly not the result of a conscientious adoption of Ḥanbalī doctrine.

One final instance of the first stage of "selection" or *takhayyur* may be of interest inasmuch as the purpose here, contrary to the general trend, was to alleviate the hardships suffered by husbands, rather than wives, under the existing law. Divorced wives who are not pregnant are obliged to observe an *'idda* period which lasts for three menstrual periods (*qurū'*) and during this time they have the right to maintenance from their former husbands. Ḥanafī law held that the *'idda* of a divorced wife who ceased to have her normal menstrual periods before the end of the *'idda* was to last until she had in fact completed three such periods or had reached the age of the menopause, set by the law at fifty-five, when she was to remain in *'idda* for a further period of three months. This rule is a particularly striking and unfortunate example of the tendency of mediaeval jurists to insist upon the mechanical observance of the incidents of a legal rule (in this case the completion of three menstrual periods) and to neglect completely the purpose which the rule was designed to serve (in this case the ascertainment of the wife's pregnancy or otherwise). As a result of it, unscrupulous divorcees could claim maintenance from their ex-husbands for excessive periods, simply by their allegation that they had not completed three menstrual periods; and to prevent such abuse the Ottoman *Law of Family Rights* of 1917 adopted the Mālikī rule that the *'idda* period of such women was to last for the normal time of gestation—i.e. nine months—plus a further three months as the normal period of *'idda* for women who had ceased to menstruate. In fact, however, as drafted in the Ottoman Law, the Mālikī period was cut down to a maximum of nine months. It may be observed that the effect of the traditional Ḥanafī rule was negated in Egypt by the procedural regulations we have discussed, under which the maximum *'idda* period, for practical purposes, was one year.

Because reform of traditional Sharī'a doctrine had begun in the Middle East, the major examples of "selection" (*takhayyur*) are naturally all cases of the superseding of Ḥanafī law by some other system. But there is no reason why the same process should not be used to advantage in certain respects in non-Ḥanafī areas of Islam. Courts in Algeria, as we have seen, preferred the Ḥanafī to the Mālikī doctrine concerning the capacity of an adult woman to conclude her own marriage contract. Tunisia, in a law of 1959 which formed a supplement to her *Law of Personal Status* promulgated in 1957, abandoned the traditional Mālikī rule that the surplus of an estate, failing any *'aṣaba* relative, went to the Public Treasury, and adopted the doctrine of *radd* or "return" (to the Qur'ānic heirs) as expounded by the non-Mālikī schools; indeed it went beyond these by allowing the spouse relict to participate in the surplus.[15] And finally Saudi Arabia, rigidly conservative enough in 1927 to defeat King Ibn-Saud's proposal to codify the law on the basis of other than Ḥanbalī doctrines,[16] has recently accepted the principle that the rules of the other Sunnite schools might be preferred in suitable circumstances.[17]

Thus far a reformer could perhaps properly claim that he had done no more than exercise his acknowledged right (as a *muqallid* obliged to follow authorities) to choose between variant opinions which jurisprudence had recognised as equally authoritative. But such a claim became more dubious as the application of *takhayyur* or selection passed into its second stage; for now the reformers could only attribute the rules embodied in their Codes to the authority of individual jurists whose opinions had preceded or were in conflict with the dominant doctrines of the four Sunnite schools as a whole.

As opposed to the Egyptian policy of discouraging child marriage by the indirect and procedural method of denying judicial relief, most other Middle Eastern countries—Jordan, Syria, Iraq, Tunisia, and Morocco—have followed the precedent of the Ottoman *Law of Family Rights* by directly adopting as substantive law the rule that no child below the age of puberty may be contracted in marriage, the minimum ages for puberty fixed by the various laws ranging from twelve (boys) and nine (girls) under the Ottoman Law to the age of sixteen for both sexes in Iraq. Between these ages and the age of full capacity to marry, usually eighteen, permission to marry may be given by the court if it is satisfied of the applicant's maturity. For these rules the only available juristic support lay in the views of very early scholars like Ibn-Shubrūma, who held that minors could not be contracted in compulsory marriage, and, at least as far as minor boys are concerned, in the opinion of the Ẓāhirī jurist Ibn-Ḥazm.

Similarly, when Syria in 1953 adopted a maximum period of gestation of one year as a rule of substantive law, only the isolated view of the Mālikī scholar Muḥammad ibn-al-Ḥakam could be adduced in support. Equally contrary to the established doctrine of all the four Sunnite schools were certain modifications of the law of divorce by *ṭalāq* introduced in Egypt in 1929. Conditional repudiations uttered solely in order to induce a wife to perform or abstain from some act and without any intention that divorce should actually take place—e.g. "If you behave thus again you are repudiated"—were declared inoperative on the alleged authority of such personages as the Meccan scholar 'Aṭā', who died in A.D. 733, and Shurayḥ, who is said to have been appointed judge of Kūfa by the Caliph ʿUmar (634–44). The provision that a repudiation coupled, by word or sign, with a number was to be accounted a single and revocable repudiation also rested on the authority of individualistic opinions such as that of the Ḥanbalī Ibn-Taymiyya.

Reliance upon isolated doctrines is an outstanding feature of the Egyptian *Law of Inheritance* of 1943. Two examples from this law must here suffice. Firstly, where a child is born dead as the result of an assault upon its mother, Sharīʿa law exacts from the person who made the assault a special kind and amount of blood-money known as *ghirra*. All the Sunnite schools regard this money as belonging to the child itself, and therefore transmissible to its own heirs, while the Ḥanafīs further maintain that the child, because its legal existence is assumed by the *ghirra* rule, should inherit and pass to its heirs any other property which it would certainly have inherited had it in fact been born alive. Under the Egyptian law, however, the child itself does not acquire and pass to its heirs either the *ghirra* or, *a fortiori*, any other property, but the mother alone is entitled to the blood-money for her still-born child, which is thus regarded as compensation payable for damage to the body of the mother herself. Rabīʿa ibn-Abī-ʿAbd-ar-Raḥmān and al-Layth ibn-Saʿd, both scholars of Medina who died in the early eighth century, are the only alleged authorities for this rule.

The second example concerns the general problem of a competition, on intestacy, between the deceased's paternal grandfather and his collateral relatives. All schools agree that uterine brothers and sisters are totally excluded from succession by the grandfather. Germane or consanguine brothers and sisters are also excluded by the grandfather in Ḥanafī law, but are allowed to share with him according to the Shāfiʿīs, Ḥanbalīs and

Mālikīs. The Egyptian Law adopts the general principle of these latter two schools that such collaterals are not excluded by the grandfather, but departs in many particulars from their rules concerning the precise mode of distribution among the respective claimants. To take a simple instance: as a general principle the grandfather is counted as a brother, and as between brothers the germane excludes the consanguine by virtue of his superior blood tie. Where, then, the deceased is survived by his grandfather, a full brother and a consanguine brother, Shāfiʿī and Mālikī law would allot one-third of the estate to the grandfather and two-thirds to the full brother, on the ground that the consanguine brother should first be given a notional share of one-third as against the grandfather and then excluded from this share by the full brother to the latter's sole advantage. Under the Egyptian law, however, the consanguine brother will be excluded *ab initio* by the full brother, who will then share the estate equally with the grandfather. In this, as in other particulars where it diverges from the Shāfiʿī and Mālikī doctrine, the Egyptian Law rests its provisions on the alleged views of the Prophet's son-in-law ʿAlī. But in order that the conflict of authorities should appear a more balanced one, the choice is represented as lying between the alternative views of ʿAlī on the one hand and those of the Prophet's secretary Zayd ibn-Thābit on the other, from whom, it is alleged, the Mālikī and Shāfiʿī doctrine was derived.

It will perhaps now be obvious that in this second phase of the exercise of *takhayyur* the mantle of *taqlīd*, which until then had been cloaking the activities of the reformers, was beginning to assume a threadbare appearance. In their search for authority from the corpus of ten centuries of juristic speculation the legislators had foraged beyond the legitimate bounds established by traditional jurisprudence. Individual and, from an orthodox standpoint, eccentric views held by scholars of bygone ages had been resurrected from the grave to which the general consensus of opinion had consigned them.

In the third and final aspect of *takhayyur*, however, the claim of *taqlīd* by the legislators becomes little more than an illusory formality. Legal rules are ostensibly constructed by the combination and fusion of juristic opinions, and of elements therefrom, of diverse nature and provenance; and to this activity is given the descriptive term *talfīq* (literally "to make up a patchwork, to piece together").

There is, however, some uncertainty as to the precise definition of *talfīq*. In one sense, of course, any departure at all from the doctrine of a particular school constitutes *talfīq*. Because of the essential unity of the individual rites or schools, the adoption of Mālikī law, say, concerning divorce, and the retention of the Ḥanafī law of marriage would, in effect, produce a composite legal system. At the more restricted level of the subject of conditions in marriage contracts, the application of the Ḥanbalī doctrine to stipulations preventing a second marriage by the husband but not to stipulations securing social freedom for the wife (as is the case in the Ottoman *Law of Family Rights*) could be termed *talfīq*. And a similar view could be held of the Tunisian law of intestate succession (page 193 above), which accepts the non-Mālikī principle of "return" (to Qur'ānic heirs) but retains the Mālikī view that cognate relatives (*dhawū'l-arḥām*) have no rights of succession; for both the doctrine of "return" and the claims of the cognate relatives together largely depend, in traditional law, on the position which is assigned to the Public Treasury. The present Tunisian law amounts to an adoption of the non-Mālikī view of the Public Treasury in relation to the Qur'ānic heirs and a retention of the Mālikī view of the Public Treasury in relation to the cognate relatives.

It was more than a simple extension of this situation, however, when the doctrine of one school was held to be applicable in certain specified circumstances and that of a different school in others. Roman law, by way of comparison, provides a good example of this in its rules concerning *specificatio*—i.e. the creation of a new kind, or *species*, of property out of existing material, such as the fashioning of an ornament from gold ore. Ownership of the created object belonged, according to the Sabinian school, to the owner of the material, but belonged to the creator of the object according to the Proculian school. Justinian, however, ruled that ownership vested in the creator if the product could not be reduced into its original state, but remained with the original owner if it could so be reduced. A remarkably parallel instance of such a compromise solution between two opposing views is contained in the Egyptian Law of Inheritance of 1943 in a provision concerning the bars to succession which apply between non-Muslims. According to Ḥanafī law, no rights of inheritance exist between two non-Muslims when one is the subject of a Muslim state and the other is the subject of a non-Muslim state, while in Mālikī law such difference of domicile raises no bar to inheritance. Under the Egyptian Law such difference of domicile is not a bar provided the laws of the non-Muslim state concerned permit reciprocal treatment, but is a bar if they do not. It would seem reasonable, then, to classify rules of this nature as the starting-point of *talfīq* proper. For in the cases previously cited the boundary between the operation of the rules of one school and another is clearly defined; whereas in the last case the views of two schools are closely fused together under the terms of the proviso in a single legal rule of restricted ambit.

In its extreme form, however, *talfīq* goes far beyond the sphere of intermediate and compromise solutions. With regard to the same question of inheritance between non-Muslims, the Egyptian law (assuming the condition of reciprocity to exist) would allow a Jew domiciled in a non-Muslim state to inherit from his Christian relative domiciled in a Muslim state. This would not be possible under Ḥanafī law because of the different domiciles of the two relatives; nor would it be possible under Mālikī law, where a difference of religion between non-Muslim relatives constitutes a bar to inheritance. Although, therefore, the reformers might claim Mālikī support for holding that no bar is raised by difference of domicile and Ḥanafī support for holding that no bar is raised by difference of religion, the combination of the two views results in a rule for which no authority exists in any of the Sunnite schools.

A particularly complex example of this extreme form of *talfīq* is found in the Egyptian *Law of Waqf* of 1946. Widespread dissatisfaction with the system of *waqf* settlement had made reform in the traditional law highly desirable. Economists condemned the immobilisation in perpetuity of vast amounts of landed property which lay, withdrawn from commerce, under the "dead hand". Moralists inveighed against the evils of a system which allowed a person to deprive his legal heirs of their rights by the simple expedient of declaring all his property to be *waqf*, reserving the use thereof for himself during his lifetime and excluding from any benefit therein all or such of his family as he might choose. As a remedy for these two principal mischiefs, the Law of 1946 provided, firstly, that all such *waqfs*, other than those for specifically religious purposes, should have a maximum duration of sixty years or two successive series of beneficiaries, whichever was less; and secondly, that all legal heirs of the founder should have, after his death, an "obligatory entitlement" in the *waqf* equivalent to their rights of succession, whether they had been expressly nominated as beneficiaries or not. The limitation upon the period of a *waqf* was formally based on Mālikī doctrine, which allows temporary foundations, buttressed by the principle that the ruler has the right to command the observance of something permitted by the Sharī'a; while the rule of "obligatory entitlement" rested on the views of the Ẓāhirī Ibn Ḥazm and certain Ḥanbalī jurists, who regarded the exclusion of some of his heirs by the founder as "oppressive" and opined that in such cases the excluded heirs should be admitted to share in the *waqf*.

It is in regard to a *waqf* in which the beneficiaries have an "obligatory entitlement" and which comes to an end under the terms of the Egyptian Law that our particular example of *talfīq* occurs. Article 17 provides that in such circumstances "the property no longer subject to the *waqf* shall belong to the founder if alive, while if he is dead it shall belong to the beneficiaries". On straightforward social and moral grounds—particularly in the light of the purpose of protecting the interests of the founder's heirs—the justice of this provision is beyond dispute. But the claim that its juristic basis lies in the traditional authorities is exceedingly tenuous. Obviously the major point at issue is the ownership of *waqf* property, for this will determine its subsequent reversion on the termination of the *waqf*. Mālikī law, certainly, held that ownership remained with the founder, while Ḥanbalī law held that it passed to the beneficiaries. The Egyptian Law, therefore, may be represented as amalgamating both these views, applying the Mālikī rule where the founder is alive and the Ḥanbalī rule where he is dead. But, arbitrary though this distinction which governs the operation of the respective doctrines may be, what really exposes the fallacy of the claim of traditional authority is the fact that the Ḥanbalīs entirely rejected the validity of a temporary *waqf*, and never therefore regarded the ownership of the beneficiaries as anything other than a nominal title.

When the traditional authorities had to be manipulated in this fashion to yield the required rule, any claim that this process constituted *taqlīd* had become nothing more than a thin veil of pretence, a purely formal and superficial adherence to the established principles of jurisprudence, which masked the reality of an attempt to fashion the terms of the law to meet the needs of society as objectively determined. This new attitude of modern Islamic jurisprudence, which is, of course, the antithesis of the classical view that the only legitimate standards for society are set by the law, was inherent in the process of reform from the outset; for, in fact, *takhayyur* was essentially the selection of views on the basis of their suitability for modern conditions. And as time went on, an increasing emphasis was placed upon practical and social considerations by the Explanatory Memoranda which accompanied the codifications of the Sharīʻa. The review of the mass of variant views which the method of *takhayyur* entailed had brought about a growing consciousness of the human and therefore fallible nature of the bulk of traditional Sharīʻa doctrine; and the validity of the thesis that the juristic speculations of mediaeval scholars were binding upon modern generations naturally began to be questioned. Traditional principles now appeared in relation to certain problems as a formidable barrier to the further progress that modernism desired. *Taqlīd* had become largely a fiction. Like other historical legal fictions it had served its purpose as a transitional device; and when its potential appeared exhausted, modernist jurisprudence inevitably passed on to a more frank and open recognition of the real purposes that had inspired it.

CHAPTER 14

NEO-IJTIHĀD

As early as 1898 the great Egyptian jurist Muḥammad 'Abdūh had advocated the reinterpretation of the principles embodied in the divine revelation as a basis for legal reform, and scholars like Iqbāl in India, pursuing the same theme, had argued that the exercise of *ijtihād* or independent judgement was not only the right, but also the duty, of present generations if Islam was to adapt itself successfully to the modern world. Such a thesis, representing an outright break with the legal tradition of ten centuries' standing, naturally engendered violent controversy. Its opponents maintained that as a contradiction of the doctrine of "the closure of the door of *ijtihād*" which had been established by the infallible *ijmā'* (consensus) it was tantamount to heresy, while its supporters replied by denying either the existence or the binding nature of such an alleged consensus. There is much to commend the latter view. Apart from the fact that the cessation of *ijtihād* is explicable as the inevitable result of the historical development of Sharī'a law, a universal consensus to this effect had never existed. In fact the Ḥanbalīs had consistently maintained the impossibility of any real consensus after the generation of the Prophet's contemporaries—on the ground that it had become impracticable to ascertain the views of each and every qualified jurist, and in the fourteenth century the Ḥanbalī scholar Ibn-Taymiyya had himself claimed the theoretical right of *ijtihād*.[18] Furthermore, the incidents and the authority of *ijmā'* had been laid down by classical Muslim jurisprudence and not by any unequivocal dictate of divine revelation, so that it might well appear that a self-constituted human authority had arrogated a legal sovereignty which belonged only to God.

In fact, however, the theoretical dispute concerning the right or otherwise of *ijtihād* was secondary and subordinate to the real and practical issue, which lay in a straightforward clash between conservative and progressive opinion. Those who saw the established law as the ideal order of things upheld the doctrine of *taqlīd*, while those who sought reform argued for the legitimacy of *ijtihād* as the ultimate and proper means of changing legal rules which rested on the unanimous authority of the mediaeval manuals. In short, the fundamental question was rather whether the law ought to be, than whether it could be, reformed. Nevertheless, because of the principles involved and the strength of the traditionalist attitude, it has not been until the last decade that modernist legislation has given any practical implementation to the principle that the interpretations of classical jurists may be wholly ignored and that the Qur'ān and the authentic example of the Prophet (*sunna*) may be construed afresh in the light of modern conditions.

Prior to the open and explicit recognition of *ijtihād* as a juristic basis of reform, a number of changes were effected which combined traditional authorities with wholly novel precepts, and thus represented a mid-way stage between *taqlīd* and *ijtihād* proper. Adopting the usual recourse of legal analysts in such circumstances, we may classify this type of reform under the head of *quasi-ijtihād*, and consider as an example of it the rule of "obligatory bequests" introduced in the Egyptian *Law of Testamentary Dispositions* of 1946.

Representation, as a principle of intestate succession, was afforded scant recognition by traditional Muslim jurisprudence. Shāfi'ī and Ḥanbalī law admitted its application in the limited field of succession by the cognate relatives where, under the doctrine known as *tanẓīl*, relatives stepped into the shoes of the predeceased primary heirs (Qur'ānic sharers or *'aṣaba*) through whom they were connected with the propositus and were entitled accordingly. A daughter's child inherited as a daughter, for example, and a maternal grandfather as a mother of the deceased.

In regard to this same class of heirs, Ḥanafī law determined the existence of entitlement by a system of priorities of much the same nature as that which applied to agnate relatives. Ascendants, for example, were in an inferior class to descendants and therefore excluded by them. But where there existed a number of claimants, all entitled by virtue of being in the same class and of equal degree, the two Ḥanafī jurists Abū-Yūsuf and ash-Shaybānī differed as to the principles governing the actual amount of the estate each would receive. Abū-Yūsuf held that distribution should be *per capita* (i.e. taking into account only the actual claimants), while ash-Shaybānī maintained that it should be *per stirpes* (i.e. taking into account the intermediate "roots" or links through whom the claimants were connected with the deceased). One of the simplest cases of the divergent results which stem from these two different principles occurs when great-grandchildren of the propositus are in competition and there is occasion to apply the fundamental rule of succession that a male relative takes twice the share of a female relative of corresponding order and degree. As between, therefore, a great grandson *X*, the child of the deceased's daughter's daughter, and a great granddaughter *Y*, the child of the deceased's daughter's son, Abū-Yūsuf would allot two-thirds of the estate to *X* and one-third to *Y*. Ash-Shaybānī, on the other hand, would apply the rule of double share to the male to the *stirpes*, or parents, of the actual claimants, which notional share would then descend to their respective issue, so that the result would be precisely the opposite to that of Abū-Yūsuf.

This partial type of representation, which determines not the bare fact of entitlement but simply the *quantum* of the share received, is in fact applied throughout the whole of the Shī'ite system of intestate succession. Apart from these restricted applications, however, representation is precluded, certainly in regard to the primary classes of heirs, by the basic rule common to all schools that the nearer in degree excludes the more remote. In particular, orphaned grandchildren are totally excluded from any rights of inheritance by a surviving son of the deceased.

It was this last result of the absence of representation which was considered to be a grave defect in the traditional law and which the Egyptian reformers proceeded to remedy by the system of obligatory bequests. Under the law of 1946 orphaned grandchildren of the deceased are entitled, notwithstanding the presence of a surviving child of the deceased, to the share their own parent would have received had he or she survived, provided that such a share shall be cut down, where necessary, to a maximum of one-third of the net estate (the recognised limit on testamentary dispositions), and provided that the grandchildren concerned have not received such amount by way of gift *inter vivos* from the propositus or, of course, by actual bequest. This same system was adopted by Syria in 1953, by Tunisia in 1957, and by Morocco in 1958, although under the Syrian and Moroccan laws the rule is confined to the children of the deceased's son and does not apply to the children of the deceased's daughter.

That this reform is essentially a matter of intestate succession is perfectly clear from its general nature and from the particular rule that, where a number of grandchildren are so entitled, the male receives double the share of the female; for the normal principle of bequests is that individual legatees of a general class share equally regardless of sex. The reformers, however, used the machinery of bequests because this offered the soundest juristic basis for their purpose. In the first place, individual jurists had dissented from the majority view that the Qur'ānic injunction to make bequests in favour of near relatives had been completely abrogated by the later rules of intestate succession. Ash-Shāfi'ī himself opined that it was still morally praiseworthy (*mandūb*) to make bequests in favour of near relatives who were not legal heirs, while the Ẓāhirī Ibn-Ḥazm considered it positively obligatory. And in the second place other early scholars supported the view that such provision for relatives in need could be enforced by the courts if the deceased had failed in this duty. With these traditional authorities, then, the reformers had combined their own particular interpretation of the spirit of the Qur'ānic provisions by specifying those near relatives of the deceased who were so to be provided for. Since the objective of supplying a rule suitable for modern conditions had been achieved without a complete break with past tradition, and since the rights of obligatory legatees, who can never, of course, be legal heirs in their own right, are supplementary and not contradictory to the established system of intestate succession, this development provides one of the most attractive and effective examples of legal modernism.

Ultimately, however, the stage was reached when no shred of traditional authority at all could be adduced to support the desired rules. At this point the reformers could only claim that their proposals were founded upon a novel but yet valid interpretation of the original sources of Sharī'a law; and the success with which they did so may be measured by recent provisions concerning those twin pillars of patriarchy which had been the unshakeable supports of Islamic family law since the days of the Prophet—the husband's rights of polygamy and unilateral repudiation.

There has perhaps been a natural tendency in recent years to exaggerate the picture of Muslim wives labouring under the heavy shackles of the traditional law. Miserable though the lot of Muslim wives may have been in practice, this was often not so much the direct result of the terms of the law itself as the responsibility of society. The customary seclusion of women, and especially the lack of educational facilities, left them ignorant of their legal rights and unable to insist upon the proper use of machinery which the law had provided for their protection. To counteract the husband's right of polygamy, Ḥanbalī law, as we have seen, regarded stipulations against a second marriage as enforceable, while the Mālikī concept of "prejudice" (*ḍarar*) was broad enough to allow an insistent wife a judicial divorce in the event of her husband marrying again. More particularly, all schools endorsed the validity of the two institutions of "suspended repudiation" (*ta'līq aṭ-ṭalāq*) and "delegated repudiation" (*tafwīḍ aṭ-ṭalāq*). A husband might thus be persuaded either to declare that divorce would become effective upon the occurrence of some event which the wife wished to avoid, or to delegate, absolutely or conditionally, his power of terminating the marriage to some close relative of the wife (or even to the wife herself according to some jurists), so that this power could be exercised if circumstances unfavourable to the wife arose. A further device formulated by the law to safeguard the wife's position was that of deferred dower. Payment of a portion of the dower could be postponed by agreement of the parties until the termination of the marriage, and if the amount so stipulated was high enough it would obviously provide an effective brake upon the capricious exercise of the right of repudiation by the husband.

Nevertheless, despite the obvious concern of the law for the position of the wife, the fact remained that the husband's established powers could not be curtailed without his free consent. Reforms in the Middle East, by the use of administrative regulations and the principle of *takhayyur*, had succeeded in whittling away some of the more oppressive features of Ḥanafī law; but the husband's basic rights of polygamy and repudiation remained secure, and whatever restrictions social and economic factors might impose upon their exercise, their mere existence under the law was sufficient to constitute a formidable obstacle to woman's real emancipation.

The first attempts to remedy this situation by way of *ijtihād* materialised in the Syrian *Law of Personal Status* of 1953. Husbands were enjoined by the Qur'ān, argued the Explanatory Memorandum to this Law, not to take additional wives unless they were financially capable of duly supporting them. Such an interpretation had in fact been given to the Qur'ānic "verse of polygamy" by many jurists, including ash-Shāfiʿī, but had always been construed as an essentially moral exhortation binding on the husband's conscience—although obviously a co-wife who did not receive proper maintenance could claim judicial dissolution of marriage, at least in Mālikī law. The Syrian reformers, however, maintained that this Qur'ānic provision should be regarded as a positive legal condition precedent to the exercise of polygamy and enforced as such by the courts "on the principle that the doors which lead to abuses must be closed". This novel interpretation was then coupled with a normal administrative regulation which required the due registration of marriages after the permission of the court to marry had been obtained. Article 17 of the Law accordingly enacts: "The *qāḍī* may withhold permission for a man who is already married to marry a second wife, where it is established that he is not in a position to support them both". A second marriage concluded in defiance of this provision, however, will not be invalid; but the parties will be liable to statutory penalties, and the courts will not recognise the marriage, for purposes of judicial relief, unless children have been born therefrom or the wife is clearly pregnant.

With regard to repudiation (*ṭalāq*), which has rightly been held to occasion far greater prejudice to a woman's status than polygamy, the Syrian Law introduced a bold innovation when it provided that a wife who had been repudiated without just cause might be awarded compensation from her former husband to the maximum extent of one year's maintenance. This reform represented the implementation of the spirit of those Qur'ānic verses which enjoined husbands to "make a fair provision" for repudiated wives and to "retain wives with kindness or release them with consideration"; but these verses, again, had been largely regarded by traditional jurisprudence as moral rather than legally enforceable injunctions. A limited practical effect had been given to them by those jurists who regarded the provision of a small gift of consolation (*mutʿa*) for divorced wives, as obligatory on the husband; but the Ḥanafīs maintained that this *mutʿa* was payable only when no dower had been specified in a marriage and a repudiation had been pronounced before consummation. In any event the Syrian Law certainly provides the first instance of a husband's motive for repudiation being subject to the scrutiny of a court, which may then penalise him for abuse of his power.

It may perhaps be felt that provision of one year's maintenance is a small price to pay for an arbitrary and totally unjustified repudiation. And the terms of the Law do in fact appear as something of an anti-climax after a resounding preamble on the need to adopt a new attitude towards the laws of divorce and to remedy the appalling lack of security in married life. Similarly, it may be argued that the provisions concerning polygamy had merely made this practice the privilege of the rich. Yet it was only natural that the first steps of the reformers in this new direction should be somewhat hesitant and tentative. In any event the real significance of the Syrian provisions lies not so much in their concrete terms as in the juristic basis on which they rest. For the first time independent assessment of the Qur'ānic precepts had resulted in a departure from interpretations hallowed by thirteen centuries of legal tradition.

Thus unlocked, the "door of *ijtihād*" was swung fully open by the Tunisian *Law of Personal Status*, 1957. Following the arguments put forward by Muḥammad 'Abdūh more than fifty years previously, the Tunisian reformers pointed out that, in addition to a husband's financial ability to support a plurality of wives, the Qur'ān also required that co-wives should be treated with complete impartiality. This Qur'ānic injunction too should not be construed simply as a moral exhortation but as a legal condition precedent to polygamy, in the sense that no second marriage should be permissible unless and until adequate evidence was forthcoming that the wives would in fact be treated impartially. But under modern social and economic conditions, declared the reformers, such impartial treatment was a practical impossibility. In short, there was an irrebuttable presumption of law that the essential condition for polygamy was incapable of fulfilment. Polygamy, therefore, was prohibited outright.

Even more radical perhaps, in contrast with the preceding Syrian Law, was the Tunisian *ijtihād* concerning repudiation, where once again reform was based on the views of Muḥammad 'Abdūh. In the case of "discord" between spouses the Qur'ān orders the appointment of arbitrators, a provision which had previously found practical implementation only in the Mālikī procedure regulating charges of cruelty by a wife against her husband. Yet, argued the reformers, what more obvious case of "discord" between spouses than a pronouncement of repudiation by the husband? And who then better qualified to undertake the necessary function of arbitration than the official tribunals? On this ground, therefore, the right of a husband to repudiate his wife extra-judicially was abolished, Section 30 of the Law enacting that "Divorce outside a court of law is without legal effect". Although the court cannot refuse to dissolve the marriage if the husband persists in his repudiation, two features of the Law are particularly striking. In the first place, the court has an unlimited power to grant the wife compensation for any damage she has sustained from the divorce; and secondly, the spouses are treated on exactly the same footing in this regard. For a wife also has the right to insist upon divorce, without adducing any specific ground, in which case the court has power to award compensation to the husband in suitable circumstances. It is noteworthy in this regard that an Algerian Ordinance of 1959, which followed the Tunisian Law in making all divorce judicial, apparently intends that a decree of divorce should be granted to the husband on his simple request, but to the wife only if she establishes the existence of proper grounds therefor.[19]

Reinterpretation of the Qur'ān had thus achieved in Tunisia reforms hardly less radical than those effected in Turkey thirty years previously by the adoption of the Swiss Civil Code. At the same time the use of *ijtihād* is still the exception rather than the rule in the

Arab world and is resorted to only where the desired reforms cannot be accomplished with the formal observance of the doctrine of *taqlīd*. And from the most recent codifications of Sharī'a law it would appear that Islamic society in the Near and Middle East generally is not yet attuned to the extremist approach of Tunisia, at least in regard to the two major issues of polygamy and repudiation. The Moroccan Code of 1958 declares polygamy to be prohibited where there is any apprehension of unequal treatment; but, since the courts may only intervene retrospectively by granting dissolution of marriage, in such circumstances the Law hardly goes beyond orthodox Mālikī practice. Compensation for the wife in cases of injurious repudiation is among the reforms introduced by the Code, but extra-judicial repudiation remains perfectly valid and effective. Under the Iraqi *Law of Personal Status* of 1959, the *qāḍī* will not give his necessary permission for a second marriage unless he is, at his discretion, satisfied, first that the husband is financially capable of supporting an additional wife or wives; second "that there is some lawful benefit involved"; and third that no inequality of treatment is to be feared. There is no provision in the Iraqi Code for compensation in the case of injurious repudiation, but a husband seeking to repudiate his wife is required, in normal circumstances, to obtain a decree of the court to this effect.

Pakistan has provided one of the most recent pieces of modernist legislation in Islam by her *Muslim Family Laws Ordinance* of 1961. This short enactment of thirteen sections represents the ultimate outcome of the proposals emanating from a Commission which was set up in 1955 to consider possible reforms of the family law. At the time they were published, the Commission's proposals were radical enough to provoke acute controversy, as appears from the forceful note of dissent published by one member of the Commission. But by comparison with recent Middle Eastern legislation, the reforms actually embodied in the Ordinance appear distinctly moderate, particularly as the recommendations of the Commission were only partially implemented.

Arbitration councils, consisting of an independent chairman and a representative of each of the parties, are to be formed under the terms of the Ordinance to deal with the two primary matters of polygamy and repudiation. For a second marriage during the existence of a subsisting one the written permission of the Arbitration Council is required and will only be given where the council "is satisfied that the proposed marriage is necessary and just". As to when a second marriage will so be considered "necessary and just", it is obvious that the consent or otherwise of the existing wife will be extremely relevant, but such factors as the sterility, physical infirmity, or insanity of an existing wife are specified as circumstances which may be taken into account. Failure to obtain the Council's permission before contracting a polygamous marriage does not render such marriage invalid, but entails a three-fold sanction. The husband is liable to imprisonment of up to one year or a fine of up to 5,000 rupees or both; he is obliged to pay forthwith the entire dower of his existing wife or wives, even where the payment of part of the dower was expressly deferred until the termination of the marriage; and finally the existing wife has the right to a dissolution of her marriage, an express clause to this effect being added by the Ordinance to the *Dissolution of Muslim Marriages Act*, 1939.

Repudiation by the husband (*ṭalāq*), the Commission of 1955 had recommended, should not be effective without the permission of the court, and this should only be given when suitable provision had been made for the wife's maintenance. The Ordinance, however, merely requires the husband, under pain of statutory penalties, to give written notice of his having pronounced a repudiation to the Chairman of the Arbitration Council and to his wife. Following the delivery of such notice a period of ninety days is to run, after which, failing the success of attempts at reconciliation, the repudiation will become effective. Since this procedure is to apply after the pronouncement of a repudiation "in any form whatsoever", the immediate effect of the various types of irrevocable repudiation known to traditional Sharī'a law is completely nullified. However, while this last result is a considerable step forward, the fact remains that the Ordinance has left the husband's power of unilateral repudiation at his discretion substantially unimpaired.

Unlike the Muslim countries of the Middle East, Pakistan did not attempt any comprehensive codification of Islamic law, but, in the English tradition, simply amended the existing law in a limited number of particulars. Moreover, it is evident from the deliberations of the 1955 Commission and from the terms of the Ordinance that the *ijtihād* on which the reforms are allegedly based is of a very different nature from the conscientious reinterpretation of the original sources as practised by the Middle Eastern reformers. Eminently "Islamic" though the system of Arbitration Councils may be, this does not appear to be a deliberate attempt to implement the Qur'ānic provision, while the rules concerning polygamy are conditioned by straightforward criteria of social desirability rather than by the Qur'ānic injunctions of financial capability and impartial treatment. As has always been the case since the first legislative interference in the domain of Sharī'a law in the Indian sub-continent, the problems of the juristic basis of reform have not commanded the same attention as they have in the Middle East. In short, therefore, the Ordinance continues the particular tradition of Anglo-Muhammadan law in a manner which is certainly practical and probably best suited to the present mood and aspirations of Pakistan.

Sectarian groups in Islam have naturally become subject to the terms of modernist legislation which has been promulgated on a nationalist basis, although in matters not so specifically regulated they have continued to be governed by their own system of personal law. This is the case, for example, with the Ithnā-ʿasharite and Ismāʿīlite Muslims in the Indian sub-continent, the Jaʿfarī Shīʿite population of Iraq and the ʿIbāḍites in Algeria. But where sectarian communities are autonomous—at least in matters of personal status—legal reform is theoretically far less of a problem than it is in Sunnite Islam, for the sects as a whole never recognised the doctrine of *taqlīd* in its Sunnite form. No real impetus for reform, however, has as yet been felt by the Zaydites in the Yemen or the ʿIbāḍite community in Zanzibar, while in Iran, the stronghold of Ithnā-ʿasharite belief, the Civil Code at present applicable largely retains the traditional family law but embodies features like the prohibition of childmarriage and the compulsory registration of marriages, which may now almost be said to be the common law of Islam.

It is recent laws affecting Ismāʿīlite communities outside India which provide the sharpest contrast with the process of reform in Sunnite Islam, for the radical changes that have been introduced rest simply on the supreme legislative authority of the Imām Aga Khan. Thus the prohibition of marriage before the ages of eighteen for boys and sixteen for girls, which was contained in the *Rules and Regulations of His Highness the Aga Khan Ismāʿīlī Councils in Africa*, required no other juristic authority than the will of the Imām and naturally superseded the law previously applicable to Ismā'īlites in East Africa—a point which was not fully appreciated in a recent decision of the Court of Appeal for East Africa.[20] On the same basis the "*New Constitution for the Shia Imami Ismailis in Africa*" of 1962 strictly prohibits polygamy, allows divorce only by decree of the Council and, contrary to all Islamic tradition, accepts the principle of legitimation *per subsequens matrimonium*. It may finally be remarked that the *Law of Personal Status* for the Druze community of Lebanon, which was promulgated in 1948, equally directly prohibited polygamy and declared repudiation to be ineffective until confirmed by the decree of the *qāḍī* of the community, who was empowered to award damages to a wife who had been repudiated without reasonable cause.[21]

For Sunnite Islam, however, such radical reforms had become possible only when jurisprudence had eventually emerged from a long period of internal conflict to declare itself in favour of *ijtihād*, at least in cases where this was deemed necessary to achieve the required reform. Strict theorists may, and indeed do, object to the activities of the reformers on the ground that the interpretation of the divine texts should be purely objective, while so-called modern "*ijtihād*" amounts to little more than forcing from the divine texts that particular interpretation which agrees with preconceived standards subjectively determined. Yet legal history shows that current social conditions had exercised a predominant influence in the formative period of Islamic jurisprudence and that, whatever the classical theory of law might maintain, the early jurists had in fact interpreted the Qur'ān in the light of those conditions. From this standpoint modern jurists might well claim not only to be following the example of their predecessors but also to be improving upon it. For it is at least arguable that traditional jurisprudence had minimised the purposes of the Qur'ān by relegating to the category of moral injunctions many of its provisions concerning the treatment of women. Modern reformers, on the other hand, have laid great emphasis upon this type of Qur'ānic precept as well as upon certain alleged statements of the Prophet such as that "Of all things permissible repudiation (*ṭalāq*) is the most abominable". And thus, it may be held, a new synthesis of law and morality has been created which more truly implements the spirit of the divine commands. But whatever view may be taken of the theoretical basis or the results of modernist *ijtihād*, its practical and undeniable effect has been to infuse life and movement into Sharī'a law. The era of *taqlīd* now appears as a protracted moratorium in Islamic legal history. Stagnation has given way to a new vitality and potential for growth.

CONCLUSION

Religious Law and Social Progress in Contemporary Islam

LOOKING to the future there are two principal features of modernist legal activities which command attention.

In the first place the current expression of the law rests upon a striking diversity of juristic criteria, which represent varying degrees of fusion between the two basic influences of practical necessity and religious principles. During the first stage of legal modernism these two influences had produced a clear-cut dichotomy in the law. Western law was directly adopted in the field of crime and civil transactions generally, while traditional Sharīʿa doctrine continued to govern the sphere of personal status. Recent trends, however, have tended to break down this firm division. In the civil law a growing emphasis has been placed on religious principles. A merger of foreign and Islamic elements is the outstanding feature of the Iraqi Civil Code promulgated in 1953. Many of its rules were derived from the Ḥanafī codification of the *Majalla* and from traditional Sharīʿa texts, while other provisions, on such matters as insurance and aleatory contracts, rest squarely on European sources. Family law, on its side, has been increasingly permeated with Western standards and values, and it is here that the juristic basis of the law, viewed as a whole, appears most complex. For, as it stands within the limits of any single modern Code, the law is an amalgam of traditional and novel elements, and the novel elements are the result sometimes of the manipulation of established principles, sometimes of a fresh interpretation of the original sources, and sometimes of the frank recognition of the needs of the time.

Economic grounds alone were thus held to justify the total abolition of family settlements under the traditional *waqf* system in Syria in 1949 and in Egypt three years later, while social necessity has been the declared basis of certain recent reforms in that traditionally most invulnerable sphere of the Sharī'a—the law of succession. In 1945 a judicial circular in the Sudan allowed bequests to be made, within the established limit of one-third of the net estate, in favour of legal heirs, and expressly stated the reason for this reform to be the need felt by testators to make additional provision for the less fortunate of these heirs. Ithnā-'asharite law, it is true, had always maintained that bequests to legal heirs were permissible, on the ground that the Tradition, "No bequest in favour of an heir", should either be read with the additional words "except within the permitted third", or should be interpreted to mean not that it was prohibited to make such bequests but that it was no longer obligatory to make them. When Egypt adopted the same reform in her *Law of Testamentary Dispositions* of 1946, a veiled and oblique reference was made to the Ithnā-'asharite view. But for a Sunnite community the direct adoption of the views of a heterodox sect could not be an acceptable juristic basis for reform; and so it is hardly surprising that the validity *per se* of bequests to legal heirs, contrary as this is to the consensus of traditional Sunnite authorities, has not been recognised by any other Muslim country save Iraq, where the adoption of the rule is due to the fact that at least half of the population is Shī'ite.

An even more radical departure from the traditional law of succession is contained in the Tunisian law of 1959 which provides that *any* lineal descendant of the deceased, male or female, excludes the deceased's collateral relatives from intestate succession; for under the agnatic system of traditional Sunnite law the brothers of the deceased, in the absence of any surviving *male* ascendant or descendant, are the primary residuary heirs. It could in fact be argued with some force that this provision does implement the general spirit of the Qur'ānic legislation. For one of the basic trends of the reforms introduced by the Prophet was the replacement of the wider social unit of the tribe by the unit of the individual family. This purpose had been largely nullified by the traditional law, in inheritance at least, by its retention of the customary tribal system, which gave superior rights to male agnate relatives. But it is obviously the concept of the family, as consisting of the husband, wife, and their issue, which inspired the Tunisian reform. No attempt, however, was made to suggest that the law rested on any other basis than that of the need felt by society. Finally, it was on this same ground that the Pakistani *Muslim Family Laws Ordinance* of 1961 directly modified the traditional law of inheritance by introducing the principle of full representation in regard to intestate succession by lineal descendants of the deceased. This last reform, therefore, stands in sharp contrast to the Egyptian method of dealing with the same problem by the system of obligatory bequests, which found its juristic basis, convincingly enough, in traditional authorities.

If the outright recognition of the needs of society which jurisprudence has thus endorsed in many respects is to be regarded as modern *ijtihād*, it is obviously a very different concept of *ijtihād* from that we have seen operating, for example, in relation to polygamy and repudiation, where reforms were based on particular interpretations of specific Qur'ānic injunctions. In sum, it appears that modern jurisprudence has not yet evolved any systematic approach to the problem of adapting the traditional law to the circumstances of contemporary society. Lacking any consistency of principle or methodology, it has tackled the process of reform as a whole in a spirit of juristic opportunism.

The second feature of modern Islamic law which is relevant to the question of potential future development is the fact that many of the substantive reforms must appear, on a long-term view, as temporary expedients and piecemeal accommodations. This is not to deny the present efficacy of the reforms in solving the immediate problems of the areas in which they have been introduced. But certain provisions, such as the partial restrictions placed upon polygamy and repudiation, point inevitably towards the direction which future progress must follow and can represent only an intermediate stage in the advancement of a society along this road. In some cases novel provisions lie in uneasy juxtaposition with the traditional law. The introduction of the representation rule in succession in Pakistan, for example, is completely disruptive of the finely balanced scheme of priorities established by the Sharī'a. It means, for instance, that a granddaughter of the deceased, the child of the deceased's son, will now exclude the brothers of the deceased from inheritance while the deceased's own daughter will not. In other cases reforms, far-reaching in themselves, disclose a root problem which has still to be solved. The restriction of polygamy and repudiation, for example, is obviously aimed at the ultimate goal of equality between the sexes. Within the structure of traditional Sharī'a law, however, these institutions appear as derivative rights of the husband stemming from the root concept of marriage as a contract of sale wherein the husband purchases the right of sexual union by payment of the dower. If the law, therefore, is to endorse, logically and satisfactorily, any system of real equality between husband and wife, it is at least arguable that this basic traditional concept, epitomised by the payment of dower, must be completely eradicated. Finally, the uncertainty which still clouds the basic conflict between traditionalism and modernism is revealed by recent events in Iraq. In 1959 the Iraqi *Law of Personal Status* adopted a completely new system of inheritance which owed nothing to traditional Sharīʿa law but was derived from Ottoman legislation, itself of Germanic inspiration, concerning succession to government lands. The purpose of this enactment was to unify the law on a national basis, and since the divergence between the Ḥanafī and the Shīʿite laws of succession was too deep-rooted to admit of compromise, a "neutral" system was adopted as the only one which would be acceptable to both the Sunnite and the Shīʿite communities. By a law of February 1963, however, this system has now been abolished and replaced by traditional Shīʿite law.

In combination, therefore, with the opportunist character of modern jurisprudential method, the nature of the substantive reforms themselves lends a general air of transience and instability to current Islamic law. The fortress of the traditional law has been breached beyond repair, but the complex structure that has taken its place does not as yet rest upon the same solid foundations, and its substance is almost volatile by comparison.

This is perhaps inevitable in the circumstances of the time. For history appears to have turned full cycle and to have confronted Islam with a situation remarkably parallel to the one she faced during the Umayyad period. Just as the law of the Medinan community, a rudimentary system of customary practice modified by basic Qur'ānic precepts, proved wholly inadequate to meet the circumstances of the new political empire, so today traditional Sharīʿa law has crumbled under the impact of

Western civilisation. And modern reformers, just like the Umayyad administrators, have managed to control the sudden surge of events by *ad hoc* measures adopted under a policy of pragmatism and expediency.

During the eighth century jurisprudence had systematically reduced the haphazard growth of Umayyad legal practice and the hotch-potch of customary, Qur'ānic and foreign elements of which it was compounded into terms of an Islamic legal system. The question, therefore, may naturally suggest itself as to whether modern jurisprudence will assume a similar function by endeavouring to assimilate and "Islamise" the mass of heterogeneous material which makes up current legal practice; and, following the approved fashion of concluding historical surveys, we may now briefly speculate upon the form such a process might take.

Fundamentally, and in its simplest terms, the problem facing Muslim jurisprudence today is the same problem which it has always faced and which is inherent in its very nature—namely, the need to define the relationship between the standards imposed by the religious faith and the mundane forces which activate society. At the one extreme is the solution adopted by classical jurisprudence, a divine nomocracy under which religious principles were elaborated into a comprehensive and rigid scheme of duties to form the exclusive determinant of the conduct of society. The other extreme solution is that of secularism, as adopted by Turkey, which relegates religious principles to the realm of the individual conscience, and allows the forces of society an unfettered control over the shape of the law. Neither of these solutions can be acceptable to modern Muslim jurisprudence; for while the former is wholly unrealistic, the latter is positively un-Islamic. Obviously, therefore, the answer lies somewhere between these two extremes, in a concept of law as a code of behaviour which is founded upon certain basic and immutable religious principles but which, within these limits, does not neglect the factor of change and allows the adoption of such extraneous standards as may prove more acceptable to current Muslim opinion than indigenous tradition.

Historical enquiry reveals that during the early period of Islam the religious precepts contained in the Qu'rān had been gradually absorbed within the framework of the existing customary law and the administrative practices of the Umayyad Empire. When nascent Muslim jurisprudence came to systematise this material, it did so, in some cases, on the basis of a loose and liberal interpretation of relevant Qur'ānic precepts in the light of existing practice—this was generally so, for example, in regard to matters of family law—while in other cases it had developed the Qur'ānic principles with extreme rigour, as, for example, in the doctrine of *ribā*. And ultimately these accretions of juristic interpretation had all come to be artificially expressed, particularly through the growth of Traditions, as manifestations of the divine command. As has so often been suggested in recent times, it must be the primary task of modern jurisprudence to ascertain the precise limits of the original core of divine revelation. And this perhaps will necessarily involve a re-orientation of the accepted attitude towards Traditions, not only as regards their authenticity, but also as regards the nature of their authority if their authenticity is duly established. Once the limits have been ascertained, it is axiomatic that these precepts of the divine revelation must form the fundamental and invariable basis of any system of law which purports to be a manifestation of the will of God.

It cannot be denied that certain specific provisions of the Qur'ān, such as that which commands the amputation of the hand for theft, pose problems in the context of contemporary life for which the solution is not readily apparent. But, generally speaking, the Qur'ānic precepts are in the nature of ethical norms—broad enough to support modern legal structures and capable of varying interpretations to meet the particular needs of time and place. And on this basis it would seem that Islamic jurisprudence could implement, in practical and modernist terms, its fundamental and unique ideal of a way of life based on the command of God. Freed from the notion of a religious law expressed in totalitarian and uncompromising terms, jurisprudence would approach the problem of law and society in a different light. Instead of asking itself, as it has done since the tenth century and still generally does today, what concessions must be wrested from the law by the needs of society, its new terms of reference would be precisely the opposite: to determine what limitations religious principles set upon society.

Radical though the break with past tradition which such an approach involves might be, it is nevertheless a break with a particular construction of the religious law and not with its essence. This, at any rate, would seem to be the only realistic basis for future development and the only alternative to a complete abandonment of the notion of a law based on religion. Law, to be a living force, must reflect the soul of a society; and the soul of present Muslim society is reflected neither in any form of outright secularism nor in the doctrine of the mediaeval text books.

NOTES

ABBREVIATIONS

BSOAS: *Bulletin of the School of Oriental and African Studies.*
RSO: *Rivista degli studi orientali.*

Part One: THE GENESIS OF SHARĪ'A LAW

QUR'ANIC LEGISLATION

Page 16, 1. This was the standard Islamic view. The complications are here neglected that arise from the apparent existence of residual matrilineal elements in Muḥammad's time. Cf. W. Montgomery Watt, *Muhammad at Medina* (Oxford, 1956), 378 ff., 292.

16, 2. G. Bergsträsser, whose observations in his *Grundzüge des islamischen Rechts* (Berlin, 1935) anticipated in many respects the picture of early Islamic legal history now provided by Western scholarship, regarded the dissolution of the tribal organisation as Muḥammad's chief political aim.

17, 3. The prohibition of usury was, of course, an anti-Jewish measure in part; cf. Schacht, art. "Ribā" in *Encyclopaedia of Islam*, first edition; Watt, *Muhammad at Medina*, 296 f.

LEGAL PRACTICE IN THE FIRST CENTURY OF ISLAM

Page 27, 4. For a comprehensive account of the historical development of the law concerning the *dhimmīs* and a detailed analysis thereof, see Antoine Fattal, *Le Statut légal des non-Musulmans en Pays d'Islam* (Beirut, 1958).

29, 5. The best account of the early *qadīs*, though limited to the *qadīs* of Egypt, is by al-Kindi, *Governors and Judges of Egypt*, Arabic text edited by Rhuvon Guest, 1912, Gibb Memorial Series, XIX. It is from this work that many of the details of legal practice which appear in this chapter are taken.

30, 6. See R. Brunschvig, "Considérations sociologiques sur le droit musulman ancien" in *Studia Islamica*, Fasc. III (1956).

31, 7. Schacht, *Origins*, 225.

Jurisprudence in Embryo: the Early Schools of Law

Page 44, 8. Schacht, *Origins*, 153 f.

49, 9. See the article of Farhat J. Ziadeh in the *American Journal of Comparative Law*, VI, No. 4 (October 1957).

51, 10. E. Sachau, *Zur ältesten Geschichte des muhammedanischen Rechts*, 723. For accounts of ash-Shaybānī's life and work see Dimitroff, *Asch-Schaibani* (Introduction), and O. Spies, "Un Grand Juriste musulman: Mohammed b. al-Hasan al-Shaibani" in the published reports of the Fifth International Congress of Comparative Law, Brussels, 1958.

Master Architect: Muḥammad Ibn-Idrīs ash-Shāfiʿī

Page 54, 11. For the text of ash-Shāfiʿī's argument see Khadduri's translation of the *Risāla*, in *Islamic Jurisprudence*, 227-9.

56, 12. See Schacht, *Origins*, 53-7.
56, 13. *Ibid.* 45 f., 48.
60, 14. As translated by Schacht, *Origins*, 97.

CONCLUDING STAGES OF GROWTH

Page 64, 15. On the general subject of the classification of traditions see Aghnides, *Mohammedan Theories of Finance*, Introduction, 1-117; also *An Introduction to the Science of Tradition*, by al-Ḥākim an-Naysābūrī, edited and translated by James Robson (London, 1953).
65, 16. *Origins*, 201 f.
66, 17. For an English translation see Majid Khadduri, *Islamic Jurisprudence, Shafi'i's Risāla*, 141-5.
72, 18. See p. 46 above.

Part Two: LEGAL DOCTRINE AND PRACTICE IN MEDIAEVAL ISLAM

THE CLASSICAL THEORY OF LAW

Page 78, 1. See p. 59 above.
80, 2. See p. 72 above.
80, 3. See, e.g., Ostrorog, *The Angora Reform*, 31. (Cf. Montgomery Watt, *Islam and the Integration of Society* (London, 1961), 243, 207.)
82, 4. For this aspect of Muslim jurisprudence see my article, "Doctrine and Practice in Islamic Law", in *BSOAS*, xviii/2 (1956).

UNITY AND DIVERSITY IN SHARĪ'A LAW

Page 89, 5. See G. H. Bousquet's French translation, in condensed form, of some of Goldziher's writings, *Études islamologiques d'Ignaz Goldziher* (Leiden, 1962), 52-6.
89, 6. See p. 71 f. above.

92, 7. See, e.g., Fyzee, *Outlines of Muhammadan Law*, 19, and Abdur Rahim, *Muhammadan Jurisprudence*, 165 f.

94, 8. See Anderson, *The Maliki Law of Homicide*, a pamphlet published by Gaskiya Corporation, Zaria, N. Nigeria.

94, 9. See p. 49 above.

95, 10. See Schacht, "Sur la transmission de la doctrine dans les écoles juridiques de l'Islam" in *Annales de l'Institut d'Études orientales*, Algiers, x, 1952.

95, 11. See p. 31 above.

100, 12. See p. 139 f. below.

100, 13. For one aspect of this question see my article "Doctrine and Practice in Islamic Law", in *BSOAS*, xviii/2 (1956), 225 f.

101, 14. See p. 182 f. below.

101, 15. See p. 88 above.

102, 16. Edmond Cahn, "A Lawyer looks at Religion", in *Theology Today*, xv (April 1958), 103.

Sectarian Legal Systems in Islam

Page 105, 17. Schacht, *Origins*, 260-8.

105, 18. *Ibid.* 260.

106, 19. For a theological account of these sects cf. Montgomery Watt, *Islamic Philosophy and Theology* (Edinburgh, 1962), esp. 20-6, 50-6, 99-104.

107, 20. Cf. *Islamic Philosophy and Theology*, 53.

115, 21. Schacht, *Origins*, 267.

Islamic Government and Sharī'a Law

Page 123, 22. See my article "Doctrine and Practice in Islamic Law", in *BSOAS*, xviii/2 (1956), 211.

126, 23. *BSOAS*, xviii/2, 219.

129, 24. Although Abū-Yūsuf (d. 799) deals with

limited aspects of public law in his *Kitāb al-Kharāj*, al-Māwardī (d. 1057) provides the first comprehensive and systematic treatment of the subject with his *Kitāb al-Aḥkām as-Sulṭāniyya.* The Ḥanbalī scholar Ibn-Taymiyya (d. 1338) and the Mālikī Ibn-Farḥun (d. 1395) are the other outstanding authors of treatises on public law.

129, 25. The word should often be translated "revelational" or "scriptural" rather than "legal".

130, 26. The phrase of al-Wansharīshī, a Mālikī jurist (d. Fez 1507), whose work on public law has been translated into French and commented upon by Brunot and Demombynes in *Le Livre des magistratures d'el Wancherisi* (Rabat, 1937).

131, 27. Brunot and Demombynes, *op. cit.* 18.

132, 28. See my article "The State and the Individual in Islamic law", in *The International and Comparative Law Quarterly* (January 1957).

Islamic Society and Sharī'a Law

136, 29. Bousquet, *Justice française et coutumes kabyles* (Algiers, 1950), 48 f.

136, 30. Bousquet, *Du droit musulman et de son application effective dans le monde* (Algiers, 1949), 91 f.

136, 31. Anderson, *Islamic Law in Africa*, Index.

137, 32. Ettore Rossi, "Customary Law of the Arab tribes of Yemen", in *RSO* (1948).

137, 33. Schacht, "La Justice en Nigérie du Nord et le droit musulman", in *Revue algérienne . . . de législation et de jurisprudence*, No. 2 (1951), 37 f.

138, 34. Bousquet, *Islamic Law and Customary Law in French North Africa* (a printed lecture delivered in the University of London, 1945).

138, 35. See R. J. Wilkinson's treatise entitled

"Law" in the series *Papers on Malay Subjects* (Kuala Lumpur, 1908), 54.

140, 36. See p. 99 f. above.

143, 37. Quoted by Mahmassani, *Falsafat at-Tashrī' Fī Al-Islām* (English translation by Farhat Ziadeh), 116.

143, 38. To L. Milliot belongs the credit for the discovery and analysis of this phenomenon of Islamic jurisprudence. See his *Introduction à l'étude du droit musulman*, 167-78. A summary of this subject, and of the place of custom in Islamic law generally, will be found in my article "Muslim Custom and Case-Law", in *The World of Islam*, VI (1959), 13 f.

144, 39. See the penetrating work on this subject by Berque, *Essai sur la méthode juridique maghrébine* (Rabat, 1944).

Part Three: ISLAMIC LAW IN MODERN TIMES

FOREIGN INFLUENCES: THE RECEPTION OF EUROPEAN LAWS

Page 152, 1. For a general account of the process of codification in the Middle East, see the report presented by G. Tedeschi to the Fifth International Congress of Comparative Law, Brussels, 1958, under the title "The Movement for Codification in the Muslim Countries: Its Relationship with Western Legal Systems".

153, 2. See Anderson, "The Sharī'a and Civil Law (the debt owed by the new Civil Codes of Egypt and Syria to the Sharī'a)", in *Islamic Quarterly* (1954), 29-46.

154, 3. See p. 136 above. Also Bousquet, *Du droit musulman et de son application effective dans le monde* (Algiers, 1949), 77 f.

156, 4. See Anderson, "The Modernisation of Islamic Law in the Sudan", in *The Sudan Law Journal and Reports* (1960).

157, 5. See Schacht, "Problems of Modern Islamic Legislation", in *Studia Islamica*, Fasc. XII (1960), 123.

159, 6. See Anderson, "Conflict of Laws in Northern Nigeria", in the *Journal of African Law*, I, No. 2 (1957).

159, 7. See A. Gledhill, *The Penal Codes of Northern Nigeria and the Sudan* (Stephens, London, 1963), ch. 23.

160, 8. See Sauser-Hall, *La Réception des droits européens en Turquie, Extrait du recueil de travaux publié par la faculté de l'université de Genève* (1938), 31 f.

160, 9. *Hassan and Gaafar Abdel Rahman* v. *Sanousi Mohamed Sir El Khatim* (1960). This case, and others concerned with the relationship between civil law, custom and the Sharī'a in the Sudan, have been analysed by C. d'Olivier Farran in a "Case Note" in *The Sudan Law Journal and Reports* (1960), published by the Faculty of Law of Khartoum University.

Sharī'a Law in Contemporary Islam

Page 165, 10. For this and the other features of Anglo-Muhammadan law noted in this chapter, refer to the standard text book on this subject by A. A. A. Fyzee, *Outlines of Muhammadan Law* (Oxford, 1955).

167, 11. See I. Mahmud, *Muslim Law of Succession and Administration* (Pakistan Law House, Karachi, 1958).

171, 12. See Anderson, "Waqfs in East Africa" in

the *Journal of African Law*, III, No. 3 (1959), 152-164. See also the most recent decision of the Privy Council in this regard, *Riziki Binti Abdullah* v. *Sharifa Binti Mohamed Bin Hemed*—Privy Council Appeal No. 63 of 1960.

Taqlīd and Legal Reform

Page 191, 13. See Anderson, "A Law of Personal Status for Iraq", in the *International and Comparative Law Quarterly* (October 1960), 550.

191, 14. Fyzee, *op. cit.* 104 f.

193, 15. See Roussier, "Dispositions nouvelles dans le statut successoral en droit tunisien", in *Studia Islamica*, Fasc. XII (1960), 138.

193, 16. See Schacht, "Islamic Law in Contemporary States", in the *American Journal of Comparative Law* (1959), 146 f.

193, 17. See Anderson, *Islamic Law in the Modern World*, 83.

Neo-Ijtihād

Page 202, 18. But cf. H. Laoust, *Essai sur les doctrines . . . de Ibn Taimiya* (Cairo, 1939), 228.

211, 19. See Roussier, "L'Ordonnance du 4 février 1959 sur le mariage et le divorce des Français de statut local algérien", in *Recueil Sirey* (April 1959), *Chronique*.

216, 20. See Anderson, "Muslim Marriages and the Courts in East Africa", in the *Journal of African Law*, I, No. 1 (1957).

216, 21. See Anderson, "The Personal Law of the Druze Community", in *The World of Islam*, II, (1952), 83 f.

GLOSSARY

of Arabic legal terms appearing in the text

ʿadāla The quality of religious probity and moral integrity which a witness must possess for his testimony to be admissible. A person of such character is called *ʿadl* and the plural *ʿudūl* is often used of persons whose profession is essentially that of public notaries.

ʿamal Practice of the courts.

ʿāqila The group who shoulder the burden of collective responsibility for compensation in cases of homicide, wounding and assault.

ʿāriyya Gratuitous loan, or transfer of the *usus* of property.

ʿaṣaba Agnate relatives.

aṣl (pl. *uṣūl*). Lit. "root". Technically, the sources of law or the principles of jurisprudence.

ʿayn The substance or *corpus* of property.

bayʿ Sale or barter.

bidʿa Lit. "innovation". Used of practices which are contrary to established tradition and therefore "bad" or "disapproved". In this sense the term is the opposite of *sunna*—i.e. that which is in accord with established tradition and therefore "good" or "approved".

ḍaʿīf Weak. Used of poorly attested Traditions or juristic opinions of slender authority.

ḍarar Damage, prejudice. In the context of divorce, cruelty.

dhawū'l-arḥām Lit. "the possessors of relationship through the *riḥm* or womb"—i.e. cognate relatives.

dhimma Obligation, undertaking, responsibility.

dhimmī One whom the Muslim State undertakes to protect in the practice and profession of his religion —particularly the Jew and the Christian.

diya Blood money or compensation due in cases of homicide, wounding and assault.

faqīh (pl. *fuqahā'*) Legal scholar, jurist.

farḍ Precept of the divine law. The form *farā'iḍ* (pl. of *farīḍa*) is used particularly of the quota shares of inheritance prescribed by the Qur'ān.

faskh Rescission, annulment of a contract.

fatwā (pl. *fatāwā*) Opinion of a jurist on a legal problem.

fiqh Lit. "understanding". The science of law or jurisprudence.

gharar Uncertainty, risk (particularly in relation to commercial contracts).

ghirra Blood money or compensation payable for the destruction of a foetus.

ḥaḍāna The care and custody of young children.

ḥadd (pl. *ḥudūd*) A specific, fixed penalty.

ḥadīth Report, or Tradition, of a precedent set by the Prophet or other early authorities.

ḥakam Arbitrator.

ḥarām Forbidden.

hiba Gift, or the gratuitous transfer of the *corpus* of property.

ḥīla (pl. *ḥiyal*) Legal device or stratagem.

ḥisba In its widest sense the function of ensuring that the precepts of the Sharī'a, particularly those of a moral and religious nature, are observed.

'idda The period following the dissolution of a marriage during which the legal rights and obligations of the spouses are not wholly extinguished. In par-

ticular a widow or divorcee is not allowed to remarry during this period.

iḥtibās The control or dominion which a husband has in law over the person and the activities of his wife.

ijāra Hire or lease.

ijmā' Consensus of opinion.

ijtihād The exercise of human reason to ascertain a rule of Sharī'a law.

ikhtilāf Divergence of juristic opinions and doctrines.

'illa Effective cause. The ascertainment of the reason or *'illa* underlying a legal rule is an essential step in the process of reasoning by analogy (*qiyās*). A legal principle established by an original case is extended to cover new cases on the ground that they possess a common *'illa*.

iqrār Confession or admission.

isnād Chain of authorities reporting a Tradition.

istiḥsān The principle of jurisprudence that in particular cases not regulated by any incontrovertible authority of the Qur'ān, Traditions or *ijmā'*, equitable considerations may override the results of strict analogical reasoning.

istiṣḥāb Continuance, i.e. the presumption in the laws of evidence that a state of affairs known to exist in the past continues to exist until the contrary is proved.

istiṣlāḥ The principle of jurisprudence that "consideration of the public interest" is a criterion for the elaboration of legal rules.

kafā'a Social equality (of the spouses in marriage).

kharāj Land tax.

khiyār Option.

khiyār al-majlis "The option of the session". The right of a party to repudiate unilaterally a contract he has concluded as long as the "session" lasts. A "session" is the period during which contracting parties devote themselves to the business in hand and is terminated by any event—such as physical departure from the place of business—which indicates that negotiations are concluded or suspended.

khulʿ A form of divorce by mutual agreement, the wife providing a consideration for her release.

lawth Lit. "suspicion". Circumstances constituting *prima facie* evidence of guilt in cases of homicide.

liʿān Lit. "imprecation". The procedure by which a husband may repudiate paternity of a child born to his wife.

madhhab School of law or rite.

mafqūd Missing person.

mahr Dower.

makrūh Blameworthy.

mandūb Praiseworthy.

manfaʿa Usufruct.

mashhūr "Well-known." Used of a Tradition which is widely reported or a juristic opinion which commands widespread support and is "dominant" among the existing variants.

maṣlaḥa The public interest.

maẓālim Lit. "complaints". The prerogative jurisdiction exercised by the political authority or his delegate.

muddaʿā ʿalayhi The litigant against whom a *daʿwa*, or claim, is made.

muddaʿī The litigant who makes a *daʿwa* or claim, and upon whom falls the onus of proving his contention.

muftī A legal scholar competent to deliver *fatāwā* (q.v.)

muḥtasib The official exercising the function of *ḥisba* (q.v.).

mujtahid One who exercises *ijtihād* (q.v.).

muqallid One bound by the principle of *taqlīd* (q.v.).

mushāʿ Property jointly owned by two or more persons.

mutʿa (a) A form of compensation for divorced wives.

(b) A marriage contracted for a specified period of time.

mutawātir A Tradition which has a sufficiently large number of independent chains of authority to guarantee its authenticity.

muzābana A contract of exchange of fruits growing on the tree (particularly dates) for their calculated value in harvested fruits of the same species.

naskh Repeal or abrogation.

naṣṣ Text. An explicit provision of the Qur'ān or the Traditions.

nikāḥ Marriage.

qadhf The offence of an unproved imputation of illicit sex relations (cf. *zinā*).

qānūn Administrative regulation.

qarāba Relationship.

qasāma A procedure of compurgation in cases of homicide.

qiṣāṣ Retaliation. The legal sanction in cases of homicide and wounding.

qiyās Juristic reasoning by analogy.

qurba Lit. "approach to God". Particularly the pious or charitable element in *waqf* settlements.

qur' (pl. *qurū'*) Menstrual period.

radd "Return." The distribution of the residue of an estate, failing any residuary heir, to the Qur'ānic heirs *pro rata* their original shares.

rājiḥ Preferable. Used of a variant juristic opinion which, though it may not be *mashhūr* (q.v.), is nevertheless deemed to be the more correct view.

ra'y Juristic speculation.

ribā Basically, interest on a capital loan. In classical doctrine, however, the term covers many forms of gain or profit which accrue as the result of a transaction and which were not precisely calculable at the time the transaction was concluded.

rukhṣa Lit. "indulgence". Used of a legal rule which represents a particular exception to, or concession from, a generally accepted standard of conduct.

shahāda Oral testimony in court.

shirka Partnership.

shurṭa Police.

siyāsa shar'iyya "Government in accordance with the revealed law". The sovereign's prerogative power of supplementing the doctrine of the jurists by administrative measures and regulations.

sunna Lit. "trodden path". Historically there were three principal stages in the development of the concept of *sunna*. During the first century of Islam the term means local custom or traditional practice; for the early schools of law it signifies the generally accepted doctrine of the school; and from the time of ash-Shāfi'ī onwards it denotes the model behaviour of the Prophet—the practices he endorsed and the precedents he set.

tafwīḍ Delegation of an authority or power—e.g. the delegation by the husband of his power to repudiate his wife (*tafwīḍ aṭ-ṭalāq*).

takhayyur The modernist process of "selection" from variant juristic opinions.

ṭalāq Unilateral repudiation of his wife by a husband.

talfīq The process in legal modernism of "patching together" or combining the views of different schools and jurists, or elements therefrom, to form a single legal rule.

ta'līq Lit. "suspension". To make the effect of a legal act or transaction dependent upon some future condition or contingency—e.g. *ta'līq aṭ-ṭalāq*, to pronounce a repudiation which will become effective upon the occurrence of a specified event.

anzīl The doctrine of representation (in succession).

aqlīd The principle of strict adherence to the law as

expounded in the authoritative legal manuals.

ta'zīr Lit. "deterrence". The power of discretionary and variable punishment, the essence of which is that it is corrective as opposed to the *ḥadd* punishments which are retributive.

tazkiya The screening of witnesses to establish their credibility.

tha'r Blood revenge. The system of private justice operating in cases of homicide and wounding in pre-Islamic Arabia.

'udūl See *'adāla* above.

ujra Lit. "remuneration". The monetary consideration payable by the husband in a contract of temporary marriage.

'urf Lit. "what is known about a thing" and loosely "custom".

uṣūl See *aṣl* above.

wājib Obligatory.

waqf A settlement of property under which ownership of the property is "immobilised" and the usufruct thereof is devoted to a purpose which is deemed charitable by the law.

walī A person authorised to act on behalf of someone else—e.g. a legal guardian.

walī al-jarā'im An official exercising jurisdiction over criminal offences (*jarā'im*) by delegation from, and on behalf of, the political sovereign.

wathīqa (pl. *wathā'iq*) "A trustworthy document"—e.g. a draft contract drawn up and witnessed by the *'udūl* (q.v.).

zakāt Alms tax.

zann Conjecture. The legal value attached to the results of juristic reasoning.

zinā' The offence of illicit sexual relations—i.e. sexual intercourse between persons who are not either husband and wife or master and slave concubine.

SELECT BIBLIOGRAPHY

General and Introductory Works

The Encyclopaedia of Islam (First edition, four vols. and Supplement, Leiden, 1913–42; Second edition, Vol. I, Leiden and London, 1960, continuing) contains numerous articles on individual legal topics; the bibliographies, especially to "Sharī'a", have references also to German and Italian works.

M. Gaudefroy-Demombynes, *Muslim Institutions*, London 1950.

Sir Hamilton Gibb, *Mohammedanism* (Second edition), London, 1953.

G. E. von Grunebaum, *Medieval Islam*, Chicago, 1953.

R. Levy, *The Social Structure of Islam*, Cambridge, 1957.

D. Santillana, "Law and Society", in *The Legacy of Islam* (ed. Sir Thomas Arnold and A. Guillaume), London, 1931.

J. D. Pearson, *Index Islamicus*, 1906–55, and Supplements, Cambridge, 1958; a classified list of articles in learned journals. Section deals specially with law.

C. Brockelmann, *Geschichte der arabischen Literatur* (two vols. and three supplementary vols.); Leiden, 1937–49; lists all known MSS. and printed editions of works by Muslims, with notices of the authors.

BIBLIOGRAPHY

PART ONE

Law in the Middle East (Vol. I, *Origin and Development of Islamic Law*), ed. M. Khadduri and H. J. Liebesny, Washington, 1955. Chapters ii and iii provide a concise history of Islamic law, and particularly its early development, written by the pioneer scholar of this subject, J. Schacht. A French version of substantially the same material exists in the same author's *Esquisse d'une histoire du droit musulman*, Paris, 1952. See also his article "The Law", in *Unity and Variety in Muslim Civilisation*, ed. G. E. von Grunebaum, Chicago, 1955.

J. SCHACHT, *The Origins of Muhammadan Jurisprudence*, Oxford, 1950. The fundamental work of modern research on the early development of legal theory.

Institutions du droit public musulman (Tome Premier: *Le Califat*), E. TYAN (Paris, 1954), 3-116, and *Kinship and Marriage in Early Arabia*, W. ROBERTSON SMITH (new ed. by S. A. Cook, 1903), deal with various aspects of pre-Islamic Arabian customary law.

Qur'anic Laws, M. V. MERCHANT, Lahore, 1947, and *The Social Laws of the Qoran*, R. ROBERTS, London, 1925, are translations of and commentaries upon the Qur'anic legislation.

M. KHADDURI, *Islamic Jurisprudence*, Baltimore, 1961. A translation of ash-Shāfi'ī's *Risāla* with an introduction on the role and significance of the work and its author in the development of Islamic jurisprudence.

PART TWO

(i) LEGAL PHILOSOPHY AND THE CLASSICAL THEORY OF THE SOURCES OF LAW

Abdur RAHIM, *Muhammadan Jurisprudence*, Madras, 1911.

N. P. AGHNIDES, *Mohammedan Theories of Finance*

(Introduction on the classical legal theory), New York, 1916.

Kemal A. FARUKI, *Islamic Jurisprudence*, Karachi, 1962.

S. MAHMASSANI, *Falsafat al-Tashrī' fi al-Islām (The Philosophy of Jurisprudence in Islam)*, translated into English by Farhat J. Ziadeh, Leiden, 1961.

Snouck HURGRONJE, *Selected Works*, edited in English and French by G. H. Bousquet and J. Schacht, Leiden, 1957.

(ii) SUBSTANTIVE PRIVATE LAW

Abdur RAHMAN, *Institutes of Mussalman Law*, Calcutta, 1907.

Ameer ALI, *Mahommedan Law*, Calcutta, 1912.

N. B. E. BAILLIE, *Digest of Moohummudan Law*, Parts I and II, London, 1869–75.

A. A. A. FYZEE, *Outlines of Muhammadan Law* (Second edition), London, 1955.

The four above works are primarily concerned with Ḥanafī and Ithnā 'asharī law as applied in the Indian sub-continent.

G. H. BOUSQUET, *Le Droit musulman*, in the Librairie Armand Colin series, Paris, 1963. A concise book which is mainly concerned with Mālikī law in N.W. Africa. It includes chapters on legal theory and modern developments and a short bibliography of the most important works by French scholars on Islamic law.

I. GOLDZIHER, *Vorlesungen über den Islam* (second edition), Heidelberg, 1925; French translation, *Le Dogme et la loi de l'Islam*, by J. Aron, Paris, 1920.

C. HAMILTON, *The Hedaya* (second edition, by S. C. Grady), London, 1870. A translation into English of an authoritative mediaeval manual of Ḥanafī law. Mainly

Ḥanafī also is J. Schacht, *G. Bergsträsser's Grundzüge des islamischen Rechts*, Berlin, 1935.

L. Milliot, *Introduction à l'étude du droit musulman*, Paris, 1951. Primarily an account of Mālikī law as applied in N.W. Africa.

A. Querry, *Droit musulman*, Paris, 1871–2. A manual of Ithnā-ʿasharī law.

F. H. Ruxton, *Mālikī Law*, London, 1916. A summary from French translations of an authoritative Mālikī text.

L. W. C. Van den Berg, *Minhadj aṭ-ṭālibin*, Batavia, 1882–4. Annotated translation of an authoritative Shāfiʿī legal text.

(iii) Public Law and Legal Administration

E. Fagnan, *Les Statuts gouvernementaux*, Algiers, 1915. Annotated translation of al-Māwardī's treatise on public law.

H. Laoust, *Le Traité de droit public d'Ibn Taimiya*, Beirut, 1948.

E. Tyan, *Histoire de l'organisation judiciaire en Pays d'Islam* (two vols.), Paris, 1938–43.

—, *Institutions du droit public musulman* (two vols.), Paris, 1954–6.

PART THREE

Legal modernism in the Middle East was first analysed by J. Schacht in *Der Islam*, vol. XX (1932), 209-36. J. N. D. Anderson has documented in detail the various modern codifications of Sharīʿa law and his *Islamic Law in the Modern World*, New York and London, 1959, provides the best introduction to the subject. The bibliography of this book contains a comprehensive list of articles on various aspects of legal modernism, to which should now be added:

J. N. D. Anderson, "Waqfs in East Africa", in *The Journal of African Law*, V, No. 3, 1959.

—, "The Modernisation of Islamic Law in the Sudan", in *The Sudan Law Journal and Reports*, 1960.

—, "A Law of Personal Status for Iraq", in *The International and Comparative Law Quarterly*, October 1960.

—, "Recent Reforms in Family Law in the Arab World", a paper presented to the Conference of the Gesellschaft für Rechtsvergleichung, 1963.

—, "Islamic Law in Africa: Problems of Today and Tomorrow", in *Changing Law in Developing Countries*, London, 1963, 164-84.

N. J. Coulson, "Islamic Family Law: Progress in Pakistan", in *Changing Law in Developing Countries*, London, 1963, 240-58.

J. Roussier, "Dispositions nouvelles dans le statut successoral en droit tunisien", in *Studia Islamica*, Fasc. XII, 1960.

—, "Le Livre du testament dans le nouveau code tunisien du statut personnel", in *Studia Islamica*, Fasc. XV, 1961.

—, "L'Application du Chra' au Maghrib en 1959", in *The World of Islam*, VI, 1959, 25-56.

J. Schacht, "Islamic Law in Contemporary States", in the *American Journal of Comparative Law*, 1959, 133-47.

—, "Problems of Modern Islamic Legislation", in *Studia Islamica*, Fasc. XII, 1960.

J. N. D. Anderson, *Islamic Law in Africa*, London, 1954. A meticulously detailed survey of the extent to which Sharī'a law is today applied in the former British Colonial Territories of sub-Saharan Africa and in the Colony and Protectorate of Aden.

G. H. Bousquet, *Du droit musulman et de son appli-*

cation effective dans le monde, Algiers, 1949. A general survey, country by country, of the extent to which Sharī'a law is applied throughout the Muslim world excepting sub-Saharan Africa.

I. MAHMUD, *Muslim Law of Succession and Administration*, Karachi, 1958. An analysis of the extent to which modern judicial practice in the Indian sub-continent diverges from the traditional Sharī'a law in the field of the administration of estates.

Count Leon OSTROROG, *The Angora Reform*, London, 1927. An assessment of the motivations behind, and the implications of, Turkey's abandonment of the Sharī'a law in the 1920's.

INDEX

(The Arabic article *al-*, with its variants such as *an-*, *ash-*, etc., is neglected in the alphabetical arrangement.)

INDEX